Praise for
Inside the Crips

"Simpson shows us exactly how and why a bright, personable kid comes to join a gang and why that same kid would choose to stay despite the lethal risks, the soul-battering violence, and the inevitable incarcerations. . . . Simpson gives us fresh, detailed snapshots of this highly disciplined supergang existence, where survival involves keeping abreast of group politics so intricate they resemble high-court intrigue."

— *Los Angeles Times*

"A colorful memoir."

—*Los Angeles Daily Journal*

"In this often enthralling and emotional memoir, Simpson takes readers inside his life with the gang, from the time he joined through his sixteen-month prison sentence and to his leaving the Crips. . . . The world Simpson evokes with Pearlman's help is fascinating, and his narrative is clearly heartfelt."

—*Publishers Weekly*

"A raw account of Los Angeles gang underworld and his life as a thief, thug, and triggerman in the bloody battle between the Crips and the Bloods."

—*Calgary Herald*

"When I read *Inside the Crips,* I'm reminded of this injustice we all experienced growing up in South Central L.A. Yes, we were violent and destructive, but all we knew was survival, and more times than not, that meant kill or be killed, do or die. . . . You, the reader, will experience the life of a gangbanger, a prisoner, a Crip Stabilizer. Crips rarely express remorse, fear, or sentiment. Instead, we relate old war stories depicting ourselves as macho soldiers who conc book, I realize I only knew Cee, the gang member. Now I know Colton, the man."

—from the foreword by Ice T.

"This book tells the story of Simpson's life, from his childhood to his adulthood. It covers abuse at the hands of his mother; his induction into the Crips, the notorious Los Angles-based gang; and his time in prison. It's brutal and filled with dramatic, nearly unbelievable, scenes."

—*The Ann Arbor News*

"Simpson's book paints a stark portrait of life in prison as the conflict between the Crips and its rival gang, the Bloods, is magnified by the claustrophobic surroundings."

—*The Washington Post*

"This unvarnished portrayal of gang life is enlightening and even inspiring about a subject badly in need of illumination."

—American Library Association

Inside the

Crips

ALSO BY ANN PEARLMAN

Infidelity: A Love Story
*Keep the Home Fires Burning: How to Have an Affair with
Your Spouse*
Getting Free: Women and Psychotherapy

Inside the
Crips

LIFE INSIDE L.A.'S MOST
NOTORIOUS GANG

COLTON SIMPSON

with

ANN PEARLMAN

St. Martin's Griffin
New York

www.stmartins.com

Library of Congress Cataloging-in-Publication Data

Simpson, Colton.
    Inside the Crips : life inside L.A.'s most notorious gang / Colton Simpson with Ann Pearlman.—1st St. Martin's Griffin ed.
      p. cm.
    Includes index (p 329).
    ISBN-13: 978-0-312-32930-3
    ISBN-10: 0-312-32930-X
    1. Simpson, Colton. 2. Crips (Gang). 3. Gang members—California—Los Angeles—Biography. I. Pearlman, Ann. II. Title.

HV6439.U7L775 2005
364.1'092—dc22
[B]

2005042704

10 9 8 7 6 5 4 3

To the Crips and Blood Army, both current and past members
and
To the men and women in prison who continue
to fight for what is right—uhuru!

Contents

Acknowledgments

JODIE RHODES, OUR AGENT, PLEADED, CAJOLED, AND DRAGGED me into this project. For that I want to thank her, because writing this book has been a terrific adventure. It's been a privilege to become close to Li'l Cee Loc and his world. More than simply a team, we will always be friends and family to each other, counted on for both love and loyalty. Working with St. Martin's and Elizabeth Beier has been easy and invigorating, made that way by her effortless enthusiasm. And I want to thank Heather Florence and Catherine Revland for their patient attention in smoothing out some rough edges.

Elizabeth Kai Hinton had a vision of what this could be from the beginning and read this manuscript in its earliest stages; her suggestions and perceptions were incorporated. James Martin Dell'Orco's insights are peppered throughout this book. Our discussions as well as his support were invaluable. Both of them provided me with what a writer needs to counterbalance the isolation of the work. Susan Beth Miller, as always, improved the prose and consistency; Dr. Moses Everett brought his psychological/sociological intelligence to the material and characters; and Mr. Timothy Kornegay provided his knowledge of history, time, language, and people. Dr. Ren Farley supplied me with source materials. My children buttressed me with encouragement, excitement, and (always) love, and they have included Colton in our circle.

I relied on the work of Eldridge Cleaver, George Jackson, and Mumia Abu-Jamal for information and perspective. The figures quoted are from *Servico Brasileiro De Justice E Paz*, Sept. 21, 1995; *Sacramento Bee*, May 25, 1989; and the *Prison Activist Resource Center*. Several books informed the pages of this work. Among them are: *The Culture of Control: Crime and Social Order in Contemporary Society*, by David Garland; *Prismatic Metropolis: Inequality in Los Angeles*, by Lawrence D. Bobo, Melvin Oliver, James H. Johnson, and Abel Valenquela; and Alejandro A. Alonso's thesis, *Territoriality Among African-American Street Gangs in Los Angeles*.

—Ann Pearlman

Infinite love goes out to all the Crips and Bloods who fought and struggled with me inside of prison for what is right. Think not that our energy and efforts were in vain; for those who have impeded our progress there has been a price. And with this book, a soldier has come!

To the symbol of beauty, dominance, and perfection: Louise DeBlanc (my grandmother), the only mother I've ever had. For catching me when I fell. You are omnipresent in my life.

To my only wife and eternal friend, Regina Leshawn Jake, the only person who covered my back through this entire ordeal. And to my "brother," Smiley, and the entire Jake family.

To Ann Pearlman, my coauthor. For your undying support and love. You are so right about us making a good team. Love and loyalty to u always.

To my editor at St. Martin's Press, Elizabeth Beier. For believing in me and Ann Pearlman and making this thing so unbelievably smooth. People told me you were the strictest editor one could encounter. They were right (smile).

To Jodie Rhodes, my agent, for believing in my work. God sent you, I'm sure.

To the most powerful woman in the word: Karen SK Bailey. For helping me transform.

To two matches made in heaven: Tracy Marrow, a.k.a. rapper/actor Ice T—my brother in faith, comrade in ideology, and mentor in spirits—and Darlene Ortiz (my younger sister); and my sister and brother-in-law, Lisa Ashby and Steven Ashby. You are living examples of what love and loyalty can create. I love you unconditionally. Your spear and shield.

To my nephew, Ice Marrow, a.k.a. Li'l Ice T. U may not know this, but when u introduced me to paintball you gave me an outlet that calms me even to this day. It opened a lane for me to shoot people for fun and not get in trouble. I just bought an electric trigger. You're dead meat (smile).

To Uncle Van, "Uncle" Timothy, Schellee Rocher, and Greg Parks. You four have had my back since day one. How will I ever repay you for all you've done?

To my longtime friends, D'Andre Clark, Steve Thompson, Brian Sims, Bentley Evans, and my cousin, Steven "Stevo" Young. Man, we've been through so much together. You guys have really had my back. Much love and respect.

To the original member of the Soledad Seven, Ruchell McGee; X–Black Panther party member Geronimo Pratt, and all the other brothers that aided me when I had no direction and no assistance. We are one. Men sharpen men—steel sharpens steel!

To my cousins, Mark Laidler (310 Motoring), Chris Mills (NBA player), and Kirt Watts. Had it not been for you three I'd definitely be in chains. Infinite love from the highest.

To my father, Richard "Dick" Simpson. And all my real family members. For your undying love and support.

To Tamara. I've never had someone be as down as you are for me. Infinite love.

To Coach Brown, vocational instructor Loren Erickson, Lt. Hunt at Calipatria State Prison, and the best university in the world, prison, for teaching me so much.

To Lunatick Frank from the Rollin Sixties. For teaching me the most valuable lesson a prisoner can learn: security!

To all the fallen soldiers of the Harlem Crips. And Cornell "Nelsie" Smith (R.I.P.) from the Rollin Sixties. Not a single day goes by without thoughts of you. You are still alive.

To Timothy "Big H" Kornegay, Louie "Three Finger Louie" Cook, Vigil "Kato" Byers, Mike "Watt Nitty" Byers, and Sheree Torres. For keeping it real when the word real was alien to our world.

To Adam Winnick. In 2002, you saved my life. I love you, man.

To those who live now in prisons across America and abroad. There is hope. There is spirit. And there is a God. Keep the faith.

To all my present and X-homeboys and homegirls, Crips, Bloods, and nonaffiliates. You know these folks are making it extremely hard for us. Life is a struggle, without that struggle there is no progress. Open your eyes wide and "overstand" that we are all from the same fist—a clinched fist. Discipline is the key.

And, finally, to the players in the false charges against me for shooting Son, including my first lawyer, the witnesses, the prosecutor, and the sentencing judge. You've proven to me that there are no such things as "rights"; they're privileges of the powerful and rich. For me, "rights" were nothing more than a mere chimera that vanished in front of me once I reached out to grab them as something real and substantial. I've finally figured out why you did this to me: to make me a voice. Hallelujah!

—Colton Simpson

Foreword

By ICE T

ART COMES FROM PAIN AND SUFFERING. POVERTY CREATES pain, so there's plenty of suffering in the ghetto. *Inside the Crips* is born from that suffering, the suffering of Colton Simpson, the suffering of the ghetto. Colton insightfully breaks down what ghetto life is like and what we've been through. Colton was devoted to the 'hood and he became a rider, jewel thief, Crip stabilizer, O.G. (Original Gangster, or General) of the Crips gang. For a lot of years, both in the 'hood and in California prisons, he was "The Man." Here, he reveals the life of many of us, not only in the South Central Los Angeles ghetto, but in all the ghettos and all the prisons across America.

I met Colton—Cee, we called him—when he was ten at Smiley's house. Cee was Smiley's boy, a skinny ten-year-old, not even old enough to have a temper, just an edge. He was small in stature, but not in heart and was resolute on becoming "somebody" in the world. He wasn't afraid of anything: he was hot, quick, and aggressive.

At that time, I was graduating from Crenshaw High, where it was mandatory to be connected to a particular set, or unit, in the gang. It just so happened that the Crip sets were the ones that I hung out with and was down with. I recruited Smiley for the game and Colton lived down the street from him. So I was four years older than Smiley and eight years older than Cee. Being an older cat, I saw the capabilities of each person. In the street zone, there are a lot of different players. Some are laid back, some more calculating, some won't fight, some are manipulators, some will get down at the drop of a dime. That's Colton. A fast fuse. He'll hurt somebody quick. I saw that in him, but Smiley was able to control it. Smiley is a two-sided coin. He's very intelligent, loyal, and more calculating than Colton. He was the guy who made the plans and Colton was the guy who'd execute.

Cee brought in over $100,000 a year when he was fourteen. That's a lot of money for a kid, enough to make you influential and powerful. I know Cee was earning that much because I knew the moves he was making. As a teen, he was a celebrity ghetto gangsta.

We were hustling. We didn't expect to live past twenty-five. It was "go do it right now and fuck whatever happens." We had all the fineries of youthful hustlers: Fila sweat suits, Porsches, gold jewelry as big as dinner plates hanging around our necks. Along with all the hustles, I would rap. Cee and Smiley always came to support me. At the Culver City Talent show, which Cee describes in the book, I rapped about our lives. That's all I could do; that's all I knew. We wanted to hear about parking cars on sidewalks, grabbing jewelry, and fuckin' a bitch, 'cause that was our mentality, our daily grind. The guys cheered, "Yeah, yeah. Ice. Ice." Cats that were basically negative gave me pump. "Yo, Ice, you're doin' something."

I rap about the streets. My songs carry warnings and predictions; if you do this, this is what can potentially happen. I can inform cats that they're getting mad at the wrong thing. It's not about being mad at everything. It's about being really mad at the right thing and together we can develop some focus. That's what I rap about.

At the Culver City Talent Show, I didn't set out to be part of the invention of gangsta rap. We were just talking about our lives with our homies in the 'hood and a new form was created.

Society has always had a love/hate reaction to the ghetto. Getting rid of the ghetto and economic inequality is never going to happen in this particular society. This is capitalism and we need our status quo. We'll always have people who haven't gotten their foot up. Back in the day, it was Irish people and Jewish people. Now the Black and Mexicans fill the ghettos. The fear factor is part of the game. Our society wants to turn a certain element into monsters, certain locations into scary places. Society wants to make you think the gangs aren't organized and don't know what they're doing. White people believe the gangs are after them. The gangs aren't even *thinking* about them.

Now, the wrong person at the wrong time can get robbed in any city in America. I could walk into the wrong White neighborhood and get robbed. Incidents of the gangs messing with outside people are isolated and rare. But a gang going after White kids or White legit business man? Never. Never. Meanwhile, the media makes it seem like gangs are invading Beverly Hills. It maintains the fear. And that prevents society from helping. "Why would we want to help them? Why would we put any money in their pockets or community? They're after us."

It's not true.

We're just trying to survive and prosper in our own way. In the 'hood, we don't have the brother who went to Harvard who makes us proud, who makes us feel good about ourselves. So we work on what we do have. Masculinity. Masculinity is at a premium. The toughest kid on the block becomes the role model. Not the richest kid, or the smartest kid. But the toughest kid. Pride is based on violence and aggression. That's how we define wealth. In the 'hood, we define wealth by strength.

In the jungle, nobody has anything to shine on each other with.

Gangs are a survival unit that happens in the neighborhood because people are tough. Young men decide: If we clique up, we're safer. That's all a gang starts out being. A protection unit. Then we decide, if three of us are tough, five of us are tougher. Meanwhile none of us has anything. Take the gangbangers' outfit. It is the least expensive clothing: A white tee shirt, some Converses, pressed jeans, a carefully folded rag. That's not by choice. That's the cheapest shit at the swap meet. So what the ghetto kids have done is take nothing and turned it into something by turning it into power. The kids in the suburbs, the rich kids, have their cars, computers, designer clothes. But here comes the gang. They can be scared of us. We get a little fun out of that. It's a way of balancing.

Most gangs are defensive units. Now if you're selling dope, that's a survival scenario as people are trying to get paper and they will defend that. There's a small portion of the ghetto who are "jackers" and that's their way to get money. When the gang decides "we're tough so we're going to move," it becomes predatory. The true predators clique up and say, "We're gonna get drug dealers and other cats." When someone is hit in gang warfare, it's retaliation. It's not an offensive move. Retaliation is a reaction to murder.

Now, you can try to tell someone not to retaliate for murder. But if I were on my back dying because I was shot, my last words would be, "Get them muthafuckas. I'm not resting in peace." Most people feel the same way. If someone shoots you, you won't say, "Peace to them." You'll say, "Get them!" Human beings were doing that in Troy. Why are we over there bombing Saddam? We had to show something. It's wrong, but at the same time it's been validated throughout all of history. That's how men react. Gangs didn't make that up. In the ghetto, when someone gets shot, the cops are going to let it ride. Meanwhile, children and mothers are crying, little sisters scream over the dead body. The family looks to the young men in the neighborhood. The young men start riding for justice. So, when someone kills someone on your side of the fence, you go to their side of the fence and retaliate. Gangbanging is a war that goes on inside the 'hood.

And then the hate grows. When you're a Crip and your friends are Crips and your brother got killed by a Blood, it's hard to sit in a room with other Bloods who may know someone who killed your brother. In your gut, hatred twists. I've been around gang situations where little children are indoctrinated by their parents. For example, your child has a red sweatshirt on and you'll be at a barbeque and people will say, "Why you got that red sweatshirt on that kid? Take it off. You know the Bloods killed his uncle." Now this child has been indoctrinated to dislike a color.

Whatever starts a war is stupid on the face of it. But once the killing starts, it's hard to stop. We, in the United States think it's easy to stop. We bomb Japan and then go there and kick it with them. What we're doing in Iraq right now, killing all those people, how do we think that's going to be okay? It's not. We've killed their families. I've been all over the world. Serbia, Croatia, I've been there. It's the same exact people fighting over something. Hate and pain and suffering provoke it. Pride is based on it. Retaliation seems crucial.

In my record, I sang, "Our color is death, though we all want peace. But this war won't end till all wars cease." Our war is no stupider than any other war.

As powerful as the Crips are on the streets, they're even more powerful in penitentiaries. Then you're forced to pick a car and become further indoctrinated into the gang. There are a lot of different gangs: Aryan Nation, Muslims, Black Guerilla Family, Crips, Bloods, Northern and Southern Mexicans. Violence is going to come to you. I've been to jail. You can't do a bid without having to get down. Everyone grinds at each other, gets on each other's nerves. In prison, everyone is hard; lightweight Crips become hard-core. Prison doesn't teach good citizenship. It teaches violence.

When I went into show business, my friends rooted for me. They knew when they came out of prison, they'd have a friend who could help them. We're all from the same place. The 'hoods all over the world identify with cats like me because I was doing the worst stuff.

When I was in Australia, I meet this aboriginal chief. He said, "The police aren't the enemy. The law is the enemy." He told me a story. Once upon a time, he could run all across the land. But one day, he got to a river and he was told, "You can't cross this river."

"Why?" he asked.

"It's the system. The law says you can't."

Now here was a guy enforcing the law, but he didn't make the law. Some of these issues end up being on the ballots. Others we influence through our elected officials. We need to vote.

The same is true with the police. I have no problems with cops; they're the same as criminals. They just have a gun and a different set of principles, but they aren't the law. They're merely enforcing the law. When I was breaking the law, they were the opponent. If they caught me, "Touché."

I'm not mad at them.

I'm mad at the system. And the cop didn't make the system. Now some are cruel and sadistic, some are on a power trip, some are homies from the 'hood with a job. When I got the job on *Law and Order: Special Victims Unit*, Dick Wolf said, "Ice, play a cop the way he should be." And that's what I've tried to do.

Without treatment, gangs, and everything they bring with them, are going to grow. They'll end up being in your neighborhood, in your face. You can't turn your back and think they'll go away. When I was in the gang truce organization, a cat came to me and said, "Ice, we want to stop gangbanging but we ain't got no jobs."

"You gotta stop gangbanging. Gangbanging and unemployment are two separate things."

But in a way, he's right. Give a man a job, give him something to do and he doesn't have time to be running around. An idle mind is the devil's workshop. Black people are finding themselves and learning how to capitalize on the music business, capitalize on our talent, capitalize on our sports abilities, capitalize on what we have. We own our own clothing lines. I got a new drink out. And when I do that, I employ my friends, my community. So we're gonna pull ourselves out of this bitch. And then you'll see different people in the ghettos.

Gangbanging is something that I did in high school. Personally, I've never been jumped into a set. I've always been a gang affiliate. I wore the blue, but I've never been a hard-core gang member. I'm as down as you can get, but I never put in work for a gang. I've never been a rider. If you're into hard-core banging, you don't have anything else so you develop a rare and slanted grasp of life. But as people get older, they want to get out and go on with their lives and raise a family. They don't want to die in prison. If they get another chance, they quit. Gangbanging is a young man's game.

People don't want to be gangbanging. Not really. But they missed their chance. We got to catch them young. In tenth grade, we should start asking kids what they want to do with their lives. Nourish their dreams; tell them they can have goals. Start talking about college. Then set up their high school program so it makes sense with what they want for their own lives. Now, in inner-city schools, there's no direction. With no idea about what you want to do, you have nothing but the 'hood. You ask yourself: Who am I? All I can be is tough and feared. So you concentrate on that and turn yourself into a little hard rock.

When I came out of the 'hood, I traveled and I saw poverty. I saw poverty in Brazil, Argentina, China, Europe. It humbles you. We have it good. We need to calm down a little bit. Gang members need to see space, to travel. When you grow up in the 'hood or a project, you think this is the only place people live. On my tour bus, cats will say, "Man. I could just live on that mountain."

"Yes, you could. You just got to be willing to get out of the zone. You need the mental change of getting out of the 'hood."

Ghettos aren't just for Black people. They just have different names. Go to the Midwest, and you see some very poor White people. There are some sad trailer parks. Black kids have never seen that. If you took every kid from the ghetto and showed him some really poor White people, then they wouldn't be so angry. So with jobs, dream-focused education, and exposure to the world, all of us together could turn the negativity in gangs around.

When you're in the street and you're a player in the gang, nobody really comes to you for help. Everyone is just worried about survival. When you become successful, you become "The Man," you become an ambassador. So when anybody goes to jail, I get the phone call. I know more about what's going on than anybody. And how I deal with that burden is a result of the kind of person I am. I carry a little guilt about my success. I wish everybody were doing well. Nobody has ever forced me to do anything. But, come on. My friend just died and he can't have a funeral and the funeral is six thousand dollars and I'm sitting here with a million. I gotta pay. I never needed anything from people, so I'm glad that I'm able to give. That's how I'll be remembered. I'm lucky to be a giver as long as there's respect and appreciation behind it. There's nothing more important than having people speak highly of you. When Colton got out of prison, I was glad I could give him a job and show him the ropes. It's been a privilege.

When you're trying to reach the hardest kids, you've got an unconventional enemy and you need to use unconventional tactics. For example, put a daisy on the cover of an album and the kids will never buy it. If there's blood on the cover, the little bad kids will buy it. Then you have the opportunity to talk. With this book you'll reach the upper-class squares. And then the kids. You'll have the Crips reading it.

When I read *Inside the Crips,* I'm reminded of the injustice we all experienced growing up in South Central L.A.. Yes, we were violent and destructive, but all we knew was survival and more times than not, that meant kill or be killed, do or die. Reading *Inside the Crips,* I learned what Cee—a cat I knew my whole life— had been through. It was like I was going through it with him.

You, the reader, will experience the life of a gangbanger, a prisoner, a Crip stabilizer. Crips rarely expose remorse, fear, or sentiment. Instead, we relate old war stories depicting ourselves as macho soldiers who conquered prison. Reading his book, I realize I only knew Cee, the gang member. Now I know Colton, the man.

Just as prison strips many Crips of life and time, it saves lives in an odd, perverse way. Conscripting to the Crips is pledging participation in a game of Russian roulette. It's not an occupation where you end up dying of old age. Who knows how long you'll survive? No one truly knows. But if you're a Crip, there's a bullet—or a prison term—with your name on it looming in your future.

Author's Note

This is a personal story of gang and prison life. Some events and conversations have necessarily been reconstructed. I have changed many of the names, yet because gang members often change their names or use multiple names, it is possible that the fictitious names I have selected will be the same as the gang or the legal name of people who are not characters in my life or the book.

Inside the

Crips

ONE

Transformation

"There is an abundance of hope, but none for us."
    —Franz Kafka

EVENTS ARE LINED UP LIKE DOMINOES FALLING SO FAST I
don't have time to think about one before the next one tumbles.
Most of my life, I've been at war. If there's a time before war, it's
the time before remembering.

And so my first memory is when I am four and in a motel room
down the street from our home. It's Los Angeles, 1969. I race
matchbox cars on a light stripe on a brown rug. The sun shining
through venetian blinds creates my road. Damon, my brother a
year older, crashes his blue car into my truck. "Bam. Krr," he
growls and knocks my truck from the road to lie on its side, the
small wheels spinning.

I look up to complain about my brother's violence and see my
mom. She stands with one leg bent, sliding the strap of a shoe over
her heel as she tilts toward the wall, supported by her outstretched
arm. The wall is in an unfamiliar room in a motel, but I don't know
why we're in a motel so close to home. This is my first memory of
my mother as she leans, her long hair waving toward her waist, a

slice of sun dazzling over a dress the same color as her beige flesh. Her face is oblivious of her splendor, of us. The only thing that exists is gliding the black strap over her heel. Nothing else is important but that moment. Not me, not Damon, not the room with the pale green walls. This moment, this brief space is my peace, her paused on one leg like that, her palm on the wall. As I notice her, I realize how fine she is, her face is that restful. Like the statues of the Madonna in church. I'm splashed with the shafts of white light and her glory. Safe. I am safe.

Wham. A man backhands her and she crumbles onto the unmade bed, hair splayed out. I only see the man's back, and then as he turns toward me, a brass buckle on his belt, his navy pants. I don't see his face; I don't know who he is. These images contain no sound, just pictures. There is no blam his fist makes on her cheekbone. I do not hear a groan, or a surprised gasp for air from my mother. She falls silently to lay on the bed over a green and gold comforter. She doesn't move, doesn't rise.

And me. And me? I cover my head with my arms and cry.

My mother sits up, wipes her nose. Her feet are on the floor, but she doesn't stand, doesn't go after him, and doesn't defend herself. Just allows him to tear away at her beauty and end our harmony. He's gone. I don't remember the door slamming as he leaves.

Why didn't she sense her danger? How could she have been so innocent?

I should have seen it coming. Something—a movement, an expression, a sound, and a gesture—must have warned me. I need to pay more attention.

Why didn't she fight?

After that I see less of my father. He's away for weeks playing baseball for the Los Angeles Angels, and brings home joy and soap wrapped with decorated paper and shampoo in small bottles from his hotels. And then my brother Marc is born light skinned, lighter even than my mother, a baby pale as a fish. Blue squiggly lines run under his skin.

I can tell Moms loves him the most.

When my father sees him, he shakes his head, sadly. The baby doesn't make Pops seem huge by contrast, but turns him frail in spite of his hard arms. My mother and father fight all the time now. Then one day, Pops calls the police. He tells them, "Her new boyfriend is always threatening to shoot somebody. I want you to witness this. The stereo system is all I want and I'm outta here."

My father has angular features, a high beaked nose, and cheeks that cave under his bones. "Colton," Pops leans his elbows on his knees so we're at eye level, "I'd take you with me. But she won't let me. And I have to leave or my temper will get someone dead or someone serving time." Then he stands. "You're my son and I love you." He places his palms on my shoulders. A baseball he's given me is clutched in my hand. "Remember. Always remember. You, Colton, are my son." He leans back on his heels. "I tried to get custody of all of you, since she's so harsh, so evil and conniving, using her beauty as a trap." Pops stands and crosses his arms. "But she flirted her eyelashes at the judge, acted meek while she cried about how much she loved her sons. So." He nods at the burgundy velvet sofa, the wood dining table, the white ceramic lamp as though counting, as though counting something, saying good-bye. Every motion resounds through his body in a dance of tendons and muscles. "It's all hers now. But, Colton, you have my temper, so watch yourself," he warns.

Pops is everything I dream of becoming—tall, respected, a celebrity. The police help him load his stereo and jazz records into his car. He drives away.

We're alone with Moms. "Your father don't care about you. He ain't no good," Moms shrugs as she winds a strand of hair around her curling iron.

Pete, a White man with a red face and soft flesh around the middle, moves in. He's not long lean and lanky like Pops, built like a tank rather than a rocket. He plays "I Can See Clearly Now" and "Witchy Woman" over and over. I miss Coltrane and Miles.

"We'll go hunting for rabbits," he booms, "but first you have to learn how to shoot." One day, he lines up tin cans on the fence of our backyard and shoots at the cans. Ping. Ping. I come out and he hands me the .38. "Here." He shows me how to sight the target, lining up the little bar between the arms of the V, and to slowly pull the trigger. When I pull the trigger, power surges through my arm, my shoulder, but my bullet topples the can. Just like that I find my mark.

"Hey, not bad." Jimmie claps me on the back so hard I have to catch my footing. "Not bad, kid."

The next one, I miss, but the one after that goes right through. The can wobbles on the fence, rights itself, and waits another shot.

After that, guns are all I think of. I save my Christmas money and my birthday money to buy a pop revolver. Damon and I shoot each other in the living room, in the bedroom, hiding under the dining room table. The burnt powder adds wisps of smoke to the tobacco and marijuana clouds on the ceiling. The startling claps add to the chaos in the house. Then I buy a BB gun and save enough money to get one for Damon, too, and we race around Ladera Heights popping at the trees, the houses, palms, each other. Skinny enough to hide behind a palm, I blast the adobe corner of our house as Damon runs. Ping, the BB ricochets off the tree.

So it sounds like we're a family—Pete and Moms and Damon and Marc and me—but like the contentment racing cars in the light bars, nothing is what it seems. Pete is a roofer and Moms works long hours as a nurse. A Mexican woman lives in the spare bedroom and she's the one who is always there. She doesn't speak English, doesn't even come out of her room except to heat up a TV dinner for us when Moms works late.

One evening, Moms works the early shift and comes home before dark. She goes into the bathroom first thing and calls, "How you guys doin'?" I smell her marijuana. She enters the kitchen and pours a glass of wine and rinses dishes. I listen to predict her mood. When I walk into the kitchen for some water, she says, "You look just like your dad," and shakes her head, nibbling on the corner of her lip. She finishes the wine and pours another. "Think I'll go out for awhile," she says more to herself than to me. "Where's my keys?"

I know what's coming. I sense it when she starts her search, sense it in her restless movements, how she scatters from place to place, never even giving herself enough time to look, searching with angry hisses instead of systematic eyes.

I try to leave the house.

"Where you goin'? You help me find those keys." I search the bathroom. In the dining room, she sees my jacket hanging on the back of a chair, a comic book on the table. "Didn't I tell you kids to keep your stuff in your room?" My book flaps to the floor. She downs the rest of the wine and places the glass on the wood. Then she peeks in our room and notices our unmade bed. "Look at this mess. Didn't I tell you to clean this shit up?"

I look through the sofa cushions.

She kicks the clothes on the floor. "Where's my keys? Why's this shit all over? You goddamn kids." She slaps me. "Look at all this shit. No wonder Pete's always mad at me."

I hold my arms in front of my face.

"It's you kids." She whacks me on my back, my legs, her arms flailing in the air before her hands land. The small slot machine Pops gave me for Christmas sails at my head. I duck and it travels through the window. "See. Now I have to fix that fuckin' window."

Moms grabs the plastic bat. *Oh, no.* I remember how it hurts, the welts it leaves. Her mouth is pulled into itself, her eyes squinting, her hair uncombed. She strikes my back and my ribs with the bat, storms from the bedroom, finds her keys in her pocket, slams the front door.

Being alone is better. Damon and I sit on our bed and listen to ourselves breathe.

I rub my back and arms. Soon my red arm will darken to a bruise.

A week or so later, Pete and she watch *The Waltons*, then *Mary Tyler Moore,* smoking cigarettes and drinking beer. After awhile, they go into their bedroom.

Maybe they'll go to sleep.

But Damon and I hear them crashing the furniture and screaming at each other. We go into our rooms, lie in our beds, but we can't sleep.

"Let's go," I suggest. We leave the house with our rifles and play cops and robbers with the bushes, the palms, the telephone poles. The darkness makes the game more exciting. *Maybe this is how families are. Just not the Waltons,* I think as I stand behind the corner of our house waiting for Damon to appear. I know he's behind Pete's truck, and then he peeps out and bam, I fire. The BB bounces off the truck and hits Damon on the shoulder.

I visit Pops at his mother's in Venice and he makes sure I'm playing Little League and enrolls me in karate. But he doesn't or can't interfere with what's going on day to day.

Two nights later, I wake up to Pete yelling, "You fuckin' nigger. I'll kill you. I'll kill you, you fuckin' nigger." I peer into my mom's bedroom and her blouse is partly open. A family friend, Wilson, is behind her, his fingers on her shoulder.

"You crazy," she yells at Pete. "Wilson brought me home from the bar 'cause I'm too drunk to drive. He's helping me."

The image freezes for a split second. Pete is red, teeth glistening, his lips stretched to say "nigger." Half in her black bra and half in a red shirt dragging from her shoulder, Moms's face is turned, hair at odd angles, her mouth loose like it gets when she's drunk. Black circles of smeared makeup turn her eyes hollow and deep. Wilson's fingers are spread, his mouth open, his eyebrows raised.

Pete turns and sees me. With this motion, the picture clatters in broken pieces and movement continues.

"I was drunk and he did me a favor," Moms protests.

"You fuckin' nigger," Pete screams at Wilson. "Trying to mess with my woman." Pete collars Wilson, punches him. Wilson's nose squirts blood and he falls. Pete hits him, straightens up to kick him in the ribs.

Wilson curls to protect himself. "No," he whimpers.

"I'll kill you." Pete picks up Wilson, drags him through the living room. A table crashes. Under the punches and screaming, Wilson moans. Pete body-slams Wilson out the front door. "You fuckin' nigger."

Pete is in my house with my Black mother and her Black children, me, Damon, and he's saying "nigger." I think of sheeted, hooded men right in my house.

Pete crashes back into the bedroom. "You fuckin' whore." He kicks a table against the wall and the lamp breaks. Sharp shards of white ceramic and bitter glass glitter from the carpet.

I sneak into the living room to the phone as Moms screeches, "He's gay, you asshole. He was just trying to help me."

I dial my father. "Come help, he's calling us nigger. Pete beat up Wilson. He's punching Moms and calling us 'nigger'." I think my father is my savior.

Pete storms into the living room, grabs the phone, and jerks the cord out of the wall. He pulls off his belt and starts swinging. He hits my shoulder, my thighs. I'm only wearing skimpy pajama shorts and the buckle rips through the fabric, tears through my skin as he whips my thighs, knees, legs. I cover my knees with my hands, but he keeps whipping, hitting now my fingers and knuckles, and that hurts more. His buckle catches my knees. The strap hits my thighs.

Pete's face is purple as the belt whirls over his head, the metal shooting blinding sparks. Moms enters the room and watches.

He doesn't stop.

My mother sees Pete beating me. She sees me crying and screaming. Her eyes fix on me like this is a movie. Her mouth is slack, lipstick smeared, the blouse hangs off one shoulder, one breast contained by black bra. She watches.

She watches as though this has nothing to do with her, as though she's glad it's me and not her. I have it coming for being born looking like my father. I have it coming for my father leaving her.

When Pete is exhausted, he stops.

Blood trickles from my wounds, patches of skin ripped from my knees. I limp into the bedroom. Damon sits on the bed, his hands beside his thighs. He looks at me and turns away.

"Help."

He wets a towel and wraps it around the wounds. My father doesn't come and get me.

After that, the fighting escalates between Moms and Pete and a few months later he moves out. *Things'll be better now*, I think as I see him load up his truck with his boxes. But Moms is more determined than ever to get out of the house and more annoyed with Damon and me.

I'm eight when Moms comes home from work and heats up Swanson's turkey-and-stuffing dinners. Damon and Marc and I eat on TV trays watching *The Three Stooges*. She changed from her nurse's uniform to a red wild-patterned dress and sits at the kitchenette table. Her legs are crossed, one leg swinging. She pulls off the band that keeps her hair back for work, puts it on her wrist, and combs slender fingers through her hair as she drinks her wine. Her being nice raises my suspicion. Then, sure enough, the beat of her leg quickens. "You kids watch TV. I'll be back later," she says. She starts looking for her keys. I go into our bedroom.

Find your keys and leave, I think. *Find them soon*.

Drawers bang in her dresser and end tables. She checks the bathroom. The bathroom door slams shut. Not in there.

Plates on the kitchen counter clatter. She rifles through my schoolbooks and papers, in between the cushions on the sofa. *The pow pow is coming*. My backpack lands with a plop against the living room wall. I try to concentrate on *The Three Stooges*.

"This place is such a fuckin' mess. No wonder I can't find nothing. Why don't you kids clean this shit up?" As she rants and paces and wildly searches, she heightens and deepens her rage. She spatters my face and head with slaps. I hear her hit or kick Damon, who's in the living room. He yelps and starts crying. "It's you fuckin' kids why I can't keep no man. It's you fuckin' kids," she yells over and over. Damon comes in the bedroom and sits next to me.

Then she slams our bedroom door.

I lie on my side on the bed.

Damon and I listen to her crash through the house. Then she comes in our room. Her hands are on her hips, her mouth clenched in such a tight line her lips vanish. Her eyes are wide and eyebrows lifted. *No one would think she's beautiful if they saw her now.*

"This room is a pit, a fuckin' pit." She shakes her head from side to side, narrows her eyes, and screams, "I tell you and tell you. And you don't do nothing but sit on your asses."

I examine the indentation on the wall shaped when she threw a bat. I see the imprint of its flight on the dry wall. The ridge in the butt end made a circle, and then, the bat hit the wall so a streak zooms to the right.

She picks up my baseball trophy from a Little League game and throws it on the floor. "I've had it. That's why I can't keep no man because of you goddamn kids." She sweeps our dresser with her arm. Damon's baseball trophy, my pop pistol, Damon's BB revolver, a baseball fly off our dresser, scatter on the floor. "Look at that mess."

She grabs a switch and starts whupping us. First Damon and then me. "That's why I can't keep no goddamn man. Because of you fucking kids." She shrieks with each stroke. The baseball rolls across the carpet, halts when it hits my tennis shoe. *It'll be over soon.*

Moms leaves the room.

She's done.

But she returns with rags in her hand. "I've had it," she says. Her cheeks are red and her hair crawls like snakes trying to escape her scalp.

She ties a rag over my eyes, ties it so tightly that I see red squiggles on the backs of my lids, ties it so fast, she catches my hair. The smell of her musk twists my stomach.

I try to loosen the rag, but she whacks my fingers with the switch. "Don't you take that rag off, hear me?"

Her coat pocket rustles and keys jingle. She grabs me by the shoulders and squashes me into the backseat of a car. I can't see a thing as the rag presses my eyes. The car starts, jerks forward, then smoothes into motion. "That's why I can't keep no man. It's you fuckin' kids."

In the backseat, in all that darkness, I bob and shift in the jerking car, tossed with the sudden stops and lurches. The rag around my head is wet from tears and snot.

"It's you goddamn kids."

The car stops. "Get out of my car, get out."

I stumble out, crying. *She's trying to frighten me. This is one of her schemes to terrify me into being good. To keeping the house neater.* I reach out in the darkness, still blinded by the rag, I reach out to touch the door handle, to open the car, to get back in with her, to tell her the plan worked, I'll be good, but she squeals away.

I lurch as I pull off the blindfold, my eyes burning from my tears. It's dark. I don't know where I am. My hair pulls as I remove the rag. I see a house with a porch light on, and a tree, and a sloping lawn. I walk to the tree and sit in its shadows, my tears blurring my vision, my snot wetting my pajama top. I'm all alone and I don't know where I am or what to do. *I hate her.*

I rub my arms. It begins to rain; the rain makes slivers of silver in the streetlight. *You can make it.* Then I bend into a ball, huddle on the prickly grass, and cry. *You can make it.*

What did I do to deserve this? Don't think that. Can't feel sorry for yourself, or you're lost. The tree shelters me from the rain, only a few drops find their way to my pajama tops, but still the wetness chills. I wipe my nose. I try to stop crying, try to stop feeling sorry and alone.

Suddenly, Damon is sitting next to me. I didn't even know he was in the car. We sit under the tree but don't say anything. The earth smells fresh, rich. *You can make it.* I curl myself into a fist, a tight fist all wound around myself. My arms hold my legs, my head tucks into my torso. I clench my muscles. *See. You can make it. I'm a fist. Stay strong.*

A woman comes out of the house and sees two scrawny boys wearing pajamas with blue rags and wet faces under her tree. Damon tells her what happened.

"Oh, my God. She put blue beanies over your face and dropped you off in a Blood neighborhood."

The woman takes us into her house and calls our maternal grandmother, Louise, who comes for us. After that we live with her in South Central. Some weekends we visit Moms in Ladera Heights, and some weekends we visit Pops in Venice. But mostly, we're with Grandma Louise, and her home on Second Avenue is at the heart of Harlem Crips, Rollin' Thirties territory, the second-largest gang territory in South Central.

Grandma Louise has already raised six children, three boys and three girls. The eldest, Albert, is an attorney who works with Johnny Cochran. Deedee, Ralph, and Robert are professional singers. Audrey is an artist and is married to Uncle Van, the cop who patrols South Central. My mom has been a model and now works as a LPN.

Louise is Creole from Shreveport, Louisiana. My grandfather was originally from D.C. After they divorced, he opened the first Black barbershop in Los Angeles, married Lovey, who owned Fatburgers hamburgers. When Damon and I move in with Louise, she's alone except occasionally for Ralph when he's between jobs. Usually, he's on the road singing.

Louise's house is white with green trim and black iron bars striping the windows, the door. Under the bars, thinner frilly white metal twirls. Two sets of bars. My mother's windows don't have bars, just blinds and curtains. Louise's house is surrounded by shrubs, some in pots with flowers like fire. When I see Louise's bars on the windows and doors, the barrier of her shrubs, I think, I'm safe.

I begin a new school, but remain in the same Little League baseball. When I come home that first day, Louise adds spices to a pot of gumbo with hot links. She cooks it. Not the maid. Not Swanson's. After dinner, we play in the living room. Her eyes are on us. I turn and she smiles from the plastic-covered sofa. "Look at them. There's my sweet, handsome grandsons," she muses and kisses the top of my head. That night, as I go to bed, she's on her knees praying. A light gleams down on a pot of African violets. Louise picks up her Bible and opens it to a page marked by gold ribbon.

That Saturday, she buys us new suits and on Sunday we go to church and she enrolls us in Sunday school.

A month later, driving home from MacDonald Aircraft plant where she's an assembly-line worker in the electrical division, she catches me shooting dice with the older boys. "Colton." Her voice is stern. Stoned from marijuana and my head buzzing from beer, I race home, arriving just as she pulls her brown Toyota Hatchback into her driveway. *Now the whuppin'll start, the yellin', screamin', throwing clocks and shit at me, beating me with a bat, breakin' windows, puttin' holes in the wall. It'll start.* I enter the house, my muscles tightened so the whacks won't hurt as badly.

Instead, she says, "Come with Grandma."

We go into her bedroom and both of us get on our knees. I want to be the Colton she wants, comforted by the predictable rhythm of the days. If I act like her, maybe I'll be okay. I press my palms together just like she presses hers. She bows her head till her chin touches her chest. Her warmth escapes from her body to mine. Beside me her pot of flowers bloom velvet purple. "Our father, who art in heaven . . ." We say the prayer together. When we finish it the first time, she stands and says, "You say that prayer three more times and don't let me catch you playin' dice with those boys no more."

But I can't stay away from the fun on streets. And the truth is, no matter how good Grandma Louise is, no matter how much I try, no matter how much I want safety, there's something between us, something I can't quite name, which prevents me from feeling the love a mother gives her son, and a son should give a mother. Maybe, because no matter how much I want her to be my mother and no matter how much she may want me to be her son, she's not. Moms keeps licking around threatening to make us move back with her.

In the fall, the fall I'm nine, I'm playing football on the street with some of the boys and go back for a pass, catch the ball, and streak for the goal with Dimitri right behind me. "That's six for us," I yell as I reach the goal the same time Dimitri tags me.

"Bullshit. You were five feet from the marker when I got you," he spits.

"I'm past the trees." I point at the two palm trees that span our imaginary boundary.

"I got you here," He points to his feet. "So shut up, punk ass. You ain't shit!"

I can't let his insult ride. I gotta crush all threats. When I was six, at my father's house in Venice, a kid rammed me off my swing. I lay on the ground gasping for air, then started screaming. Pops heard me, grabbed me under my arms, pulled me till I faced him. "You gotta stand up for yourself. Don't you ever let a man disrespect you." He wagged his finger at me. "You fight till you knock him out or he gives."

I wiped away my tears, staring at my tennis shoe to avoid his strict glare.

"Look at me."

I raised my chin.

"Now go over there and fight or you'll have to deal with me!" Pops's arms were thicker than my body. I didn't want to deal with him. I fought the guy and beat him up. My swing was stronger than I looked.

"He'll never mess with you again, Cokey, and he'll think twice 'bout bullying another boy." Pops ruffled my hair. "I'm proud of you, son."

This was the beginning of using violence against those who disrespect me, my family, friends, or space. So when Dimitri starts talking crazy, I know what I have to do.

After I smash Dimitri, he gets his big brother.

Around the corner Smiley strolls, a dark blue flag hanging from his shirt pocket, pants slung low on his hips, blue shoelaces, striding slow, one shoulder low, stroll-roll, all Cripped down. I've noticed him gliding around the 'hood, one hand swinging slightly behind his back as though nothing and no one can hurt him. That slow. That careless. Studying how he walks, I've admired the exploded muscles on his shoulders and upper arms, his forearms and hands covered with scars. He's a brown-skinned roughneck. As he comes toward us, the other boys back up and fall silent, staring at him and waiting. The sun is behind him, just beginning to set, so his face looks dark.

Smiley measures me and asks, "How old are you, cuz?"

My chest is bony, my arms skinny. "Nine."

"Did you jump my brother?"

I don't lie. I meet his gaze and tell him.

He turns to Dimitri, "He's more 'en four years younger 'en me, and two years younger than you, and you want me to beat him up?" He shakes his head.

And then he smiles and it's as if the light, the sun behind him, fills me, fills each and every one of us standing there before him. His smile melts his tough face and with just a grin, white teeth gleaming, he's transformed. Then, he turns toward Dimitri. "You disrespect this cuz and then he whupped you' ass, that's what you get. If you wanna fight, you fight him back, don't come around here to try to get me." Smiley stroll-rolls back around the corner, a flag hanging like a bright arrow to his knees.

And that's how I meet Smiley. I don't know he's going to change my life forever.

The next day, I see him rollin' down the street and he picks me up in his blue Chevy; we shoot dice together, and then I go to his house.

Smiley and his family live in a house painted the color of the sky with white trim. The bushes in front of his house are trimmed like blown-up lollipops on sticks. The bars on his windows are painted white to match the trim. His mother, Curly, sets the table, sees me, says, "One more, uh?" and arranges my place. There are six kids, four boys and two girls. His dad comes home from work, hangs up his cap, sits down, and reads the newspaper while Curly tosses pork chops in a paper bag of seasoned flour. His father has thick shoulders, neck, and arms from his boxing days. When dinner is ready, we assemble around the table, me between Smiley and his sister, Gina, and pass the greens, corn bread, and chops.

Everyone lives in the same house, eats at the same table. With a father. Everyone functions as a human being. After that Smiley and I start hanging together. Some days, I take a shower there. Some nights I sleep there. They treat me like a son.

After school, we play football, roll around in a stolen car, listen to sounds, and smoke marijuana. Louise's gentleness doesn't cut through the fact that I'm a tough kid, tough from my mother's beatings and the results of my own temper. But Smiley has the heart of a lion. "You're like me," he says. "Just like me. Both of us middle sons. We think the same way, want the same things. You're not as aggressive or smart, but you're younger." He pops me upside the head, gentle like. "Don't worry. I'ma toughen you up, though. Make you hardcore."

I'm ten that spring and am admitted into the majors for Little League, determined to seal my chances of making the all-star team. Sure enough, the Ladera team makes the playoffs. The day is hot, not a cloud in the sky, peaceful and spooky quiet. But I'm on edge. The day before, Smiley asked, "What ya' doin' tomorrow night, cuz?"

"I'll be at Moms's after my game."

"I want you to claim the set. I got love for you like a brother, cuz."

"Cool." Working at being nonchalant, I shrugged one shoulder like he did. But think, *I belong somewhere.*

"Way I figure is, you got the heart to be a down 'Rip."

"Tomorrow night, cuz."

I'm in my uniform and ready for the game. Coach Montgomery pats my back, leans to my ear, and whispers. "I'm counting on you. So's the team. You can do it. You're Dick Simpson's son."

He says that before every big game so I expect it, but this time I flinch. *Is my skill a simple reflection of my father's? Do the hours I spend practicing my swing and catching fast balls count for nothing? Well, by tonight, I'll be a Crip. Different from Pops.*

The ballpark is surrounded by chain-link fence. Houses border the park. Scarce palms and poles from the tall fence lend spiky shade. The stands are filled. Moms and Grandma Louise are there. It's the bottom of the ninth, there are two men on base, and my team—the Yankees—is losing by two runs. The count is 0 and 2, and, Greg, the pitcher, is one of the best in the league. He's a good enough friend and he knows I have a habit of trying to knock curves over the fence as opposed to making contact with the ball and placing it in the field.

As I walk to the plate, I see my father leaning against the fence as if it waited for him. He fits so perfectly, so inevitably.

I didn't know he was here. I swing the bat, practicing my swing.

Pops nods at me and slants a smile. "Be strong, Colton. Be strong and stay focused." He doesn't move from his position on the fence. Then he pulls his baseball cap lower on his forehead, slides his palm in his pocket, and acquiesces to watching. The fence submits to holding him.

Ten years before he'd been in a similar situation at Dodger Stadium while he was a rookie star playing for the California Angels. He'd gotten behind the count 0 and 2, but hit a solo shot over the right-field wall.

I tighten my grip on the aluminum bat and hear Coach Montgomery's words. *Dick Simpson's son.* I hear my father's voice, too. *Stay focused. Be strong.* I inhale. And then Greg winds up and pushes his head back, gazes hard at me as though he knows all about who I am and sees right through my cool. He's going to pitch me a curved ball. I swing the bat to loosen up my shoulders and appear fierce.

Focus. Stay strong.

The ball is off. It spins in slow motion as it enters my space. I lean toward it. When it connects with the ball, the bat vibrates through my hands, arms, shoulders. I nail it for a three-shot blast over the right-field fence that wins the game.

As I trot to the bench, Pops nods. He takes off his cap and wipes his forehead with the back of his hand. The coach says, "What'd I tell you. Simpson's son." He hits his hand as though he's wearing a mitt. "Let's go eat some pizza at Shakey's."

I want to be more than Dick Simpson's son. I don't even live with him. He doesn't protect me. He can't save me from anything.

Moms brings me to her house and enters the bathroom. I tear off my uniform and cleats. One leg is in my jeans.

"Cokey, don't you leave this goddamn house without cleaning up your funky bedroom."

I pull my pants up, revolve my feet into tennis shoes.

"And make sure you take out the trash, help Damon with dishes . . ." her words follow as I dash out of the house, jump on my BMX Bicycle, peddle to Thirty-ninth, and bunny-hop the bike onto the sidewalk.

As soon as he sees me, Smiley extends his hard hand. "Hey, whassup, cuz?" and spreads his smile. I'm home.

We walk to the alley. The alley is as long as a football field, flanked on one side by telephone poles like rifles pointed to the night sky. Plastic garbage bags, one topped with wire hangers, border the other side. Fences of iron spears guard brief backyards. A mattress sags against a graffitied wall tagged with CRIPS in blue, outlined in black. Several Crips shoot hostile stares, trying to figure out who I am and what I'm doing on their turf with Smiley, one of the Harlem Crips's most elite soldiers, known for hustling and fighting.

The hair on the back of my neck rises. *Stay focused.* With a wide-grin, I try to appear indifferent. I nod to T. J. who is sixteen, six feet tall and studies martial arts. The week before, T. J. stole a blue '70 Chevy and took Smiley and me for a ride down Rodeo Drive.

"Here you go, cuz," T. J. passes me a joint. Smoke expands in my lungs.

Big T, who I've seen around the 'hood and lifts over three hundred pounds at age fifteen, glances at me sidelong and then frowns. He's light skinned, about my complexion, tall, with a thick Afro. His eyes, the same color as his skin, give him a startling appearance, especially since his brows are thick. It's almost as though he can't see anything, or can see everything. He's second in command and has a lot of say-so, which means he could have someone hurt. "What's yo' name, cuz?" Big T asks.

"Colton."

"You the same Colton that knocked out that fool Be-Bop from Black P. Stone?" Black P. Stone is a Blood gang and the Crips number-one enemy.

I relax a little. I knew word had spread, but didn't know it held any weight with the Crips. "Yeah."

Big T gives me a slow once-over and shakes his head. "Shit."

He's trying to figure out how skinny me had knocked out Be-Bop, one of the Black P. Stone's elite fighters.

"What's up, homie? I'm Big Mel." Mel is dark and known for stealing cars. He's too overweight and slow to be a fighter, but his outgoing, easy personality wins respect. "You down, uh?" He passes Smiley a brown bag.

"Man, cuz might be small, but he's got heart. Me and Smiley want him to claim the set," T. J. says.

"Yeah. With the right guidance, he could be a down 'Rip." Smiley bolsters and takes a long swig, then passes it to me. His genuine grin makes me think this is easy. I suck on the bottle and pass it to Big T, who doesn't drink, but gives it back to Big Mel.

"Crippin' ain't easy," Smiley says, "You gotta stay down and represent to the fullest. You know what this means, cuz?"

I don't get to answer because Big T interrupts. "Means every member gotta fight, stab, shoot, and whatever it takes to destroy the enemy. We're at war with the Bloods. They try to kill us. So we kill them first. It's them or us." Big T rocks back on his heels staring down the alley. "Either you with it, or you get got. And whatever you do, you can't be a buster."

"Buster?" I ask.

"Coward. Gotta stay hard and fight," T. J. says.

"You wit' it?" Big T asks, but he doesn't look at me.

"I'm down," I tell them, waiting for the discussion of my worthiness and loyalty to begin.

"When I say run, run down the alley and don't stop," Smiley orders.

I take a quick glance down the alley. Only a dim light lends a gloomy vagueness. The telephone poles have disappeared into the sky. The iron bars are a striped shield. *What kinda shit is this?* Then I turn to the group. Terry is loading guns.

"Run," Smiley orders.

I take off fast. There's no streetlight. I can't see. *Stay in the middle. Otherwise, I'll crash into fences, the trash, or the poles.*

My legs thrust. *Don't stop, Smiley said.* I gasp for air.

Boom.

What's that? Car backfiring. I jerk from the sound.

Boom.

Gunshots. They're shooting at me. Fuck. In spite of the night's heat and my sweat, I'm cold. *I could die. Right here and now. No. Can't be a buster. Be hard. Run. Just run.*

My heart hammers in my chest, my ears. My legs hit the cement as fast as they can, faster than my heart thumps. Another shot slaps behind me. My arms pump. *Keep running. Stay strong. Focus. Stay in the middle. Run faster. I can do this. I can.*

A clap and then sparks fly from a hit electrical wire. Darkness is thick.

Am I halfway through? What if they hit me?

Don't think that. Don't be a buster.

I can't get enough air.

A bullet hits a wall.

I pant. Darkness diminishes. Almost at the end. It's quiet except for my gasping, my heart. *There, a car. I'm almost there, at the street, on the other side.* I stop, lean my palms on my knees to grab some air. *I made it.*

Smiley and T. J. appear out of nowhere. Smiley punches me in the face, knocks me to the ground. Dizzy, I start swinging wildly. Big T rounds the corner. Three on one. My swing connects with a torso. Then T. J. lands five flush punches on my chest and I'm on the pavement struggling for equilibrium. Kicked in the stomach, the wind is knocked out of me. I gasp and force my eyes to center.

"Squab for yours, cuz," someone says. I'm snatched by the collar, forced to stand. A solid kick to the chest whips my head back.

The world swims as I receive another kick and a strike. Hard spitting-punches come from all angles. I'm tossed by blows like a speed-punching bag. They have the control. Stars swim before my eyes again.

Stay strong and focus.

Now I know. Courting means to be physically "jumped in." It's up to me to prove my courage.

Lashing out through my anger with all my strength, I counter-punch Big T and land my swing in his chest. His mouth opens and closes like a fish. He's lost his air. Assured of my power, I swing at anyone within arm's reach.

Outsized and overpowered, I can't secure consciousness for

long. But I can convince them of my bravery, my worthiness of being a soldier.

As if there is an invisible signal, the blows stop. Instantly, I regain consciousness. My nose bleeds. My face and chest throb. Blood pounds in my neck. My arms and legs are cold. A headache turns my stomach. Standing again, I throw a flurry of punches.

"That's enough," Smiley commands.

I stop swinging. The world stops spinning. For a second we're quiet in the pitch night.

Then Smiley's arms are hard and warm around me. "You in, cuz. One of us, Li'l Cee," he says. I am dwarfed and sheltered by Big T's massive chest, arms, height as he embraces me. T. J. hugs me and pats me on the back. "You alright, li'l homie?" Big Mel asks.

Big T is beneath the car retrieving weapons, two .38 specials and a 12-gauge shotgun with a sawed-off barrel and pistol-grip handle.

"Here, Cee." Smiley hands me one of the .38s.

"Pass these." Terry furnishes Big T a number of joints and a can of Old English beer. I light a joint and pass the rest to Big Mel.

"Check this out." Smiley stands a little separate from the rest of us. A porch light goes on. His face glistens with sweat so his skin looks like molten bronze. "We're gonna blast some Inglewood faggots tonight." He spits out "faggot" to emphasize his disrespect for the Blood opposition.

"'Right." My heart's tattoo is slower, but still fast. My head hurts.

"Them fools blasted on Nelsie's car yesterday," Smiley continues, sucks on his joint, a scar like a crescent moon graces his knuckle. "And we gonna serve they ass for that shit. We gonna let them clowns know there ain't no busters from over this way."

Nelsie is a Crip from the Rollin' Sixties set and reputable as a ghetto celebrity. I heard about the drive-by through the school grapevine.

"We goin' chop them fools down." Smiley says.

We tie royal blue bandanas around our faces like bank robbers from the Old West.

Smiley gives us our instructions. "All of us gotta have aliases in case we get busted. Mine is Johnny Carson."

"I'm Raymond," T. J. says.

"Colton?" Smiley asks. "What's your name?"

I reply with Damon's birth name.

"If we get caught, none of us know each other," Smiley orders. We nod our heads just as Vic, with a blue bandana tied around his head, pulls up in a white ice-cream truck. Vic's father owns Spike's Liquor. During the day, Vic drives the truck around the 'hood, playing the silly *do to do, do to do do to doddle do to do* Mr. Softee jingle and selling drumsticks, popsicles, and creamsicles from the window. Pictures of drumsticks chunked with nuts and an orange creamsicle are on the side. ONLY TEN CENTS in black letters blurts across a red Popsicle. He's turned the song off so the van travels like a phantom of itself.

"Let's roll." Smiley stuffs his .38 special in his waistband. My barrel is cold against my stomach as I jump in the back of the van.

The truck drives. My heart resumes pounding. My hands tremble. The world spins. We're heading for trouble. I take another drag on the joint. We're going to shoot somebody. I think about my orders from Smiley. My heart hammers quicker than my home run earlier in the day. The game is far away. I was another person then. *There's no turning back. I'm in this.*

I can do it. If they can do it, I can do it. This spins over and over as I take another long drag on the joint, suck on the beer to wet my dry mouth. *I can do it. I can do anything with Smiley.*

We ride around the Blood 'hood. I can't see anything in the back of the truck sitting on one of the freezers, but I know where we're going and our prey.

"There they go," Smiley whispers. We look out of the window at Bay, one of the Inglewood Bloods, pumping gas into a burgundy car while two Bloods sit in the front seat. "Look. Them fools don't even see us comin', cuz. They sleepin'," Smiley says.

Bay is sixteen or seventeen, a brown-skinned medium-built cat with long hair. He's wearing red.

We pull around the side of the gas station. Smiley and I get out of the truck. "We're gonna creep up behind the gas pumps so they can't see us, and then jump in front of their car and bust." He checks my weapon to make sure it's fully loaded and ready. "Got it?"

"Yeah."

We duck down like we're using a pump.

This is my chance to prove myself.

We sneak up on them according to plan until we're five feet from the Buick.

If Smiley can do it, I can.

A piece of gravel crunches, Bay turns, and sees us. His eyebrows lift and his eyes widen. He pulls out his weapon, aims for Smiley, but it fails and Bay takes off running.

I jump from behind the gas pump and fire several shots.

The shots miss.

Smiley jumps on the hood of the Bloods' Buick and fires at the men in the front seat. The windshield fractures.

I leap to the hood, face the interior. I take a deep breath, hold the gun with both hands. And fire. It's easy. Like playing with Damon. Like shooting bottles off the fence.

Then one of the men, the one behind the wheel, grabs his chest and moans, "Ah. Ah." Red spreads over his chest.

I fire two more shots.

The other Blood grabs his shoulder. "Oooooh." My ears ring with the blast. The Bloods' bodies react to the puncturing bullets. Everything is slow. People run every which way and shriek, "Help. Help. Oh my God." But they move in slow motion and their screams echo as if underwater.

Smiley leaps from the car hood and chases Bay, who makes a dash from behind a parked car toward a liquor store.

I keep firing. Burnt powder fills the air. My ears echo with the shots, with the screams. The men in the car twitch and groan.

Smiley runs Bay down and beats him in the head with the butt of the pistol. Bay falls to the ground. "That's for Nelsie, punk," Smiley shouts.

Click. Click. My .38 is out of ammunition.

Now, the bodies in the car are quiet. They don't moan. The spreading of their blood, fractured like a kaleidoscope by the diamonds of the windshield, is the only action.

We run down the alley and Vic speeds up the ice-cream van to meet us. My heart pounds in my neck, my arms and legs are cold. But I am exhilarated.

I can do anything. Adrenaline and the intensity of the battle amp me up.

We drive back to Thirty-ninth Street and the alley where I was initiated.

"Cee handled his business," Smiley takes a gulp of Hennessy and passes me the bottle.

Big T and Big Mel have returned from their mission. Big T glances at me, sidelong, and draws on a joint, hands it to Smiley. "Yeah. Right," he snorts.

He doesn't believe in my ability.

"I told y'all. Colton is down." T. J. looks directly at Big T.

Smiley hands me the joint. "Li'l Cee is from the set now. Cuz's part of us." His eyes meet each of the men, stopping at Big T's. He's used to Smiley's admiration and love.

I draw on Smiley's joint though I have my own. We pass them anyway; we're homeboys.

T.J. gives me a ten-dollar bag of marijuana; Big Mel gives me a commemorative L.A. Dodger bat and another hug with his big belly. Big T gives me a blue bandana.

"It's yours now." Smiley nods at the .38, back in my waistband. "Don't get caught with that. It has shootin's on it. Now you from the set you gotta be packin' 'cause muthafuckas don't like us." I'm part of the gang, and inherit the war and the killing.

I fold the bandana and stuff it in my pocket.

"Bangin' is for real. It's a full-time job." Smiley continues.

"You'll be claiming twenty-four-seven and havin' no love for the other side. Understand, Li'l Cee?"

Patting the blue flag, I say, "I know what's up. I won't get caught with the gun." And I never do.

From that point on, Smiley is my "road dog"—a running buddy, best friend, someone I'll do anything for, including kill. He's my mentor.

Marijuana and alcohol buzz in my head. Adrenaline and anxiety abandon me to exhaustion. I go home to Grandma Louise's and am asleep as soon as I pull up the covers.

When I wake the next morning, I'm Colton again as if last night never happened. I'm Grandma Louise's church-going grandson. My mind is clear. I brush my teeth and eat a bowl of Cheerios. The TV plays *Kimba* in the next room.

I drag the garbage out to the curb. A bird sings. I hear the rhythm of a basketball dribbled a few doors away. Then Vic's ice-cream truck sings the Mr. Softee melody, *Do to do, do to do do to doddle do to do*. The stupid song reminds me. Men moan and clutch bullet-torn flesh. Hole-ridden bodies slump behind the dash of the red Buick. My stomach turns. I clench my eyes to obliterate the splashing images, but they play behind my lids. I can't escape.

I'm going to vomit.

Blood creeps over a white shirt.

I walk toward the back door. I never thought I'd be able to shoot somebody. This isn't the person I thought I was. It's not how I imagine myself.

The red flowering bushes have barbs. The garbage cans scrape against the cement so chills crawl up my spine. I enter the house and pour myself a glass of water.

How am I going to get rid of what I've done?

The water is clear, empty. I swallow all of it without stopping for air.

But nothing changes. *Who am I?*

I can't take back what I've done. I have fallen into an abyss of terror and fear for myself. It's not forgivable.

I'll never be able to shoot someone again.

But I'm here now. Located in this void forever.

The song from the ice-cream truck fades. I crawl back in bed. Smiley's warm laughter from the night before fills my head. The remembrance of my acceptance embrace soaks me in safety and love.

I can't tell anyone of this feeling of guilt. To do so will shame me.

I'm part of the Crip army. A comrade.

I am Li'l Cee. I am ten.

TWO

Gangbanger

"Streets like the one she lived on were no accident. They were the North's lynch mobs."
—Ann Petry, *The Street* (1946)

THE FEELING OF GUILT PASSES. IT'S LIKE BEING A VIRGIN.
The first time, you're swept with emotions, but the next time you know how to prevent guilt and shame from overwhelming you. After awhile, the conflict is not there and the behavior becomes second nature. My guilt remains something to be brushed away. After all, somebody is out to get me. Somebody violated the code on the streets. I'm a Crip. You're a Blood. I see you. I'm going to kill you. You see me; you're going to kill me. I'm not ready to die, so I'm going to kill you first. It's all business.

There it is. War.

That summer, Louise decides to bus me to the predominately White Orville Wright Junior High School in Westchester.

"Can't I go to Audubon or Folshay? I want to stay in the 'hood."

"No. No, you ain't growin' up to be no damn thug." Louise pulls the vacuum from the closet. "You and Damon are both going." She turns on the machine and there's no use arguing.

Plagued by asthma, Damon can't run or play without stopping to use his inhaler. I'm his little brother, but I take care of him. While riding the bus home from school, two White boys give us the finger as they peddle flashy bikes away from campus. The next day, I arrive thirty minutes early. Black Ant, who's my age, dark skinned, huskier than me and bitter about his South Central L.A. broken home, accompanies me. Black Ant and I locate the two White boys and run them down.

I grab one with sandy hair and an AC/DC tee shirt. "This is for giving me the finger." I hit his nose, shoving him to the ground.

His face is red. His lips are stretched as though he's about to say "nigger."

As I hurl my punches, Pete screams, *I'll kill you, you fucking nigger.*

I straddle him, whipping his head back and forth with my fists until he's unconscious.

Pete's belt whirls over my head, the buckle rips my knee.

I shake the boy awake and beat him more, venting the pent-up resentment and racial rage of my short life.

The next morning, my hands are swollen the size of cantaloupes. "Damn."

Damon sees me trying to flex my fingers, moving my hands as though they're not part of me. "What happened?"

I give him the details of the beating, leaving out how the boy turned into Pete under my fists.

"You crazy, Colton! Loco." I know *loco* means "crazy" in Spanish.

The name sticks and is shortened to Loc and added to Li'l Cee. Li'l Cee Loc becomes my gang name, a symbol of my transgressions. I have to live up to it.

One afternoon, Black Ant and I drive my motorcycle from the repair shop. As I zoom past Seventh Avenue on Rodeo Road, I spot T-Bone from the Black P. Stone Bloods. Before I can react,

T-Bone throws a brick at me. I jerk from the impact, lose control of the cycle, and it rams into a parked car. The collision sends me flying to land halfway down the block on my back in the middle of the street. I can't stand. *T-Bone caught me slippin'*, I think as bright flashes burst before my eyes and then fizzle to blackness. *I can't ever let my guard down.*

Black Ant grabs the .38 special from my waistband and bolts after T-Bone.

I wake and I try to rise, but pain streams through my arm. I must have broken it. I should get off the street, but dizziness prohibits me, then blackness returns.

Black Ant shakes me. "Damn, Cee. You alright, homie?"

"You get him?"

"Chased him to Tenth and planted two slugs in his chest."

"Call my grandmother." My voice is weak, even to my ears.

I have a concussion, a sprained arm and knee, and abrasions to my arms, shoulder, and back. T-Bone manages to survive the two bullets and I hear he's looking for Li'l Cee Loc and Black Ant. I have been "served" by the enemy. Only a fool waits for the enemy to find him. When two soldiers gun for each other, the one who's quicker on the draw survives. This much I know.

With my arm in a sling and my knee in a brace, Black Ant takes me to the jungles—Blood territory. Our 'hood is bordered by palms. Palms march down each side of our street. They're tidy trees, like soldiers standing at attention, the fronds well away from houses and street action. In the jungles, leaves block vision and rustle like snakes' rattles with each breeze. On our moped, we search block after block for T-Bone. But can't find him.

We spot a group of Bloods at Sherm Alley. Pay Dog and Li'l Ru have shot a Crip's house a few days before. Li'l Ru has a scar that bubbles from his forehead, across his left eye, and into his cheek. The Bloods huddle in the mouth of the alley, laughing and passing a joint.

My heart quickens as adrenaline amps me up. "Whassup, Blood?" I ask Pay Dog.

He's seventeen. A red bandana is tied across his head. He hands his joint to Li'l Ru and says, "Where you from?"

My strategy to put the opposition at ease worked. Now they're vulnerable. I pull the .38 special, shade it with my left hand. "Get a little closer," I murmur to Black Ant.

He feeds the moped some gas and it lurches.

One of Pay Dog's hands moves toward his waistband.

"Fool. This is what's up!"

Boom.

And we drive away before Pay Dog hits the ground. I've defended myself.

I'm captured a week later, charged with conspiracy to commit murder and taken to juvenile hall. No witnesses appear for my court appearance and the case is dismissed. Gang members are reluctant to testify against the enemy because we want to judge our own fates, control our own justice. We don't snitch because snitches end up in body bags. This is our resistance to America's justice system; gang members settle their own battles.

I'm released into the custody of Louise, who takes me home. "Boy, you hangin' out with those damn hoodlums on the corner and now you acting just like 'em. I told you. I warned you."

I stand quietly in front of her.

"I see those blue bandanas and those shoes like potato sacks. I hear you running in and out of the house all times of night." When she shakes her head, her soft curls jiggle. She wears a navy dress and oxford shoes. Her light-brown skin is darkened by annoyance and her features look exhausted and blurred instead of gentle. "Don't think you're foolin' me. You keep those thugs outa your life and away from here."

At home, I am Colton. I attend school and clean the house. I say *please* and *thank you*. I go to church on Sunday and observe the minister pass plate after plate for money. One Sunday I count the plates that are passed. Five. Seems church is more about money than God. But at home, God sometimes seems present in Louise's voice repeating the soothing prayers, in the light that shines in the windows, in the food that she buys and cooks and blesses each night, in the iridescent violets. I am Louise's grandson.

I keep Smiley, Black Ant, and the set away from her house. But on the streets, Li'l Cee Loc gathers fame with fist and gun.

I start smoking cigarettes because they add to my gangster appeal, my style, my look. Every Crip has a hustle; everyone needs money to wage war. The hustle is circumscribed by resources. I don't have a car so jobs are limited to what I can do on foot. I sell marijuana in my White school and steal. I start out small—grabbing purses from people leaving the bank. But just like everything else in America, you start small, work hard, and business expands. You invest your capital so your business grows. If you stay focused and are smart, you move up the ladder. Just like my father told me.

Everyone has a responsibility to represent the Crips and fight the war. I hit the Bloods by doing walk-ups—spot a Blood, walk up to him, and bust. I ignite from new recruit to dedicated soldier, busy following Smiley's orders to push the enemy violently away. Smiley understands my hunger for ghetto celebrity status. I'm his rider. Riders are the soldiers—fighting, stabbing, shooting. All gangbangers are gangsters, but not all gang members are riders. There are three things I need: reputation, power, and respect. I'm geared to accomplishing each feat and nothing can stop me.

In the winter of 1979, Smiley and I get a tip about a truckload of liquor at Ralph's Market. We go see *Apocalypse Now* and, when we leave the theater, it's pouring and cold. A newspaper headline tells us Carter has pardoned Patty Hearst and some cat named Khoumani is head of Iran. Seems like it has nothing to do with me. I grab the paper to use as shelter on the way to our car. We stop at Big Mel's to pick up the truck he obtained.

We transfer boxes of Olde English 800 from the delivery van to the truck. Our clothes are wet by the time the boxes are loaded. I'm handing the last of the cases to Smiley, shivering slightly.

"Now. For the fun." He rubs his palms together in anticipation. We've already decided how we'll invest the money.

Sirens scream. Lights whirl on top of the black-and-white police car zooming through the dark rain. Slammed car doors punctuate the vicious sirens. Police walk toward us with drawn guns.

"Hold it right there or I'll shoot," a burly White cop growls.

I jump from the truck and take off running. Smiley bolts in the opposite direction. We're both caught and Smiley, eighteen, posts his bail. I'm in juvenile hall before my trial, during which I plead guilty and am sentenced to six months in camp.

Camp is just a different battlefield, a new place to further my reputation of danger and bring me a sense of security. Kids are forced to sleep next to people they've chased, fought, stabbed, shot. It's as if Nazis, the Black Panther Party, and the Jewish Defense League live under the same cramped roof, day after day, night after night. Gang fights continue. Two bunks from me is a Blood who's part of the Black P. Stones—T-Bone and Pay Dog's set. For six months, we're at each other's throats. When I leave the camp, I'm ten pounds heavier, three inches taller. My fighting skills are honed.

I'm released back to my 'hood to discover doing time solidified my reputation by proving I'm rugged and raw. While I was gone, the war between us and the Black P. Stone Bloods reached fever pitch. One of their generals was killed by a Crip rider during a party. In retaliation, our homeboy, Amp, was caught slippin' at Audubon High School and stabbed in the chest. The war is fought inside the school as well as on the street. Two of our set saw the assailant run away wearing red pants and shirt and an all-red kufi.

Smiley calls a meeting of the Harlem Crips and the Rollin' Sixties Crips.

The next day, I'm reported for selling marijuana on campus. The dean of students removes me from class, escorts me to the principal's office. I'm searched, pot is discovered, and I'm expelled. Louise enrolls me in Folshay. Two days later, I jump the fence, meet up with Big Mel, drink liquor, and smoke weed until school lets out. Louise enrolls me in Audubon, which is filled with Crips. I attend for week and that's the end of my school career. I'm in eighth grade.

Meanwhile, in retaliation for Amp's stabbing, a new recruit from Black P. Stone is ambushed on Crenshaw Boulevard and Santa Barbara, shot six times and killed by the Crips Rollin' Sixties. The Bloods stab and beat a Crip at Flipper's Skating Rink. This is the second homie to be stabbed in a matter of months. A day later, a Crip is shot and killed at the Reseda Skating Rink by a Blood.

There's no "I don't wanna get involved in gangbangin'." If you live in the 'hood you're in it—victim or perpetrator, the choice is yours.

Men who aren't committed to gangbanging avoid handling their responsibilities. Some join other gangs. Black Ant's mother sends him to live with his aunt in Montebello. "The 'hood is lethal," she tells him. Vic stops banging and drives his ice-cream truck. A Black P. Stone jumps gangs and starts riding with us, but Smiley never trusts him. The Harlem Crips split into three squads, or "sets." In my set, the Avenues, we gangbang half a day and hustle the other half. I get conditioned to being rocked to sleep by ambulance sirens and hovering helicopters. I'm awakened by gunfire as the sun rises over the stiff palms.

One evening, I pull on new Chuck Taylor shoes bought with some money from a robbery Smiley and I had done. I lace them with blue strings, pull on a blinding white shirt and khaki pants. My

flags are neatly folded and pressed. I've sewn two bandanas together and my crisp slice of royal dangles to my knees. I check
myself in the mirror as I pick my hair long. I'm "Cripped down,"
playing a position for my team. This is my army uniform, the bandanas my medal of honor. The blue is me. I'm no longer Colton,
abandoned by his father and abused by his mother. I locate myself
in this world as Li'l Cee Loc.

The energy shimmers thick on the street. I polish the barrel of
the .38 special till it gleams. Its sights are flawlessly aligned. I
stroll the same cool stride, but hair prickles on my neck, and my
ears stretch down the block till I hear a car before it turns the corner. I know by its velocity if it's hunting or driving to a destination.
My .38 special is reassuring in my waist. When I hold it, I have an
invincible shield. I can change the world with one bullet.

Smiley and I drive to Freeway Records picking up some Rick
James and Parliament. We run into Huckabuck checking out
sounds. I've seen his skinny dark self in the neighborhood, a Crip
from Denker Park, but have never talked with him.

He buys a Funkadelic tape and we stand outside discussing
music and hanging out. His words are sparse and pertinent, but he
pops energy, jumping, flashing his arms. It's a clear night without
a moon, but the lights from the city waste the stars.

A squeal of tires turns our heads just as Santa Claus, wearing
his red uniform, bends the corner in a '64 Chevy. His rider, K. B.,
spits fire at us. Powpowpowpow. Popcorn steel against metal. Bullets bounce off the walls, puncture one of Freeway's windows.

I check myself and give a thumb-up.

An explosion of air sighs from Smiley. He hasn't been hit.

"You okay?" I ask Huckabuck.

He nods, passes his palms over his thighs and arms.

"Them slob niggas can't shoot." Smiley grins.

"Man," Huckabuck says, "we gotta hit a lick so we can buy better guns. These fools ain't bullshitin' wit' us." Huckabuck's brows
form one line above his eyes, as if he wears a helmet.

Smiley leans back against the wall of Freeway's. He lights a cigarette and then smiles one of his slow smiles, promising all the time in the world. "Don't trip. Me and Li'l Cee goin' get with Big T and shake shit up around this muthafucka."

"We gotta smash those Piss Stain and Twinkie Bloods." Huckabuck looks back and forth between Smiley and me. "If we don't get them fools, Santa Claus and K. B., they get us." Huckabuck's arms are ridges of muscles and sinew as though he's cartilage and bones with no waste. Face flushed with zeal, he jumps with the hostile vitality of a soldier resolute on shooting himself through enemy lines. "Let's go. Do or die."

Do or die. "I'm down," I say.

The destruction of the Bloods burns in me like an oil fire. You can pour water, you can spray it with retardant. You can fight it all you want, but inevitably it's going to burn.

As though he needs to discharge his energy, Huckabuck picks up a rock and heaves it across the street. "Let it rain, let it drip, sock a Blood on his lip." He laughs and his laughter carries anger throughout South Central Los Angeles, home of the body bags, where people live and die in dog years.

Smiley and I are behind Spike's Liquor Store on Van Ness. Letters from the red and white sign have long been smashed so only the *L, I,* and *O* are left. By the time Spike buys new letters, the old ones have faded to pink. Smiley, Huckabuck, and I plan our next mission, plot revenge on the Bloods, drink liquor, and shoot dice. We ride in the jungles, but we don't see Santa Claus or K. B.

Spike, collapsed cartons in his arms, frowns when he sees us. "What's wrong with you youngsters? You don't have any incentive. You act like everything will come on a silver platter. You should go back to school."

Rather than return home to eat, we walk to Ralph's Market to steal food. There's a newspaper stand in front of Ralph's. After the store closes, Huckabuck and I pick up the newspaper stand and heave it through the plate-glass window. We run through the window and grab steaks, Remy Martin, and Olde English 800. We drink the liquor and sell the steaks to Spike. We purchase guns with the loot.

The next week, we're hanging out at the Laundromat when Flinn strolls by. "Man, you draped," Smiley says, nodding to his neck full of gold chains and rings on every finger. "What you been up to?"

"I've been hanging out with Tray hitting jewelry licks."

Tray raps under the name of *Ice T*, practicing his flow behind Spike's.

Lethal weapon, bump-bump-bump, lethal weapon, bump-bump-bump-lethal weapon, now assassinate if the people ain't steppin'!

Spike hears the rhymes, comes out to listen, shakes his head, and says, "So much talent going to waste."

After that conversation, Smiley and I start serious planning. We consider every strategy, anticipate all consequences. We visit malls. Smiley checks ideas with Tray and Flinn.

We pick a store in Delamo Mall for our first job. Mission Mary, Smiley's girlfriend, cases the store. Flashing a wad of cash in her purse, she buys a thin chain. The cheap stuff is in the front, the gold watches are in glass cases in the back, just like Tray predicted. There's no security guard in the store. The Rolexes are in the cases in the left rear. The store is next to an exit. Perfect location.

"Trip," Smiley says. We finished eating dinner and are in Smiley's attic above his garage. "We're gonna roll to the store in gees." Gees are stolen vehicles shortened from Grand Theft Auto. Smiley reaches into his father's tool chest. "Li'l Cee, you walk in with this." He hands me a sledgehammer. "And smash the jewelry cases."

I swing the hammer. My baseball practice will pay off. "What if somebody tries to play superhero?"

His smile stretches across his face. "Don't worry. I got a new equalizer." He bought a new 12 gauge from Big T with money we made robbing a Mexican homosexual who propositioned us in the park.

Mission Mary drives the stolen car. Flinn, Smiley, and I walk quickly to the store. We pass a newly opened Gap and Walden-Books. The smell of Mrs. Fields cookies mixes with the fragrance of *Charlie* being sprayed onto cards and presented to women. Then we arrive at cases of thin gold chains with a sign saying SALE, 50% OFF at the entrance to the jewelry store.

My heart pulses a surge of adrenaline. I'm ready.

A blue-suited man shifts his weight behind the glass counter; a couple leans over a case, studying earrings. A woman examines a ring on her finger, then holds it up to catch light.

Smiley jerks his head, signaling Flinn and me to move from the entrance. With two steps, Smiley is inside the store. He shoots the 12 gauge at the ceiling. The blast ricochets around the room.

People dive for the floor. The woman covers her head with her arms. The suited man cowers under a case.

Smiley motions for me to enter.

My ears ring from the gunshot. I swing.

Crash. Glass fractures. Jagged splinters fall into the case. Just like that.

One step to the next case. Swing.

Crash. Another case is cracked.

It's so easy. The glass is a flimsy membrane under the force of my hammer and my swing's power.

Step, Swing. Smash. Step swing smash.

The woman is frozen as though she holds her breath until I'm finished. The man under the case huddles in a ball.

Here I am, skinny little me, just a child fourteen years old, and they're afraid. Wow.

Flinn, a step behind me, scoops out the contents with gloved hands and throws them in a gym bag. Smiley stands at the en-

trance, his 12-gauge pointed into the store. He wears a black
leather jacket and jeans. His face is darkened with fury, eyes narrowed, lips tight.

When I'm finished, I watch for security at the entrance of the
store while Flinn gathers the goods.

In less than a minute, five cases are relieved of their merchan-
dise and the three of us race down the mall walkway.

We open the door to bright daylight.

An unarmed security guard jumps from behind the door. I jerk
in surprise.

He's a White man in his midthirties, well muscled, but a
middle-aged paunch already tightens his uniform. "Hold it right
there and put your hands in the air."

"Throw that muthafuckin' walkie-talkie," Smiley barks, "and
shut the fuck up."

The guard tosses the walkie-talkie. His face drains of color, his
eyes pop wide. "Please don't shoot, please."

Smiley uses his free hand to unzip his fly. He pulls out his meat
and flashes it at the guard. "Suck my dick, White boy," he says and
snorts.

While Mary drives us to the motel, I think about Smiley's startling action. It's as if he got off flashing his dick at him because
he's White, as though he's saying, *Today, I have the power, White
boy. And you the one that ain't shit.* Maybe he's saying, *You think
we're hung. I'll show you how big I am. Be intimidated. Be unsure
you got what it takes.* But he's also saying, *you just got fucked.* He's
saying all of it by one gesture.

At the motel room, we rip off the price tags and I flush them
down the toilet. They swirl like confetti before disappearing.
Mary and Flinn stuff the jewelry in white socks. Smiley laughs.
"Fuck. We did it."

"Didn't we, though." A gold watch dangles between Flinn's fingers. "Look at all this shit. I'm holding four thousand with this one
watch." And then he packs it in a sock.

A legit car waits with its hood propped up. The loaded socks are packed where the air filter had been.

We drive the jewelry to Smiley's brother, G, who has a serious connection to underworld people who wear suits and drive expensive cars but don't frequent the 'hood. The hammer, guns, and gym bag are stashed in the trunk of a second legit car. We separate the loot from the armaments so if we're stopped, a robbery can't be pinned on us.

G takes 10 percent. We split a hundred seventy-nine thousand between the four of us. The forty snatched Rolexes yield one hundred and sixty thousand.

Smiley buys a Cadillac Eldorado and two 1964 Chevys. Mary gets a Duster and a Honda Civic. Flinn purchases a 1964 Chevy and a gold Cutlass Supreme. I have twenty-five thousand dollars to blow. I can buy whatever I want, splurge on stuff I've only dreamed about. It's more fun than Christmas. I buy a white Cadillac and a gray 1964 Chevy equipped with custom rims and hydraulics. I park the Cadillac in the parking lot of Marla's Memory Lane—owned by actor Marla Gibbs—on Second Avenue and Santa Barbara so my grandmother won't see me getting in and out of it, start asking questions, surmise that it was stolen, and tell my uncle, who is a Los Angeles police officer. I park the Chevy inside the preschool parking lot around the corner from my house.

At last I have a gangster car, squared off in front and back, long and lean on the sides, jerking and twitching like a cat about to pounce when I ignite her, the ideal low rider. I like the minimal gray color almost like air. A ghost color. I spend the rest on gangbanging attire, guns, marijuana, a little cocaine, and alcohol.

I've done it. I'm totally equipped, totally down. Fourteen years old and on the way to achieve my celebrity. Consumption and violence are my validations.

Gangsters do what they want; civilians do what they can. During the robbery, adults did what I told them. Stores across L.A.

are lavishly crammed with glimmering gold and sparkling stones. Twinkling glass waits to be smashed. Money on the vine to be harvested.

A week or so after the Delamo Mall heist, we're hanging out by the alley when Tray rolls up. Smiley flags him down.

"Yeah, homie. Whassup?" Tray checks out our new designer shirts. "You looking tight."

Smiley hugs Tray and we bust out laughing.

"Hey, man, there's a talent show in Culver City at Veterans Memorial Auditorium. You should go." Smiley's thumb is hooked over his new khaki pocket.

"Yeah, I know," Tray's eyes veer to the side. "Thinking about it."

"You gotta go, cuz." Smiley nods as though it's been decided. "Gotta hear you be Ice again."

The next day, Ice T and Smiley and Huckabuck and I go. Summer days in South Central heat up the streets. Shit's hot and shit happens. This day starts scorching and doesn't stop when the sun goes down. Everybody who is somebody in the Crip gang world is at the auditorium. Every known hustler and known gang member. We walk in together and I hear a whisper, "That's Ice T."

And then he's is on stage singing, *Crippin', never-slippin', everyday wit a blue-rag swangin' 'cause we like it that way.*

"He's representin' our 'hood, our lives," Huckabuck says. "singin' 'bout us, cuz. Keepin' it real." He laughs in quick starts, like he moves.

A girl with painted-on clothes dangles from the shoulder of a dealer in a black-and-white shirt. The auditorium is packed with hustlers wearing Fila sweatsuits or silk shirts, gangsters in blue, and a smattering of pretty girls now moving to his beat.

Cops freeze, when they see my strap, 'cause I'm Ice T, nigga, The first Crip-in-rap. Did a bid in the pen 'cause it's like that.

"Hey," I nudge Smiley, "he made up that shit behind Spike's."

You wanna be my friend, you gotta claim my set, hang wit the homies, keep ya strap in yo' lap.

"Yeah, celebratin' the Rollin' Thirties, our 'hood," Smiley says.

I ain't thru, cuz, you gotta wear all blue, and when the cops roll by holler: fuck you.

The crowd roars and Tray wins second place.

After Tray ripped the mike, the throng begins to leave, but tentatively. No one rushes for the exits. The fun is over, and a mass of hoodlums on a hot night creates caution. Smiley, Huckabuck, and I stroll toward the door when two men give us the once-over. We don't know they're Bloods, but anybody foolish enough to shoot mad-dog stares can't be Crips.

Huckabuck is the first to draw heat. "Whassup wit' you niggas, cuz!" Huck demands.

Before they answer I'm on the second cat, "Pop, pop, pop." Firing three shots, not to kill anyone as the crowd is thick with civilians, but to let the men know we mean business. The first shot hits the wall and plaster splats across the room. The second shot soars over everyone's head. The third shot takes the brim hat off the cat and sends it flying.

"Where you niggas from, Crip?" Smiley demands, his hand on the trigger of his .380, once the shots' echoes cease.

"We don't bang," the cat replies.

"Yeah, right!" Ice T cuts in. "That's Li'l Man from VNG (Van Ness Gangsters Bloods). But he's alright. Stall cuz out, y'all. I fuck wit' him on the music. He ain't here to trip."

With that, the three of us look at the cat. As if we'd practiced it a million times, we pivot in unison and shout, "Alright, cuz. This Harlem Crip nigga!"

We stroll, side by side, our feet touching the ground simultaneously until we reach the parking lot. It's cooler outside than in the auditorium.

Pop, pop, pop.

"Blood gang!" Someone yells from a moving car.

We're all on the ground, fingers on triggers, poppin' again. No one is hurt, but the lesson is well received. Summer time, shit's hot! Too many things going on. Too many heated egos. Too many hot tempers. Too many hot, smoking barrels.

Smiley and I pare down jewelry licks to the essentials and we're in and out of a store in less than thirty seconds. My skinniness and youth create the advantage of surprise. When we're working together, we're in a zone, breathing as one, anticipating each other's moves. Smiley flashes his stuff only once, but each time he does something crazy that keeps me prepared for the random. Once, a manager locks him inside the store. Smiley runs full speed through the plate-glass window to escape. He slashes his face and his neck, but keeps on running. Another time, the police circle the mall. We light firecrackers at one end and run to the other and complete our job. We're finished before they are.

I love doing jewelry licks. I love the power I wield over adults. I love the rush of adrenaline and learn to harness it. As we obtain better equipment and experience, our business expands. It gets so I go in alone, ask to see a Rolex, grab two, dash out of the store, turn them around, and have eight thousand dollars stuffed in my pocket. Not bad walking-around money for a fourteen-year-old.

Our own transportation allows us to enlarge our hustles and our visibility in the 'hood. Smiley and I pick up Huckabuck and Big T and roll four deep through enemy territory. We do so many shootings in our cars that we paint them a different color every two or three months. After we get tired of spending money on repainting, we start stealing cars. Then, we're able to damage the enemy more; we don't care if they see the car. We don't do drive-bys, we do drive-ups—get out, walk within firing range, and shoot. We're only interested in hitting enemy soldiers, not civilians. But we still don't see Santa Claus or B. K.

"Big T says you too young. And too little," Smiley tells me one evening. We've finished dinner at his house and I'm sitting on the floor. Gina sits behind me on the couch, cornrowing my hair. Her fingers flash, twisting strands around each other. She hangs out with us like one of the guys, except she does most of the cornrowing.

Big T looks the perfect gangster; the twenty-inch arms, the six-foot frame, as though he can do real damage. He's light skinned and has a hooked nose like me. I don't see it then, but I resemble a younger, shorter, skinnier him. He and Smiley were always together until I was initiated and Smiley and I start to do jewelry licks. Big T is our procurement man. We go to him for guns. He belongs to a car club and he sells us wheels. But when we hunt in the jungles, he never leaves the ride.

I turn toward Smiley, tilt my head so I can stare in his eyes, my own eyes steady as I meet his. "What do you think, cuz?"

"You do what you need to do."

"I walk my talk." I hope Smiley gets what I'm saying.

G walks in. Though he's older, he's shorter than Smiley and doesn't have their father's husky build. Like their father, he seldom smiles. Smiley got all the potential for grins in the family. Gina's are tentative, like she hasn't been given full permission. "Big T's jealous that you pay attention to Cee." G jerks his head toward Smiley who changes the channel on the TV. "Big T wants all the attention."

I know this is right.

"And his sister, Tookie, has a thing for him," G nods toward me.

Gina's hands stop flying through my hair and she shoves my head. I look back at her and say, "Nothin' happenin'."

Gina squints. I turn to Smiley. Her fingers resume their rhythmic working.

Smiley watches a basketball game.

But G continues. "We were shooting craps and things got heated. Everyone waited for Big T to prove himself, he being so harsh looking with those twenty-inch biceps. We said, 'Now we're gonna see him in action.' But when the time came, he was knocked out cold by Jelly, the smallest guy on the block."

"That cat can jump," Smiley says as Magic makes his shot.

A few weeks later, Smiley and I find his mom, Curly, crying in their living room. Her brother called her a bitch and tried to hit her. "Don't worry, Moms." Smiley leans down and wipes a tear from her cheek gentle as if he's touching the petal of a flower. "I'll make it right for you." Smiley beats his uncle up.

The next day, I spend the night at my mother's. Before I wake up, I hear her witch voice. "Why haven't you folded the laundry? Didn't you see this mess of clean clothes?"

I pull on my khakis.

"You should be in school, that's where you should be. When're you going to grow up and be a man so I don't have to see your shit all the time? Clean this fucking room."

A shoe sails past me.

I slam the door and go to the 'hood, walking to get the Cadillac. A boy rides his bike, meandering down the middle of the street. Palms feather the blue sky. The lawns are tidy, the doors closed and locked. It is supernaturally quiet.

If someone called Moms a bitch and hit her, I would shrug and figure she has it coming. Smiley risked jail for his mother.

Moms didn't write or visit me when I was sentenced to camp. She was glad I was gone. I see again her smug eyes when Pete beat me. I think about Smiley's family sitting around the table to eat. Curly makes certain she cooks something everyone likes. She asks her children how their day went and kisses them goodnight.

The scrubbed sky mocks me. I figured Damon and I had been through Moms's evil together. He would understand. One night, at Louise's, I asked if he thought about Pete. He knew I meant the beatings.

"Nah," he turned over in bed.

"Don't you wish we had a normal family?"

"Feel sorry for yourself, punk." He told the kids at school, who teased me.

I try to let Louise become Moms since she's the woman who shows me motherly love. But that tissue wall hangs between us.

The kid on the bike turns the corner. Nothing moves. As though the 'hood is frozen.

A red '67 Mustang convertible eases to a stop at the corner of my block. Bloods.

I reach for my weapon.

Then, Smiley's voice calls, "Cee Loc. It's me."

The car is stolen.

"Get in," Smiley demands. "That fool Li'l Ru from Black Piss Stain is at Hamburger City."

I'm looking for refuge and Smiley cites an enemy. Fate.

I climb in the car and we zoom.

Earth Wind and Fire, soothing me from the radio, promises all my dreams will come true. I lean my head back on the seat. "This morning, Moms started that—clean-your-nasty-funky-room—screeching, threw a shoe at me." I pull out the .38 special.

"Cee, don't trip off that shit."

With a rag, I polish the barrel.

"That still Ma."

"She takes all her anger at my pops out on me. Her boyfriends beat her, she beats us, and we get blamed." I didn't realize I knew that.

"People gonna do what they gonna do. Everybody's gonna get what's coming to them. God gonna get them in the end." He chuckles as though everything is alright. His hand rests on my shoulder.

My mother's behavior has nothing to do with me. We stop at a light and he smiles his love at me. A Porsche hums in the next lane.

"She blames us that she can't keep a man. She used her pregnancies with us to get a man. But she couldn't keep one and blamed us."

"She'll gonna reap what she sows." The light changes, the

Porsche bolts ahead, and we roll across the intersection, driving through the arching trees.

"Don't even worry."

But I keep talking. "Half the time, she tries to act White, wants to date White men. Everybody in her family is light and she could pass except Damon and I give her away. She acts like we're her maids." I can tell he's listening because his mouth is still. He isn't smiling and isn't flashing angry eyes. "She takes Marc everywhere, though." No one has listened before.

I tell Smiley about Moms blindfolding me and dumping me in Blood territory. In spite of rubbing the .38 with each word, once again, I'm the boy sobbing under in the rain telling myself, *You can make it. You're a fist.* Cee and Colton slide together.

Smiley wets his lips. "When it's your moms, people like that, your family, it's not for you to judge. It's not for you to do something to them. It's your mother." He squeezes my shoulder. "Hear me, Li'l Cee? Don't worry."

I light a joint.

"Hey. We got each other. We got the 'hood. We don't need nobody else." His face is open, not with the intent enthusiasm that is there when he grins or the callous conviction when his lips are firm. "We're cool."

He's right. *His family is my family. Crips my last name.* I feel, and maybe for the first time, like I'm known and safe. The barrel of my weapon is snug as I return it to my waistband.

"We brothers anyway, Li'l Cee, don't you know that?" *See. He knows what I'm thinking.* He gently knocks my head. His hand is warm. The sun streams in the car as it rocks down the street. Right now, in the rolling car, the sun sharpening up the edges of everything, Smiley driving, I'm at peace.

We arrive at Hamburger City.

"Hey, Blood," Smiley leans out of the driver's window, calling Li'l Ru, who has just left the restaurant.

Li'l Ru turns toward us. He's gotten larger since I last saw him. The bumps in the scar across his eyes are deep black.

"Where you from?" Smiley grins.

"Black P. Sto—"

Before he completes his word, we're out of the car squeezing triggers, blasting him in the chest.

Bangin' is more than my career. It's my refuge, the ultimate getaway. The choice is mine.

THREE

Out of the Ghetto and into the CYA

What white Americans have never fully understood—but what the Negro can never forget—is that white society is deeply implicated in the ghetto. White institutions created it, white institutions maintain it, and white society condones it.
—Kerner Commission

All the gods are dead except the god of war.
—Eldridge Cleaver, *Soul on Ice*

WE'RE AT WAR WITH THE BLOODS AND BOTH OF US ARE AT war with the police. The Black-pig war is fought all over L.A. With the Rodney King beating on March 3, 1991, America witnessed police brutality. The world was shocked. But for me, the Rodney King beating was a common event that happens to get taped.

In 1971, when I was six, visiting my father in Venice, I had finished playing softball and strolled back to the apartment, carrying my bat and glove. Dusk was falling. The streets lights had just come on.

A blare of sirens stopped my return home as police exited their cars, moving into the park carrying billy clubs.

"Don't move," one shouted, gun drawn.

"Up against the wall."

"Spread 'em."

The teens, and some of the boys who'd been playing softball with me, lined the chain-link fence, legs spread, and hands stretched.

"Cokie, get in here right now," my father's mom shouted out the window.

The cops worked down the line, pushing, then frisking my teammates, and looking for an excuse to get them into the system.

One of them, Ivory, thirteen and the slyest defensive basketball player, scratched his shoulder.

"I told you not to move." A cop hit his skull with the club and smashed another kid in the back.

"Get up these stairs," my grandmother yelled.

I scampered up the stairs and peeked out her curtain.

"You niggers, don't you fucking move," growled one of the cops.

The teens faced the fence.

White paper was wadded in a cop's hand. He reached in Ivory's pocket. When he pulled out his hand, he displayed the paper to the other cop. "Looky here. Just as I thought. You the one." He shoved Ivory to the ground. "I knew we'd find someone with drugs here."

"I didn't have no drugs," Ivory protested.

The two pigs kicked his head.

"Get away from the window, boy," my grandmother said. "You don't need to see that." She pulled the blinds and shut the curtains.

I snuck another glance as they shoved Ivory, arms cuffed behind his back, into their car. This was my first image of police, this nightly scene, right before the TV news, when the pigs bully Black youth visiting the park to play softball, shoot hoops, and be themselves.

By the time I'm twelve, I'm the one getting harassed. One night, in Denker Park, hanging out with Smiley and Big T, three cop cars drive up, sirens screaming, guns drawn. The cops order us, "Get on the fuckin' ground and put your hands behind your back." Smiley is elusive enough to escape. I see the drawn guns and freeze before flinging on the ground.

"Spread 'em," the cop hisses. As if he has a personal vendetta against my private parts, he kicks me in the testicles. "Move, and I'll kill you, motherfucker," he hisses and kicks again.

Pain rides up my body and I can't breathe. *Why'd he have to kick me?* I did just what he said. He's a six-foot-tall coward with a drawn gun. *He ain't shit,* I think, but I can't move a muscle.

The police bust down the door to Smiley's cousin Johnnie Mae's apartment and shoot her. Her fetus takes a bullet to the head and dies. Johnnie Mae survives, but will never have another baby. She sits in her house not talking, just staring out the window. We're sad, then furious when the cops aren't charged. But we're not surprised. For the next few days, Smiley mutters, "Kill the fucking pigs." "Retaliate." He makes plans, but we don't carry them out.

A week later, Smiley and I cruise down Santa Barbara in a stolen car on the way to the jungles to hunt Bloods. Two cops pull beside us.

"Pull over to the curb right fuckin' now." The cop's ice-blue eyes glint at me.

Smiley's face darkens. This is his chance.

"Did you hear what the fuck I said?" The cop's upper lip is drawn back, his teeth glisten.

Smiley draws a .357 Magnum and points it at the cop's head.

They stare at each other, having a conversation. Smiley's weapon says, "I'll kill you." And the cop's eyes plead, "Please don't shoot."

Then, the cop ducks under the dashboard, his car peels. I smell burnt rubber. Smiley presses the accelerator and zooms across the center divider, bursts a sharp right on Fourth, and speeds down the block.

In the rearview mirror, I see the pigs round the corner. "Make a left," I tell him.

"Man, let me do this shit." Smiley swerves around an oncoming Toyota and spurts left.

Police sirens.

We cut across a lawn, speed halfway down Forty-second Street, zip down an alley.

"Get ready to jump," Smiley shouts.

We leap out and sprint in different directions, the car rolling, its engine still on.

Amped by combat, I run two blocks, dart down an alley, hurdle a fence, and land in a plot of wild ivy plants. I lie on the ground and pull the vines around my body to camouflage myself.

The cops speed down the alley and skid to a stop. I hear them jump out, slam their doors, and bolt after Smiley.

It's quiet in the ivy. I wait, listening to the street, listening to my breathing. If they haven't found Smiley by now, he's free.

I count my breaths. The ivy tickles, but I don't move.

Dusk approaches.

I stay in the vines. I don't scratch my itchy nose. After two hours, I hear a pig trot to the patrol car and climb in. The door slams. He says something to his partner, but I can't hear his words. The car starts and speeds in the direction of the station.

They're gone. I stick my head above the irritating green. I'm safe. I brush myself off.

"Hold it right there," a different cop demands.

And I thought I was free.

I dash to a fence and jump to another backyard. I scan for a place to hide, but there's none. Clothes hang from a line. I grab a change of clothes and stride to a corner of the house. The pants are too small. I unbraid my hair so it's long and wavy. I crouch along the side of the house.

"Hey, get outta my yard."

I run to the sidewalk toward Third Avenue, dashing down the street, and cut through the bushes to Grandma Louise's backyard, retrieve the key from under the mat, unlock the door.

Home. Safe.

Sirens race down the block.

I lock the back door and go to the living room, lift the curtain to peek outside. Spotlights illuminate the block. A helicopter hovers above the palm trees. No sign of Smiley.

The searchlight teases the asphalt street, the lawns. The helicopter's propeller rustles the fronds of the trees and drowns out the sounds of the patrol car. Hovering, whirling. The customary South Central sound of death and evil.

The helicopter flutters away.

"Boy, what the hell you done now?" Grandma Louise's hands are on her hips.

How does she know? I stand shell-shocked.

"What's that green stuff on your shirt? Didn't I just buy you that for school? And why's your hair such a mess? And you all shiny from sweat?"

"That's from the bushes," I say.

"Don't you lie to me. You know Grandma ain't no fool. You and that Smiley been running from the police."

"I—"

"Aut. Aut." Her hand rises above her head, ready to strike. "Don't tell me no lie about you runnin' from Peggy's dog. That's a house dog."

After awhile, she wears herself out screaming at me. And the war between the Blacks and the pigs resume. I concentrate on being Colton, hiding deeper my life as Li'l Cee Loc.

Gina, Smiley's younger sister, is two years older than me. She's petite, just slightly over five feet, with a bitter personality, tough and eager. As a kid, she's the best girl fighter on our block; she got her fighting skills from her dad. She hangs with us sometimes, just like one of the set.

Then, during a summer, she grows a woman's body. Gina gets a job and keeps to herself. Sometimes I see her when I'm at Smiley's, plotting our next lick. She's short and slim, attends school, is drug and alcohol free, and is not a gangbanger. Usually Gina is at work. When she's home, I'm out on the grind, hustling and gang-banging. I'm nighttime; she's daytime. Both of us being in the same place together is rare. She appeals to my Colton side. I appeal to her wild side.

I'm always on the go being a hustler, not really into women. Money, power, wealth, being able to do whatever you want to do is liberation. No one controls me. I'm in love with the streets. When I drive down the street in a nice car, in the mix with my homies, a ghetto celebrity wearing designer clothes, big gold watch, gold chains, gold earrings, people see me, praise me, and I lap it up. That life is my love. I can't be in love with a woman. The camaraderie members share is a known thing. "It ain't no fun if the homie can't have none," we tell each other.

I'm at Smiley's house waiting for him. Parliament's *Bop Gun* plays on the stereo. Gina scans me up and down with her bright eyes and says, "Every time you pop up you got a new car, different designer clothes. Every day it's something bran' new." Gina wears blue jeans and a white tee shirt, bright red lipstick that shows off the orange tones in her smooth brown skin. I guess every woman is attracted to a man who has nice things. It's an attention-getter.

Next day, I bring her some diamond studs from a jewelry lick and her eyes widen. She puts them in her ears, turns her head back and forth for me, then runs to see herself in the mirror. "Oooooh," she squeals.

Day after that, she calls and says, "Cee, Smiley and G aren't here and Moms needs help taking out the trash. She ask me to call you."

I bet, I think, but say, "Be right there."

I pull the trash to the curb and start to leave and Gina puts her hand on my shoulder. "You want a drink or something?"

I act like I'm thirsty and exhausted from that little bit of work.

I might as well wait for Smiley at his house, I figure, and we settle back to watch some *Dukes of Hazzard* on her water bed. Her parents don't pay me any mind. I'm like a son.

I don't kiss her. I'm fifteen and she's seventeen and her age intimidates me. We lay on her bed with waves rolling every time one of us shifts and listen to the TV noise, the TV flicker behind my lids. I fall asleep with her warmth curled like a tight ball next to me, a child for me to protect.

The phone wakes me. "Hey, Cee. Meet us at the alley," orders Smiley. So I leave.

The next week, she's off work, and I'm at Smiley's again. "Let's go to a movie," she asks.

"I'm waiting for Smiley." So Gina and I cuddle on her water bed. I still don't kiss her. I rehearse a jewelry lick I'm doing the next day. The store is next to an exit. The gold in the back on the right. But the watches in the midleft. *How am I to get both cases at once? Maybe we need two smashers.*

Gina is warm in my arms, her head snuggled on my shoulder, and I see cases with their bounty of regal gold. *Or maybe I can stand in the middle and smash both and do this one alone.* Then, Smiley peeks his head in her door and says, "Cee. Let's go."

The next day Gina and I go see *Raging Bull* and stop to get our pictures taken in one of those booths where you get a strip of four pictures. When I see the photos, there's Smiley's happy grin on her skinny, big-eyed face.

I bring her money to get her hair done, get her nails done. I buy her a diamond ring and gold chains. Once, almost by accident, I kiss her and her lips are firm and moist under mine.

I tell her I love her, but that's easy. It's like telling Smiley or Curly I love them. And I tell her casual, as I'm saying good-bye. Not when it could be important when we're on her water bed.

One night, waiting for Smiley to go on a mission, I fall asleep in her bed. Best Products is having a grand opening at Torrance near the Old Town Mall. I learn later that Smiley is smoking PCP so I get Wham-O to take his place. When I tell Gina my plans, she looks at me with those black eyes of hers luminescent and serious. "Don't go. Please. Don't go."

I buckle my belt, "You just freaked 'cause Noodie gone." Two days before, Noodie was killed by Bloods outside his classroom at Manual Arts High. I'm doing this job to buy guns to retaliate. I'm on gang business, not personal gain.

Gina acts like she knows things about the streets. "Gotta strange feeling, Colton. Something weird. Something different. Wait."

"You older than me, but you don't know shit. Smiley wants this done."

"I'm beggin' you."

I shrug her away.

I obtain a stolen car from Big T, pick Wham-O from the fish market where he's worked for two years for minimum wage. The Salem in his mouth mingles with the smell of mackerel. I stay close to my side of the car, open the window, and light my own Marlboro.

We clean out two display cases and we're outta there like clockwork, thirty seconds and the smash-and-grab is done. A piece of cake. During the getaway, the clutch goes out. We ditch the car on a side street and run for the bus stop full speed. Brakes squeal behind us as we bolt through a red light. Then another light turns red. *Damn, we're getting 'em all.*

We dash through the second red and close in the final block. Our destination, the bus stop, is within our grasp.

We're spotted by a motorcycle cop. "Get to the curb." While he's writing the ticket, the bus passes our stop. My heart falls at the sight of it, my hands cold from adrenaline.

The cop gives us a worn-out speech about it being dangerous to cross the street when the light is red. It would be funny if not so frustrating.

"You're free to go," he says, finally.

As Wham-O strolls away, a Rolex falls from his pocket.

The cop pulls the gun from his holster. "Hold it right there and put your hands in the air."

Wham-O complies, but I run. Another cop arrives driving a patrol car and catches me. He cuffs us both, stuffs us in the back, and drives us to Torrance, where we're booked for armed robbery. Wham-O wasn't supposed to grab the loot, just be the gunman. Not playing his position got us busted. It's 1981. Wham-O is twenty-four years old and sentenced to five years. I'm fifteen and sentenced to seven years in California Youth Authority.

At Central Juvenile Hall, I break a White boy's nose for calling me "nigger" and am sent to lock-up. I stay there for a month before being hauled off to Youth Authority and to the Fred C. Nelles School for Boys to begin serving my seven-year bid.

The institutional transportation bus rolls through the sally-port gates, two fifteen-feet-high steel gates that swing open and then are bolted by hand. The mad-dog stares of youths, who stop cutting grass and sweeping asphalt, pierce the windows. The fifteen-foot gate is closed, a thick chain wrapped around it several times and secured with an arm-sized padlock. A series of razor-sharp wire wound in columns of three top the gate. I'm locked inside, secure from society and the inner-city streets that sucked me away from my grandmother and her ideals.

As the bus ventures farther, the landscape reveals itself. I've never seen anything like this except in the photographs that Smiley's older brother sent home from Jacksonville State University. A football field of evenly mowed green grass is surrounded by a 440 track. Huge trees and lawn are separated by a curving street that connects cottages, a gym, infirmary, culinary, an official high school–sized baseball field, and an Olympic swimming pool. The sun plays on the grass. Trees grace the buildings. All is quiet. No bars. No helicopters. It looks like my image of Eden.

I'm assigned to Cleveland Cottage, a large room of fifty beds, and enter carrying my gear.

"Rollin' Sissy killer," shout several Eight Trays as I stroll down the long aisle to my assigned bunk.

I'm not from the Sixties so I don't respond, just keep on walking, slow and easy. I'm stopped short by Big Bat from Eight Tray. He's older than me, stocky and muscular. I know his reputation as a fighter. "Nigga, roll yo' shit up. This is Rollin' Sissy killer, you can't stay here." His eyes are glued to mine as if we're connected by a supernatural power. Other men surround me in a circle that reminds me of being jumped in. The cottage has a preponderance of Crips from Hoover and Eight Tray Gangster. These sets are enemies of the Rollin' Sixties, my set's ally. Several Hoovers and Eight Trays hunt my brother Damon and some of his homeboys, all Rollin' Sixties, for the death of Lucky and attempted murder of Tit Tit. Tit Tit was shot in retaliation for the shooting death of Tyrone, the little brother of a Rollin' Sixties' OG, which is short for original gangster, slang for general. The Crip-on-Crip rivalry changes the entire atmosphere of the streets. Colors are not a simple sign of brotherhood anymore. Sets pledge alliances depending on their prediction of the war's outcome. The Rollin' Thirties, my set, select the Rollin' Sixties. So, I'm the closest my new cottage mates will get to Damon and his homeboys from the Sixties and equally appetizing. They set up shop for my arrival.

My heart beats like a bass drum. My mouth is dry. I fight off shock to muster an aggressive response. This isn't Eden after all. It's the 'hood in another guise. I can't be a buster. "Fool. I ain't from the Sixties. I'm from Harlem, I live in the Avenues."

"What street you live on?"

"Second Avenue." I try to hold his stare, not showing a sign of weakness, but he looks straight through me as though I'm already a ghost.

The others slowly close in on me. I don't turn. I grab air, puffing out my chest.

"Who you run wit'? Who put you on the set?" demands a short

cat. He looks familiar, but I can't think clearly enough to place him. It's a death challenge; they're interrogators and I'm the subject. Give the right answer and I live; tell a lie and I die.

"Smiley, Big T, and Terry," I say. The bodies of the other men touch me on all sides. I can't move.

"Man, how old are you?"

"I'm—"

River Rat from East Coast pulls a knife from his waist and raises it to my throat. The blade is cool.

"Fifteen. I'll be sixteen next month."

"Shit," River Rat roars in my ear. "Smiley is twenty. You don't know him."

"I live around the corner from Smiley. His sister, Gina, is my girl." A sliver of blood trickles down my neck.

"Hold up, Rat," the short cat demands. "Smiley do got a sister name Gina."

Sensing some hope, I counter, "He has two sisters."

A Black counselor with an Afro and glasses peeps in the dorm because of the commotion and shouts, "Break it up, break it up."

The circle disperses except for the short cat, who extends his hand. "What's up, cuz. I'm Baby Rock from West Side Harlem Crip, Denker Park side." He's dark, almost blue-skinned. When I shake his hand, his grip is iron. Baby Rock was the first person from the 'hood to kill a Black P. Stone.

"They call me Li'l Cee Loc."

"Crazy Colton?" A puzzled look passes his face. "You with Smiley when he shot that fool Li'l Ru from Black Piss Stain, right?"

"Yeah."

He spreads his arms and we embrace.

"You the little homie," he says.

The other boys standing by their bunks watch. Then the counselor calls me into his office for an interview, and when I return to my bunk, all my property is gone. Soap, toothbrush, lotion. "Which one y'all fools stole my girl's picture?" I couldn't care less about the other things; they're replaceable. But Gina's pictures are all I have good from home. I squint to glare at the men.

The dorm is silent.

"Who crossed my set out on my shower shoe?" Dee bellows. Dee is the only Blood in the cottage, a shot-caller from the Denver Lane Bloods, who earned respect by being a fierce fighter. Crossing out the name of the set is an act of blatant disrespect, punishable by death. In the 'hood, graffiti crossed out announces war's escalation.

"That new booty did it," someone yells.

Bat eases over to me and whispers, "Dee is the person who stole your stuff."

"We gotta get 'em up." Dee crouches, his fist punches the air.

Here I am, first day in the cottage. A knife's been pulled on me, people think I'm from the Rollin' Sixties, someone stole my property, and now I'm set up to fight a shot-caller for the Bloods.

"Fuck yo' momma," he spits at me.

Despite my dislike for Moms, I can't let that go. I leap from the bunk and rush him. I'm slim and quick with my hands. He's buff and has forty pounds on me. If I'm hit, he'll knock me unconscious. He swings and I duck, but his fist skins my head. He can't swing his thick arms. He strikes again and I crouch, counter-punching him in the face with a left cross, and knock him to the ground. He rises and I move in, swinging relentlessly, striking him in the torso, head, and face. When he falls, I back up to take advantage of my long arms. He staggers to his feet and assumes a martial-art stance. His blood is up; he fights for his reputation, his pride. "I know karate, fool."

I'm no expert in karate but can decipher a student from an actor. He's an actor.

I sidestep him and catch him in the jaw with a right uppercut. Bam! He falls for the third time and doesn't rise. He crawls to his bunk, grabs his state boots, and throws them at me. I dodge them and one cracks the counselors' window. They rush to us and wrestle me away.

I'm handcuffed and escorted to Ad-Seg (administrative segregation), isolated from everyone, my life limited to cell living for three days.

When I return to Cleveland, Bat and Baby Rock greet me. "Yeah, Li'l Cee, you down, homie," they say in unison as if they practiced it while I was in Ad-Seg.

"Here you go." Bat hands me a box containing my property, including Gina's pictures. It had all been a setup to see if I'm a soldier or a buster. I pass their test.

The next week I see Gina's handwriting on an envelope, hearts on the back. I stuff it into my shirt, saving it. I open it later. *I told you Colton, I told you I had a funny feeling that you were gonna go to jail!! But no, you wouldn't listen to me. You always talk about how much you love me but you never listen to me! I told you! I told you!*

I believe I love her, but she competes with my drive for power and she can't win. I don't know how to tell her this and I don't understand it myself.

A few months later she writes, *Colton you wouldn't listen to me when you were out and I found someone who would. I've another man and I got a job working at Standard Brand Paint Company with my father so you won't be hearing from me anymore. Smiley sends his love and says to call him.*

I climb to my bunk, pick up our pictures, and lay on my thin mattress. I hold our strip of photos over my head and hunt for a sign that she would dump me. We look so happy. I'm sitting and she's behind me wearing a blue dress, her hair straightened and fluffy, her bangs covering one eye. Her slender arms are surrounding me as she leans her face next to mine, wearing Smiley's wide beam. There's no indication of wavering devotion. Just her thrilling happiness smiling at me.

How can she do me like this while I'm in jail? Gina knew what *I was doing on the streets, and the money I gave her was okay then. She must be a calculating person, playing me.* I tear her out of the picture, leaving just her arms and the gold bracelet I gave her for her birthday.

I try to sleep off the heartbreak.

The next weekend, my father comes to see me. It's my first, and only, visit. He brings a bucket of Kentucky Fried Chicken and we sit at a picnic table. Real food. I hungrily gnaw on a drumstick when he clears his throat and says, "Colton."

The tone of his voice is so serious, I stop eating and look at him, the meat still in my fingers. "Sir?"

"You're a man, almost, now so it's time I tell you the truth." The hair on the back of my neck shivers. "You've always known I'm not Damon's father and I don't believe I'm Marc's father. I think that White man, Pete, is Marc's father. He looks just like him and has straight hair. Your mother was fooling around with him when she was with me. And Damon was born before I ever met her."

"I don't understand."

"Your mother was very beautiful. She was a model when I met her. Men threw themselves on her. They thought, I guess, her soul was as beautiful as her face, but all her goodness was in her looks. She never introduced Damon to his father, just took his child support. Then, after you were born, she started seeing Pete and named his child Marc Simpson."

"But Pops . . ." He's telling me something I always knew, but never wanted to believe. We, my brothers and I, are merely accessible tools used to draw in child support or as revenge. She prefers Marc, with his white skin and straight hair. He fit in around Pete.

"She's been lying all these years."

"But I love my brothers."

"You're supposed to. Nothing is more important than family. But you, Colton, you are my son. You have to understand who you are."

I don't know what to say to my father, my father whose wife

cheated on him, so I grab another piece of chicken. His head is turned from me, his eyes on the ground as though he's still ashamed.

I know from family history that Pops's great-grandmother was a slave and her slave master raped her. The rape resulted in the birth of my father's grandmother and accounts for our light skin. A black-and-white photograph of her hangs on his wall. She wears a dark head wrap with black eyes still fierce in spite of the settled hands folded on her lap. My father had to work twice as hard and be twice as good to get ahead in the White world—the world of baseball. All this and his wife cuckolded him with a White man. Pete beat me and humiliated my father.

I think of Gina. Women. They act like they care about you, but they're in it for themselves. It's all about them and what you give them. You can't trust them or their loyalty.

I don't know what to say to Pops. He's trying to set things right between us and regrets his part of our history that brought me here. He hopes to make my life better. So I keep eating for awhile. And finally say, "I hate Pete. And I hate her." But I don't know if he interprets that as my understanding him or my temper.

Then he picks up a drumstick and says, "I used to wish I won that custody suit." He looks around the Nelles School for Boys, "But this place looks like a camp. You're smart, Colton. And athletic. You can get outta here with a chance. Just take it, my son."

The best thing about transferring from one facility to another is the view. After being behind the fifteen-foot gates at Nelles for two years, I'd forgotten what the "free world" looks like. As the bus climbs the Number Five Freeway headed for Fenner, I ride past Magic Mountain. I haven't seen it since I was a child. I spot a new rollercoaster, the Colossus, which I'd seen on TV. A Mercedes Benz convertible filled with women in their twenties drives toward it. One laughs, her blowing red hair licking her face. Another's tan legs gleam from lotion. They see me watching and give me the finger. When we drive through Antelope Valley, the acres of landscape, mountains, waterfalls, dirt roads seem so tranquil, at harmony with each other and the blue sky. Weird to think that over the hills of the peaceful countryside is a city at war. Then the paved street comes to a dead end at Fenner Canyon. My new home.

There are four cottages, each designed like giant cabins that hold two dozen prisoners in a dorm setting. We have board games, television, radio, and an outside visiting area designed like a campground with log benches, a barbeque pit, and a playground. A school connects to a gym. Several garages contain green fire-crew trucks. There's a dining hall and administration building. The prisoners are mainly Crips and Bloods, and some Hispanic men from South Side Thirteen. Blacks and Hispanics are in the majority.

These cottages are named after Viet Nam units instead of presidents like in Nelles. I'm housed in Charlie Cottage and placed in a fire crew.

As soon as I enter, I'm approached. "Where you from, homeboy?" a man almost as tall as me asks. He has a knife scar across his forehead.

"I'm Cee from Harlem." I hold his mad-dog stare.

"I'm Li'l Quake from Sixty-second Street East Coast." He shows me to my assigned bunk. We learn his older brother is a Crip, my older brother is a Crip. We're both athletic, Geminis, on fire crew, our girlfriends dumped us while doing time. We both love basketball.

Coach Brown, a heavyset Black man with gold chains draped around his neck, asks us to try out for the team. I win the starting forward and Li'l Quake the guard.

"As long as you abide by the rules and respect me, I'll go to the brink for you," Coach Brown tells me.

Over time, I open up to him and tell him about my abnormal

relationship with Moms and the pain I feel over Gina. She hasn't faded from my mind, popping up sometimes with her eager smile, or I'll turn my head and smell her. I think about her more in custody than I did on the street. Then there were more important things on my mind.

That fall, 1983, Coach Brown pushes me to sign up for GED classes. Some nights, he stays three hours past his shift to go over American history and math with me.

"If x plus x2 equals 110, then x2 equals what?"

I stare at the meaningless symbols on the paper. *I have enough unknowns to decipher. Am I going to live past twenty-one? Will Gina come back to me? Which one of my set will be killed next? Is there a strategy I can construct to prevent it?*

Math can't stop a bullet, or put money in my pocket. I shake my head. *What am I doing this for? I'm conditioned to simple things. You shoot me; I shoot you. You make money; I take it. You play the pig and I play the criminal. You yell "Stop!" and I run. Life in South Central is uncomplicated. It doesn't take a brain surgeon to figure out what to do during a war.*

"You're not the same person that ran the streets," Coach Brown says. "You have to prove it. The GED and remaining discipline free will prove it to the parole board." Coach Brown's brows knit together; he pounds his fist in his hand. He's so sure this works.

I'm not convinced.

"A basketball scout, Mr. Grant, will be at the final game. With that GED you could get a scholarship." He leans back and smiles, an expression of satisfaction, like he's just eaten Thanksgiving dinner, on his face.

We advance to the final game, beating our opponents by twenty-five points. Li'l Quake and I are unstoppable. We read each other as though we're one mind figuring strategies, completing plays by grasping each other's skills and compensating for slight weaknesses.

Usually my mind is saturated with gang life. All day, I'm surrounded with people who're part of the 'hood, My mail from Huckabuck is filled with news of the set. One letter tells me that Mouse shot Santa Claus, shot him good, so he won't be ridin' through our 'hood no more. And K. B. moved to Inglewood. At night, before I sleep, my mind sorts through my homies, planning tactics to aid each one. Every now and then, my conscience steps in, Colton stirs, and that stomach-churning, sick feeling washes over me.

But the night before the championship game, I dream I'm in the NBA. I play all night, my throws swooshing through the net.

At halftime the score is 53 to 42 our favor. Coach Brown introduces me and Li'l Quake to Mr. Grant, who tells me to take my time and don't force anything. "Play your game your way," he says. "And don't be intimidated by the size of your opponents."

While he talks, I wonder how I can give up gangbanging to go to school where it's easy for enemies to find you. I see myself going up for a jumpshot. I'm three feet off the ground and a bullet hits me. What could I tell my enemies? How could I stop the bullet? I'm in the thick of things—shooting people, robbing people, assaulting people. My past is who I am. No smooth talk or new attitude can change that.

Yet, basketball is a release, another refuge.

The entire second half, I'm double-teamed. I only manage to score twenty points. Then Li'l Quake sprains an ankle. With him out of the game, the final score is 83 to 103.

Two weeks later, I hear from Huckabuck that Crazy Q, who I initiated, is dead. After being chased by some Bloods, high on PCP, he crashed into a bus.

Because of attending GED classes and remaining discipline free, I'm given a furlough pass. Moms and my youngest brother, Curtis, born while I was in Nelles, pick me up and take me to Louise's house. As soon as I step out of the car, I seize a good whiff of L.A.'s pollution. Before I exhale, a gunshot rings out. Ten seconds later, a police car races down the block, siren screaming, tires screeching. It stops on Thirty-ninth and Second, a Crip hangout for the Avenues.

I smile.

I love the 'hood, its violence, false sense of security, even the fickle serenity. When the decibels of hostility slow and people relax in an interval of peace, police revive tension simply by driving through.

When I get back to Fenner, Coach Brown tells me how proud he is of me. "You're the first guy on the team to win a furlough. Don't you know that gangbanging isn't for you, Cee? You gotta understand that you have choices. You're aggressive; you need something to occupy your time and your mind that provides release for that bottled-up energy. But you have choices how you use it."

I don't understand him then. Not really. But later his words come back.

"I heard about your homeboy, Crazy Q. Sorry."

"Yeah. Sometime I don't know why I keep going on."

He looks at me hard, narrows his eyes.

"I wish I were dead."

"What are you talking about? You've your whole life ahead."

I want to take my words away. This time I showed him too much. I shrug, "I just lose it sometimes."

"We all lose it sometimes. That's part of life."

The man is like a father to me, I think, and I smile at him. *He'll be here for me. I can count on him.*

"Hey, I'm gonna be gone for a few days. Stay outta trouble."

"Alright." I slap him five and his gold jingles.

"If 50 plus x2 equals 110, what's x2?"

"Ten," I say. "Ten."

He gets small as he walks away. He shouts back at me, "Remember, stay cool."

The next day I receive a letter from Huckabuck. *I was rolling to the store when one of them punk-ass Twinkie fools shot through my car window with a .30-.30 Winchester. I got hit in the arm, but I'm cool. Man I can't wait till you get up outta there so we can bust on these fools. Two thumbs, three fingers, Huckabuck.*

Everyone I know is under attack. My eyes wet and tears stream down my face. Every other week someone is dying, getting shot, or going to jail.

I sit on my bunk, holding his letter, tears blurring the words to irregular dots. Huckabuck was shot, but takes it in stride as if he knew it was coming. A realist. A lot of cats get shot and quit bangin', but not Huckabuck. No one else is as down for the set. He's with it win, lose, or draw. Like he said, "Do or die."

Moe, an OG Pueblo Blood, sees me. "Look at the fool, he's cryin' like a bitch."

I storm out of the cottage and find Li'l Quake shooting dice on the sidewalk. He'll cover my back. "Quake." I shake him by the shoulders.

"Whassup?" His eyes are glued to the dice, his forearms rippling as he rolls.

"I need to talk to you."

He watches the cubes hit the wall, tumble back to the cement.

I grab them before they rest. "Man, what the fuck you trippin' off of? I need to talk to you."

He stands up, pulls his head back, the scar on his forehead evident. "Whassup." His eyes meet mine and I know he's focused on me.

"Lure that fool, Moe, round to the back of the cottage."

"Cee, Moe bigger than you, let's jump him." He wants to assure my play succeeds by being part of the action.

"No. I'll handle it." I stroll behind the cottage and hide in the bushes.

Li'l Quake walks past me first, Moe behind him. I jump from the cover and start punching.

"Hold up, Cee, hold up," Moe shouts.

"Shut up, punk." I knock him to the ground and stomp him out.

"Wait a minute, bro', we all Black," he pleads.

"Fool, don't give me that Black bullshit. You know what you did." I crack him across his head till he's unconscious.

Because Moe is a Blood, our skirmish escalates and I'm met with hostile stares till I fight another Blood, putting him in the hospital.

The very next day, Coach Brown returns and pulls me from the cottage during count. "Cee, what's going on with you? I thought we had an understanding. This is how you do me, huh?" He's flushed, his forehead shining.

"I—"

"You call yourself my friend and then turn around and front me off when I'm gone?" He clicks his tongue in the roof of his mouth like a woman. It's such a sad sound how he does it, clicking with each shake of his head, it's as though he carries the world's sorrow.

"Coach—"

"No. Don't open your mouth. I asked you to be cool while I was gone. I'm not going to tell the parole board, but you're cut from the team. Man, get outta my face."

I stomp back to the cottage, sit on my bunk, and write Huckabuck a letter. *Shit don't stop up in here. These people don't understand. They think bangin' shit is part time. Muthafuckas act like we kids or something, Huck. Like this is all a game. Man, I can't wait to get out of this sorry-ass spot. I can't wait.*

In March 1984, I earn early parole after serving three years and three months. I'm almost nineteen. Moms and my three brothers come to pick me up. Before I leave, I meet Li'l Quake at the pay window and hug him. He's more rock hard than ever as he claps me on my back. We've both turned into men during my time. He hasn't even made furlough yet and I'm going home. My glee at winning freedom evaporates. I press him to me. As much as I want my release, I don't want to leave him behind. I'll miss playing ball with him, thinking as one, knowing I have someone to count on.

"Stay strong in this madhouse, Quake," I say.

"Don't trip. You know I'm gonna stay down, Cee."

I smile at him and give him five. "Here's my number. Call me when you get out." I hand him Louise's number. My throat is thick.

"I'm gonna call you, too. So you better still be out," he tells me.

"Man, I ain't goin' back to jail. Bet on it."

"Yeah. We'll see."

I hug him again and make the short walk to Moms's car. Once I'm inside, I turn to look back. He stands watching me leave. His moist eyes and settled lips make him look like he wants to crawl in my pocket. I form the Crip sign with my thumb and index finger and hit it hard across my chest.

As Moms pulls away, I stick my head out the window and shout, "When the West Side ride the East Side hide."

He salutes me with the East Coast sign and yells, "East Side is the best side."

That's the last time I see Li'l Quake.

"Boy." My mother slaps me across the neck. "Get your goddamn ass in this fucking car."

She hasn't changed.

FOUR

Road Not Taken

And if that ain't enough, you love yourselves. Nothing in this world loves a black man more than another black man. You hear of solitary white men, but niggers? Can't stay away from one another a whole day. So. It looks to me like you the envy of the world.
—Toni Morrison, *Sula*

WHILE I WAS AWAY, CRACK WAS INTRODUCED TO THE 'HOOD. Smiley is in jail, arrested for murder. He robbed the local ice-cream man who, during the robbery, had a heart attack and died. "What the fuck is he trippin' on, doin' some small shit like that?" I ask G, his brother.

"It's the crack, cuz. The crack." G talks fast and his eyes don't meet mine. He snaps his fingers after each word. Thin now and wearing gold chains, he looks around nervously. His forearm muscles flicker as he moves with fits and starts. "The crack and that PCP."

I shake my head.

"He was out on bail. Crack had him and he robbed a bank and got caught."

I can't imagine Smiley committing nickel-and-dime crimes to support a habit. We did our share of freebasing in the late seventies. After a successful robbery, we'd buy an ounce of cocaine, rent a suite, invite some women, and smoke and have sex all night. The next day we'd get up and head back to the war zone to put in work for the set. Now Smiley is pawning his jewelry and committing ridiculous crimes. Kato was on PCP and confessed to a crime he didn't commit. Big T is smoking "premos"—mixed marijuana and cocaine—and talking volumes. Shit is out of control.

Byron, who was with Smiley during the bank robbery, was gunned down by police. The cops claimed he jumped over a fence with a gun in his hand and aimed at an undercover cop during the getaway. When the investigators arrived on the scene, they couldn't find a gun. Just a bright white bag filled with money.

"Hey, Li'l Cee," G looks up at me, "You a man now, for sure. Not no Li'l nothing no more."

I return to Louise's and sit on my bed, elbows on my knees, thinking about my set. My conscience starts rolling, scolding, and I hear my father say, "You're an animal." I guess he's right, from the time I was initiated till now. Regardless of whether I'm acting out of aggression or survival in a war, my past does make me look like an animal.

That sick-stomach feeling shames me. *I'll be somebody, not an animal*, I tell myself. *You have choices*. I hear Coach Brown's words and the Colton part of me says, *You can do it*. I resolve to play basketball when my anger fumes. I'll be Louise's grandson. I move back to Louise's, get a job at my stepgrandmother's hamburger stand, Fatburgers, and enroll in Hamilton High School located in a quiet community exempt from gang violence. I start working for my mother's maintenance company washing windows. I'm working two part-time jobs and going to school. I'll try this life.

I drive by Huckabuck's house and talk to his dad, but Huckabuck isn't there. Finally I see him round a corner near Spike's. When I hug him, I feel his gun. "You been busy, uh, Crip?"

"Gun's still smokin', cuz," he says.

He's been gangbanging hard and selling drugs.

"Cuz, take a break, my nigga. Let's meet at the skating rink."

"Tomorrow night, cuz." He looks over his shoulder and I know he's gotta go.

He hugs me again. "Do or die, cuz. Do or die." Same Huckabuck.

In the school cafeteria, I meet a girl named Beauty. Her hair is in dreadlocks, her skin so smooth it looks liquid. One afternoon, we sit on the edge of the basketball court and she tells me her father was a cocaine dealer, selling powder to be freebased to the Black community. Now, in prison, he discovered that cocaine is being brought into South Central by the United States Government to destroy the Black community. Crack is genocide, she tells me. Her dark popeyes bear in at me as though to push her words into my brain. The government purposely distributes it to minority communities to reduce the Black population and finance political campaigns, she says.

That's crazy, I think. "No, they allow crack 'cause they don't give a fuck about us and would be glad if we wipe each other out. Or commit crazy crimes so they can throw us in jail."

"No. I'm tellin' you. My dad knows. It's the CIA bringing it in from Latin America," Beauty insists.

"Bullshit. It's some nigga from Hoover named Ricky Ross, but homies call 'em Freeway Rick." I don't much believe in the benevolence of the government, but that's too far fetched.

"My dad knows." She stands to return her tray.

Besides Beauty, I hang out with friends I've known from elementary school. These men have graduated from school and were once square as a pool table and twice as green. They held jobs, but after seeing thugs making three and four times their yearly income in one week, they start selling. Dealing is an opportunity for big-time money. Capitalism in action. They offer me drugs to sell and pot to smoke.

"I'm cool on that bullshit," I tell them. I'm that determined in this new life.

No one considers the future; everyone is here-and-now. Getting rich today is all they want. A Black man selling drugs to another Black man is equivalent to shooting a Black man, only a bullet is speedy and crack slow and more painful. What's the difference between me gangbanging and them selling crack? They kill for money. I kill to stay alive.

All my friends from the set are running around like a bunch of chickens with their heads chopped off. High.

Smiley's family moved out of the 'hood after his arrest. The police kicked down the door, looking for him. Knowing how the police hound a family once they peg a house as a gang member's home, they moved.

As I pull into the driveway of the new house, Gina sprawls on the front lawn playing with a baby. I do the math and realize he's the son of the man who won her from me while I was in Youth Authority. My blood races, pumps in my neck, but I inhale slowly and tuck the anger deep. She had sex with him. I don't want to provide any indication that I care.

"Is G here?" I ask.

"No," she says and then immediately calls for her younger brother, John John.

He walks to the car. "Damn, what was they feedin' you in jail? You got muscles and shit now."

I can tell he's glad to see me. "Ah man, you know how jail is, they be workin' a guy like a slave," I reply. "What's with Smiley?"

His brows come together and he sighs. "It ain't lookin' too good, Cee. You know what happen, right?"

"Heard he was in jail, but how's he doin'?"

He lowers his head. "Man, they gave him twenty-two years to life for the murder and now they charged him with Byron's murder."

"I thought the pigs killed Byron."

"They did. But because him and Smiley were crime partners,

they charged Smiley." John John's eyes are narrowed. He stares into space as if dazed by the thought.

"They can do that?"

"It's some new law. If you commit a crime and your crime partner gets killed, you get charged with his murder. We're trying to raise money to get a lawyer." John John sighs.

"Damn." I can't watch Smiley lose his freedom over some shit he didn't do.

"Tell G I'll be back here next week, when I'm off work, alright?"

"Alright," but his eyes are lost as he drifts further into worry.

I start the car engine and slowly back out. As I pass the curb and roll down the window, Gina asks John John, "Who's that? He's fine."

Before I hear the response, I'm down the block, rounding the corner.

Hour after hour, I mash meat. Sweat trickles down my face, my back, my sides. Little rivulets of moisture, like the fat and blood coursing down the grill. Same random dribbles. Grease seeps through my gloves to my hands, slicks my face, stiffens my apron. Even after a shower, the burger-grease smell clings to my hands and grips my hair. Gina with that baby crawling over her and her laughing at the sky. Smiley arrested for a murder the police did. Everyone else getting high and making big-time money. All the shit I do for my classes. Even talking with Beauty gets old. I goad myself to go through my days, but move with weights dragging. Each event looms like a major chore. Nothing is easy. Time drips, drips, drips like the grease on the griddle, the sweat on my back. I'm confused by what time it is. It feels like it's tomorrow and it's still afternoon. I'd rather pull the covers over my head and drift in sleep.

———————

I'm behind Spike's. The new letters on his sign still have not faded as much as the old ones.

G pulls into the Shell gas station next door. I creep up behind his car and bang on his hood. "Fool. This is a jack."

He jerks with shock, then sees me. "Cee, ah, nigga, I didn't know who in the fuck you was," and gets out of the car to embrace me. "Man, they tryin' to do my brother," he says.

"Nah, our brother."

"Sure, that's right." His palms are on my shoulders.

"You still freebasin'?" I ask him.

"I'm through with that shit. That's what got my little brother caught up."

When he says that, I know he's sober.

"Get in." He jerks his head toward the car. "Let's roll to the 'hood and get at the homies."

I haven't seen them. They're employed as drug dealers and armed robbers; I have a legitimate job trying the straight life. They hang out on street corners, getting high; I'm in school.

They don't know I've avoided my obligation to the set. I promised duty on my conscription, but since being released from Fenner, I allow several enemies to breathe who I caught by surprise, alone, with no witnesses.

To the gang this is treason, but to me, I give them a pass.

I have more important things to do than take a man's life because he wears a different bandana color. It doesn't take a man to fire a gun.

Don't get me wrong. There're still those I'll kill and those I'll kill for—Huckabuck, Smiley, Big T. The flame of hatred for Bloods still burns. But, if I'm going to take a human life, there has to be a just cause, for instance, he killed my companion, my family member. He shot at me. Then, it's an eye for an eye.

But Smiley needs help. The homies and I have a common passion.

G frowns. "You comin', or what? Let's roll."

I climb into the passenger seat and we drive to the 'hood to re-cruit soldiers. It looks the same, the houses painted, the flowers blooming. Smiley's old house has thick black bars on the windows. There's more graffiti on the walls of the alley where I was initiated.

Our plan is to make two hits. The proceeds from the first will go to Smiley's attorney. The proceeds from the second will be di-vided among the crew.

Goofy Vee is with it and so is J-Dog. We need a getaway driver. Women make good getaway drivers because cops are slower to pull them over. Mission Mary, Smiley's girlfriend, our normal driver, was captured for robbery, turned state's evidence, served three months, and is now in hiding.

We drive around looking for Sabrina Smith. I have a crush on her, though I never told anyone.

We catch her strolling down Thirty-ninth Street, her beige pants clinging to her revolving ass. Her black ponytail bobs slightly as her legs slide her to her destination. Just watching her walk is a symphony of percussion.

G pulls beside her and tells her the plan while I check her out from the passenger seat. She's aged a bit, lost some weight as a re-sult of smoking crack cocaine. Her eyes shine when she sees me. She piles into the car with the rest of us.

The plan is for Goofy Vee, J-Dog, and me to drive to the store in a stolen car. When the three of us finish the robbery, we'll meet G and Sabrina waiting in another car to turn over the goods. They'll deliver it to G's fence. G will take the money to his father's house and we'll divide it there.

The first part of our plan runs smooth as silk. We're in and out of the jewelry store in sixty seconds. Goofy Vee is knock-kneed and has the most ridiculous walk on the block, but when he's do-ing business, his hands zip. When we arrive at the parking lot next to the freeway, a patrol car enters, driving slow, obviously making its rounds. "Stay cool," I warn Goofy and J-Dog. "Walk easy. They're right over there." I nod to G's car.

But G panics and orders Sabrina to take off.

This changes the complexity of things; it's bad enough we're in a stolen car. Now, we're in possession of stolen property. If G had taken the jewelry, we'd only have to ditch the car. If captured, we'd be charged with GTA (Grand Theft Auto), G could still fence the loot, and the money used to bail out Smiley.

Now, capture means jewelry will be found; we'd get GTA and robbery charges, and we'll all be stuck. Smiley included.

I can't believe this nigga, I think, as G's car spits pebbles racing away.

I return to our stolen car. J-Dog, who's driving, opens the door for me. "What the fuck is cuz trippin' off of?" Goofy Vee is in the backseat, looking dumbfounded.

"Musta got scared when he saw the pigs."

"We gotta get the fuck outta here. Close the door and duck down."

I curl under the dashboard and J-Dog drives out of the parking lot, hits the freeway, and heads for L.A. We dump the stolen car and drive nonstop to Smiley's father's house.

As soon as we enter the house, G says, "Where's the jewelry?"

The TV shifts colors and fills my head with drone as I squint in his doorway. *Fool, you left us for dead and all you have to say is, where's the jewelry?* I fling this thought to him with my narrowed eyes.

He looks away, but doesn't give up the bone he's chewing as he waves his arms with his words. "Where's the jewelry?"

"Nigga, you must be crazy." I pivot and march out of the house as he turns to the TV.

J-Dog and Goofy Vee follow.

Eventually, we fence the jewelry and split the money three ways. I give Smiley's mother money and four pairs of diamond earrings for her granddaughters. I use a few thousand on clothes and guns and save the rest for Smiley's attorney. Goofy Vee and J-Dog blow their cut on crack cocaine.

Beauty is right; crack is destroying the 'hood.

A few weeks later, I visit Smiley. All the way there, I play soft tunes, sit back in the car, and try to prepare myself for the racist onslaught that looms. The waiting room's greasy windows dim the light. Gray smudges darken the walls. A toddler bats a dust bunny until his pregnant mother looks down from her magazine and pulls him away. Paper, soda cans, Styrofoam coffee cups, cigarette butts spangle the cement floor. A child stacks cans, unaware that she's at a jail instead of a playground.

As soon as I enter, a burly officer narrows his eyes at me, walks over to another pig, eyes still on me, and whispers. I wait in a line for three hours. Finally, I reach the window.

The officer at the window barks, "ID." She grabs the ID and runs it in the computer. "Who you here to see?"

I tell her Smiley's real legal name.

Smiley's name comes up with a flag on the computer, indicating he's a gang member. Her mouth tightens as she shakes her head.

"You on parole?"

"No."

"You got any cases pending?"

"No." Fuck you, I want to say, but I'm determined to maintain politeness.

She jerks her head toward another officer and calls him on her phone, telling him I'm here to see a gang member.

The officer comes over and pats me down. "You got on the wrong colors today?"

I'm wearing jeans and a white tee shirt. I don't say a word.

I can almost feel him thinking, "Look at this nigger. Who's he think he is?"

He radios another officer who moves toward me, inspecting me as I stand in another line and begin another long wait.

I wait for two hours, watching the kids play with the garbage, listening to the rudeness of the officers, thinking about Smiley until I hear a male voice announce his name over the PA system.

Smiley is behind Plexiglas and chained to the table, but in spite of the attempts at dishonor and control, he grins from ear to ear when he sees me. This is why I came, to see this expression, his smile.

I shake my head at him, happy and sad stirred together, and pick up the phone. "What up, cuz?"

"You know what's up, Cee Loc. 'Do or die.' It don't stop." His baritone voice reverberates in the phone, as though we're in a recording room. His eye, just one corner, twitches slightly.

"Hey, you know G left me and the homies for dead?"

"You bullshittin'?"

"I ain't trippin'. We made it back." I lean toward him as if I can travel through the plastic.

"I told you before about fuckin' with cuz. He ain't like us. That's my brother and I love him, but you gotta understand, ain't nobody real about this shit but a few. Huckabuck. Big T. Everyone else on their own kick." He sits straighter in his chair, uses his teaching voice, which increases his sense of control.

"Yeah. But shit is crazy."

"Whaddya mean, Cee?" He frowns.

"Look at you. You got life for some bullshit and now they trying to give you another case. How'd this happen?" I shake my head. My love for him and his constrained future seem so disconnected.

"It's that dope, homie. That crack and liquor. It ain't like the seventies when we was smoking that shit to high-sign to show off a huge diamond on our fingers. Crack is cut wit' chemicals."

"I got some ends for the lawyer situation." I want to give him another chance to be the admirable Smiley before he started chasing the crack dragon.

"I don't need no lawyer. I got a plan."

"Uh?"

"You know me. Just be over Pops's house in the morning."

I nod.

His mouth forms a thin line. He looks around the room. The scar on his neck from running through that plate glass on one of our licks has keloided smooth and shiny. Other men talk on their phones, pressing the receivers into their ears, tilting to the glass to create a private room. "You sure I can count on you, Cee Loc? John John told me you was workin' and goin' to school. Homies say you ain't been coming around."

"Ain't nothin' over there no more. Just Huckabuck. Everyone else is dead, in jail, or on crack." I lean back, drum my fingers on the shelf. I know what I'm saying when I say it. I know the cards I'm taking away from myself. "But I'm wit' you, cuz, 'Do or die.'"

"Tomorrow, then."

"Tomorrow." I hang up the phone. We sit staring at each other. I give him two thumbs up, the Harlem Crip sign, he flashes one back.

On the way home, I think of his smile when he saw me, the love so thick it washed over me like warm water. Then my mind flicks to all the different selves of Smiley. I see him nod at me and his face flashes different aspects of the man he is. For my eighteenth birthday, Smiley risked incarceration to bring me marijuana, throwing it over the fence when I was in Youth Authority. Diamonds from the wire fence shadowed his face as he caught me up with the news. His easy smile was my present. Smiley listened without teasing me for my soft feelings. I see him tucking his mom's hair behind her ear to comfort her, his mouth set soft with sorrow. I carried him into his house, removed his jacket and shoes, lay him on his couch when he was comatose from liquor and PCP. Then, the obliviousness of his face was unsettling. His astute energy replaced with a child's naïve exposure.

It was Smiley who trained me as a killer. He set me up with the girl who skirted my virginity, and he gave me my first gun, a .38 special.

Returning from a robbery, the highway patrol started chasing us. He drove a mile down a freeway ravine against traffic. Then we jumped from the getaway car and ran for a bus.

He's my road dog.

I've never met anyone like him.

I can't let him spend the rest of his life in prison.

So just like the old days, I'm back at Smiley's waiting for him. Just like the old days, Gina brings me a soda and starts braiding my hair, me sitting between her legs, the TV playing. Just like the old days, her fingers soothe my scalp, make my worries go away. She's still seeing Earl, the square guy who's the father of her baby. "It's just for sex," she tells me.

Me, I'm there for the emotional connection and her hands warm and soft. Being so close to her family makes it easy to forgive her. I love them all. Just like the old days, I fall asleep in her soft waterbed. I don't even kiss her.

I reach over her to answer the bleating phone. A deep voice asks, "Cee there?"

"Speaking."

"I'm Lunatick Frank from the Rollin' Sixties. Callin' for Smiley."

"Whassup?"

"Get a G-ride, two homies, and three guns. He'll get back wit' you in a couple of days."

"Right." The phone cuts off.

I immediately call Steve and D'Andre and they agree to help me secure guns. I ask Big Mel to steal a car and park it in Marla's Memory Lane parking lot.

Thirty minutes later, Steve, D'Andre and I drive to Royland's Hotel and drink beer till night falls. D'Andre's easy laugh makes everything seem fun. The swiftest runner in the 'hood, he loves velocity, fast rides, and rollercoasters.

At eleven o'clock, we pile into D'Andre's Datsun B-210 and drive to Big Five Sporting Goods in Torrance. I sling a bumper jack through the plate-glass display window. The glass just falls away, giving me my door. I jump inside the store, grab guns from the display rack. I hurl them to D'Andre and Steve, who toss them into the trunk of the car.

In twenty seconds we're got enough guns. I leap through the window.

We pile into the car and D'Andre flies down the alley toward a main street, makes a left turn. Red light. We wait. My heart thumps with the growling engine. I inhale slowly. Then we drive on.

"We cool now, cuz," D'Andre says.

"Piece of cake," Steve laughs.

It's too simple. The hair on the back of my neck prickles.

As soon as I think this, spotlights beam, sirens scream. The police are behind us with guns pointing. "Pull over to the curb. Get out with your hands above your head."

We're handcuffed, stuffed into the backseat of the patrol car, driven to the station, and booked for breaking and entering. My intuition was right. It was too easy.

The next morning, D'Andre's father bails him out. An hour later, Steve is out. Louise is called, but she's not home. The detective contacts my parole officer, who puts a hold on me.

I'm not given bail and transported to Los Angeles County Jail.

I wonder what Smiley's plan was. How will I tell him I was arrested getting him guns?

FIVE

Crips Module

Three in ten black men between the ages of eighteen and thirty-five will have served time in jail or under criminal supervision in their lifetime....We built prisons to provide housing for the black poor. And yes, of course, we have come to accept better-educated blacks who have made it. Prison is for blacks who haven't. Is this progress?
—Jerome Brunner, "Do Not Pass Go"

INMATES PATCH TOGETHER A BUSINESS BARTERING GOODS OR favors. Since I'm housed in a dorm and given a job in the kitchen, I steal coffee from the storeroom, which I trade for cigarettes to support my habit.

To make coffee, you ignite a plastic milk carton, hold a second one over the flame till the water boils, and then add a cap or a sock filled with grounds. Homemade coffee in your cell is a little bit of home, a little hit of caffeine, a luxury.

I'm packing coffee grounds in a cap.

"Hey. I know what you doin', homeboy." John crosses his arms over his protruding stomach, leans into the doorway of the store-room.

Sliding the coffee wad into my pocket, I brush by him on my way out.

"You're stealing my customers, homeboy. You better stop sell-ing, or we're gonna have a problem," he hisses to my back. He's stealing coffee, too.

"You threatening me?" I turn toward him.

"I'm promising." He steps toward me, his face inches from mine.

I slam the sneer off his face, but, outweighing me by more than forty pounds, he punches me hard enough to knock my air out. Never one to lose a fight, I grab a steel mallet from the giant-size stove and whack him. I break both his arms, his jaw, and knock him unconscious.

A few days later, a confidential informant snitches on me and I'm thrown in the hole for ten days. Rats scurry on the floor of the dark cell and my skin crawls. "Joot balls"—yesterday's food ground up and scooped on a plate with an ice-cream scoop—are slid in the slot in my door. We had stew yesterday and minced and compressed it smells like Alpo dog food. The bars are steel, the bed, ceiling, and walls are cement.

As I'm escorted to court line, Tweety Bird from Compton Crip tells the deputy that I'm a Crip. Now I'm rehoused in Module 4800. Cripville. It is a brand-new testing ground and training station.

First, I stand against the wall in Operation Safe Streets (OSS) interdepartmental office, holding a one-and-a-half-foot square placard with my full name, birth date, set name, and 'hood for a series of Polaroid pictures. The pictures are distributed among the pigs and sent to FBI headquarters. I'm permanently labeled a threat to the security of the United States, issued a gray jumpsuit, instead of the blue that the other inmates wear, and then sent into the module.

I'm just nineteen and a security threat to the entire United States. Wow.

I'm housed on Baker Row in a six-man cell. A command booth is situated in the middle of the module. A glass catwalk runs the length of the tiers so the pigs can observe us.

At first, there's such a racket I can't distinguish one sound from another. Men scream out their sets, slap signs, yell through the vents, curse the prison guards, beat on the bunks. One man beats percussion on the bunk and raps. Down the tier another starts a different beat.

A man shouts across the tier, "You a punk, fool. A bitch. I'ma beat yo' ass."

Someone bellows back, "Bring yo ass home to Cripville." When I step into my cell, my stomach rolls.

From the next cell, I hear, "Hey, is that Li'l Cee?"

It's T. J., from my set, finishing up a county lid—a one-year term. He assures me he'll contact the homies so a lawyer can be hired to represent me.

"Yeah. What module is this, cuz?" I ask him.

"Forty-eight hundred. The homies call it 'forty-eight hours'."

"Why y'all call it that?"

"'Cause If you survive the first forty-eight—the racket, the assaults, the constant chaos—then you worthy of representing Crip and living in Cripville. But, Li'l Cee, you got heart, cuz. Plus you got laced by the OGs, like Smiley and Big T. So this ain't gonna be shit to you."

T. J. tells me that 4800 is the latest project created by the Los Angeles County Sheriff's Department Operation Safe Street to curb gang violence and restore order in the jail. "But shit," Terry says, "instead, it's our training station. Cuz, I've learned all kinda shit in here with the homies. I learned how to resist the pigs. I've learned the philosophy and history of being a Crip. My head is where my heart always was, Cee."

The module was set up because of the 1984 rebellion, T. J. continues. During that year, Big Heron, a Compton Crip, was thrashed with batons for a minor infraction. Numerous Crips had been beaten by the police and the sheriff's department when arrested. But the brutal beating of Big Heron becomes the last straw in the long and violent sequence of pig violence. Twenty Crips seized the chow hall. First, the deputy sheriffs were attacked, and then the Crips turned on the khaki trustees and hammered them for being pigs' servants and shortchanging them on their food. One pig was held hostage and used for negotiation after the rest ran out of the chow hall.

T. J. stands close so I can hear him in spite of the din, the shouts, a radio blasting *Beat it*.

"So what happen', cuz?"

He tells me the pigs barricaded the doors as we began making demands for clean clothes, better food and treatment. The siege lasted for hours. The sheriff's department told the media the "riot' was due to the breakdown of the air-conditioning system. The inmates were videotaped from an elevated Plexiglas tower. Meanwhile, Module 4800, which sat adjacent to the mess hall, was evacuated.

For half a day, the resistors demanded that they be given clean clothes, access to the law library. "And the pigs," T. J. hisses, "said, 'Okay. We're all men here; let the deputy go. Then we'll talk.' " T. J.'s voice raises, loses its urban twang as he talks like a White man. "The resistors were manipulated into leaving the chow hall naked. Walked through a gauntlet of deputies dressed in full riot gear. Fuckers were armed with batons, or those one-and-a-half-foot-long flashlights made from aircraft metal. They whacked away, forcibly directing Crips into Forty-eight hundred." The resistors remained naked with no bedding, no clothes no showers, no toilet paper, no visits for seventy-two hours. After that, they were given gray jumpsuits.

"That's the birth of the Crip Module, cuz. Li'l Cee, don't get caught slippin' when you leave here to go on visits or court." T. J. warns. "Our enemies, the Bloods and the pigs, are out there layin' in wait to bum-rush us. Everywhere we go we're shackled from the waist down and blanketed with escort. I mean every time you leave the module. We're even chained during visits. And our gray jumpsuits give us away. Everybody knows we're Crips."

"Shit."

"Whether you goin' to court, a visit, or the doctor, you're marked."

Guess I won't be able to steal my coffee and do my hustle, I think.

"Check out everything you hear. The pigs tell one homie a lie about another to start fights. They like to see us fighting each other."

That night, a voice shouts, "Ma-chine in motion."

My five cell mates stand at attention facing the tier. They inhale as if one and shout simultaneously:

> Ma-chine-in-Mo-tion
> C-R-I-P, C-R-I-P
> Crip, Crip!
> One mile.
> Two miles.
> Three miles.
> Here we go,
> All the way,
> Up the hill,
> Down the hill,
> Through the land,
> Kill a klan,
> Through the fog
> Fight like dogs.
> No food. No shoes
> In our houses,
> Full of mouses.
> Baby dying.
> Mothers crying.
> Got to struggle to survive.
> Got to Crip to stay alive.
>
> Who say?
> C say.

Who say?
C say.

In sixty-nine Crip was born,
Sixteen years and going strong.
East Side, West Side,
North Side, South Side,
Nationwide, Unified,
Crip. Crip.

Raymond Washington did his best,
Cripped for years, now he rests.
Big Tookie, be like him,
Let us fight like Africans.
Mac and Saity, they were down,
Compton Crip, strong and proud.
Hoova Joe, he was right,
Cuttin' throats day and night.

The fellas have made this up and I haven't heard it before. This
time I shout the chorus with the others and belong to the throng.

Who say?
C say.
Who say?
C say.
Who the greatest?
C the greatest.
Can't stop. Won't stop.
Won't stop. Can't stop.
Refuse to quit,
Ride or die.

Keepin' busters on the run,
When you catch 'em cut his tongue.

Uptown. Downtown.
Blue flags all around.
C-R-I-P! C-R-I-P!
Whata'ya want? (Freedom)
When'da'ya want it? (Now)
How'daya get it? (Power)
When'da'ya need it? (Now)

Who say?
C say.
Who say?
C say.
Do or die.
Make 'em cry.
Do or die.
Won't stop
Do or die.
Can't stop.
Crip. Crip.
Crip. Crip.

I sing with my brothers, five hundred voices strong. Their voices and power fill my chest. The Crip Nation lives. Unified and strong. Here I'll have the camaraderie of the streets, Crip love— homie love.

The pigs hate it.

The next day, T. J. is released. "I'll have the homies get you an attorney," he shouts at me as he exits.

Treatment in the module is different than in the rest of the jail. It's as if I'm a mouse in a cage and the pigs are the scientists. They use the Plexiglas windows to monitor our strengths and weaknesses. They never make contact with us other than to handcuff us or beat us. I can't walk around freely, unattended to canteen, other modules, and visitors. There's no coffee or other items to steal and sell, no reading material, full-course meals, or access to the law library.

Two days later we're on lockdown. When the trustee delivers my sack lunch, I ask, "Why're we on lockdown?"

"Security," he growls.

"They just tryin' to fuck with us," my cell mate sighs. "Happens all the time."

We're on lockdown for four days. And then we're let out of our cells.

Finally, I can go to the yard. A sign says, STOP HERE. My toe crosses the line and a deputy screams, "Can you read? Can't you read that sign?" He tries to slam me into the wall, but the other Crips on the chain close in and the pig gets intimidated.

The Crip Constitution, what we call "paperwork," maintains order and rules for the module. The Consolidated Crip Organization (CCO) and Blue Note Organization (BNO), for which my homeboys, Big BJ and Big Tookie, are generals, organizes classes. CCO ideology is attributed to the Black Panther Party and is pro-Black. The BNO is more centered on Cripism and not involved with Black nationalism. They're both created to stop "set tripping" (Crip civil war), supply us with guidance, and teach us sophisticated ways to influence the pigs for food, phone calls, showers to make our time go by smoother.

Smuggled books such as *Soledad Brother* by George Jackson, *Art of War* by Sun Tzu, *The Autobiography of Malcolm X* as told by Alex Haley, and a book on slavery become our bibles. We're our own nation run by our own laws and leaders within the system. The leaders set about educating us.

The next week, I receive a letter from T. J. that the homies are broke, trippin' off PCP and crack cocaine. No one's in a position to hire me an attorney. I'm forced to go to my mother and father. Meanwhile, I know Smiley is in jail; I ask where he is, but no one knows.

And then I'm escorted to court, shackled from the waist down, shuffling as I walk since my wrists are cuffed to my waist and the chain between my feet is only two feet long. I sound like a dog rattling his chain.

When I arrive at Torrance, a cop says, "You're a Crip, uh? Think you're tough, uh?" He jerks the chains on my wrists. "You tough? Tighten up his cuffs. He can handle it. He's a Crip." Another cop constricts my cuffs. Then, I'm thrown inside a giant-size holding tank with prisoners from the general population. Seeing me in gray, they bunch together and study me warily as though I'm Charles Manson.

The tank smells like body waste. My stomach turns. I use my teeth to pull the jumpsuit over my nose and sit down on the cold cement bench. Even then the odor is strong. I close my nostrils and try to breath through clenched teeth. The other prisoners in blue jumpsuits stand together laughing, joking, and shooting the breeze as if they're at a party in a penthouse suite, comfortable with the piss, vomit, and shit marinating on the floor.

The tightened cuffs cut off my circulation and my forearms swell. The skin rubs from my ankles and the red flesh oozes.

"Simpson?" bellows the deputy. I jangle to the drill gate, moving so quickly that the other prisoners stop talking to watch.

The deputy escorts me to the second floor to see my attorney, who has been hired by my mother. He's an older Black man, his hair in a short Afro, graying in a patch near his forehead. I sit on the steel bench next to him.

"Hi, Colton. How're ya' doin?"

"I'm alright." I inhale fresh air.

He has a clutter of files on his lap, the smell of his cologne welcome after the holding tank. "Well, your mother asked me to represent you as a favor that I owe her."

He opens one of the folders. "I've had a chance to review your file and see that you're recently paroled from Youth Authority. If it's alright with you, I figure it'll be best to plead guilty to receiving stolen property." He chews on the inside of his lip. "You'll receive sixteen months in the state prison as opposed to four years in California Youth Authority."

"Sixteen months?"

"Don't worry. You won't do the entire sixteen. You'll do half, as long as you get a job and remain discipline free."

He talks about months like they're hours. Some lawyer. Meanwhile, I weigh the consequences of going to trial and being found guilty. I don't have an alibi. Four years in CYA? Hell, no. "Okay. I'll take it." I look down at my shoes on the linoleum floor.

A little later, I'm in front of Judge Cecil J. Mills for sentencing. I stand in my gray jumpsuit, shackled from the waist down. He's draped in black king's robes, sitting on a platform high above me. He peers over his glasses, reading my file, gawks at me, and shakes his head.

"Well. Now. Mr. Simpson. Don't you dare look at me like that."

My forearms are swollen to three times their normal size, the blisters on my wrists seep, the heavy chain around my waist hurts my back. I still smell the odor of the fermenting cesspool of the holding tank. I feel like an animal. I don't understand how he thinks I'm being antagonistic. I stare at the desk in front of me. Must be the gray jumpsuit.

"I'm doing you and society a favor. Now, I'm going along with the plea bargain agreed between the district attorney and your lawyer. But I'm cautioning you. Should I ever see you in my courtroom again, I won't be so easy." He wags his forefinger at me and clenches straggly eyebrows. "You must be responsible for your actions. If not, then it's my duty to familiarize you with what it means to be responsible." His eyes strive to penetrate me. "Do we have an understanding?"

I nod.

"Okay." He slides his glasses from the bridge of his nose to rest like empty eyes in the middle of his forehead. "You are sentenced to sixteen months in the California Department of Corrections.

You are to be remanded to the custody of the Los Angeles County Sheriff's until you are transferred to Chino Prison forthwith."

I can do that, I think. I've done longer in Youth Authority. My forearms throb. *All I really like doing is gangbanging and I can do that in prison. Maybe I'll see Smiley.*

I'm escorted back downstairs to the same holding tank. The drill gate opens and there's T-Bone from Black P. Stone Bloods and two of his homies.

"Where're ya from, Blood?" One of his homeboys asked.

He knows that I'm Li'l Cee Loc from Harlem Crip. It's only been ten years since I shot Li'l Ru at the bus stop and only seven years since T-Bone hit me with a brick while I rode down Rodeo with Black Ant behind me on my moped. I'm shackled from the waist down, defenseless, and wearing gray. Obviously I'm a Crip. Why the questions? An enemy is an enemy. Kill or be killed. Do or die. His rules are the same as mine.

My mind works in rhythm with my pounding heart. He's playing the test game, asking me where I'm from to see if I'm a soldier or a coward. If I lie and tell him that I don't bang, he'll pump me for information. Who killed so-and-so? Where does your homie live?

If I tell him the truth, that I'm a Rollin' Thirties Harlem Crip, I'll get beat. Adrenaline surges through me. My hands cold, my throat pulsing, I weigh my options. Three against one. They're free from chains and I'm in chains. These fools gonna jump me regardless.

I rush T-Bone head first, knock him to the ground. Then, I spin and drop-kick the cat doing the talking and he hits the wall. My momentum takes me to the ground where the other homie kicks me in the head and ribs. T-Bone rises from the cement and the cat doing the talking recovers from the wall and stomps me like a soda can. I roll from as many kicks as I can but don't avoid punishment to my testicles, head, chest, and shoulders. The grief is so intense, I don't hear the deputies enter the tank swinging.

Whack.

"Break it up." Whack.

By then, I'm unconscious. When I wake, I'm in the infirmary back in LACJ, my head being stitched up. I don't feel a thing. I remain in the infirmary, the walls pulsing, the slightest sound reverberating in the tunnels of my brain. It seems like three days, but it's only six hours, and then I'm back at 4800.

Tweety Bird comes to my cell the next day. "You alright, cuz?"

"I want some get-back," I tell him.

"Don't trip. The homies handled that shit. Ronnie-T, from West Boulevard Crip, came up with a handcuff key, passed it around the holding tank at court, and we beat up three Bloods. We told them busters, 'This is for the homie Cee, punk.'"

I'm avenged. I thank those who mounted the response and assure them I'll return the favor. That's what's homies are for. Families for each other.

I want to get word to Smiley that I'm here. I continue hunting for him. Because only Steve and D'Andre know about the plan to free him, no one in Smiley's family knows that I'm in LACJ. I look past the fact that Gina left me in Youth Authority and had another man's baby. I don't know why I keep thinking about her so much. I don't know why I don't just ask her where Smiley is. Finally, I write her. Before I get a response, my brother visits me; he wants to see me before I leave for Chino.

Going back to the module after the visit, I see Smiley under heavy escort. He's shackled from the waist down but wears a blue jumpsuit.

"Smiley," I call.

He turns to me, his eyes widen. "Cee Loc. Wha' the fuck you doin' in here? What happened?"

"I got arrest—" But before I finish, the pigs snatch him through a thick steel door across from the visiting area. His face is toward me, his lips in a straight line as he's pushed through the door. His eyes turn down in a mixed expression of sadness and surprise and, somehow, bleakness. On the door is a sign that says 1750.

When I get back to 4800, I ask Three Finger Louie what it means.

"That's high power, cuz. Maximum security. That's where they send the high-risk homies."

"Smiley?"

"The pigs say he's a threat to the population."

The next day, I board the bus for Chino Prison to commence my sixteen-month bid.

SIX

The Ultimate Test: Chino

There is a tendency in democracy not to draw men together, but...make them run away from each other and perpetuate, in the midst of equality, hatreds originating in inequality.
    —Alexis de Tocqueville, *Democracy in America*

CHINO CENTRAL IS A WAREHOUSE WHERE THEY CATEGORIZE you to decide your custody. I go through medical tests, IQ tests, personality tests, and visit a counselor who reviews my case, computes my time, and makes recommendations for placement. This takes a week before I'm sent to Chino West, Chino Prison's minimum-security yard.

It's here that I'm introduced to the politics of California's prison system. I hold a placard with my last name and number for a photograph that is laminated to a two-by-four-inch card. This ID is like a civilian's driver's license and I must carry it to gain access to the library, canteen, or recreation. The prison number becomes me, takes precedence over my last name. Everywhere I go, I must recite the last two numbers: nine one. Nine one becomes another name in my list: Colton, Cokie, Li'l Cee, Nine One. I don't hurry when I say it. I don't rush the One as though I'm ashamed. Instead, I enunciate each consonant, pronouncing the words so they hear what I've become. Nine. One. At last the system has turned me from a human being to "just another number."

Both staff and veteran prisoners assess weakness and strength, stupidity and intelligence, in their observation of new arrivals. Those convicted of sex crimes, or considered homosexual or cowardly, are labeled "inmate" by staff and "buster" by prisoners. They're preyed on by prisoners who beat, rob, rape them. "Buster" is the worst thing one can be. A coward. The ultimate loser. I learned this on the streets; it's an important lesson in dealing with prison. Prisoners respect those proven righteous and courageous, but staff labels them "convicts" and considers them threats to safety and security. No one gets off easy.

The label "convict" must be earned. Action speaks louder than words and, in prison, words are considered bluster and braggadocio. Each prisoner is judged by his "walk," not his "talk". One of today's politicians wouldn't last a week.

I enter Chino West as a foot soldier under scrutiny like all the rest of the Crips from the module. I'm determined to advance in the ranks. I promise myself to approach each war with ardor and vitality. This is my arena, like baseball was my father's. I'll stay focused, just like he told me, work hard, and embrace the goal of becoming an elite soldier with dignity and pride. This is my choice. I focus on being my own hero, on gaining celebrity in the world I've been handed.

Just as in the larger society, race and nationality divide prisoners. Each race has a different clique, and each clique has its own army with foot soldiers, sergeants, lieutenants, captains, enforcers, stabilizers, and generals. The correction officers are stratified similarly.

The largest group is the Southside Mexicans' Southern United Raza (SUR) under orders from the Mexican Mafia. These are Mexican Americans who live south of Fresno, California. Their allies are the Whites. The Whites blatantly validate themselves as racists by covering their bodies with tattoos of swastikas, "100 percent Honky," lightening bolts, Hitler. Blacks ally themselves with Northern Mexicans under the orders of the Nuestra Familia. The Northern and Southern Mexicans are at war, just like the Crips and Bloods. Ironically, Mexican gangs distinguish themselves by bandana color similar to that of the Crips and Bloods. The SUR wear blue and the Northern wear red.

Blacks from Northern California—San Francisco, Oakland, Palo Alto—are usually under orders from the Black Guerilla Family (BGF). They maintain a weak alliance with the Bloods and call themselves Four One Fives (415s), which is the Bay Area telephone area code.

Wars are most prevalent between the Crips and Bloods, and between the Southern and Northern Mexicans. Like the Arabs and Jews, the Protestant and Catholic Irish, the Bosnian and Serbian Yugoslavians, wars within ethnic groups seem to intensify cruelty, revenge, and momentum. It's Cain and Able through the centuries.

Sophisticated cats wearing bifocals may be incognito shot-callers utilizing a nerd camouflage to elude identification by the pigs, who believe that all gang members wear sun glasses, have bulging muscles and have "Loc" in their name. Some of the men with reputations as elite soldiers are snitches working for the pigs who give them telephone calls, radios, drugs, conjugal visits in exchange for information. If snitches are discovered, they're robbed, stabbed, and oftentimes murdered.

So, though race and home neighborhood let me know who's affiliated with which army, I don't know who is at what rank, or who is righteous. Everything seems apparent, but under the façade of transparency lie layers of treacherous veils and masks. You're in peril if you assume things are as they seem.

Immediately after being processed, I introduce myself to Big Silky, general of the Crip Car in Chino. His name embodies his being. A big man, about six feet four, his hand easily palms a basketball, his chest thick and wide. Rumored to be part Indian, his hair falls in sheets of silk, and he moves through the air soundlessly.

He stares me up and down slowly, as though appraising each muscle, but actually pushing me to flinch, look away, shrivel. I meet his gaze. "Hear you on the way, cuz." His voice is melodic.

"Yeah."

"Some Bloods stabbed and beat Insane to death with weights." His lips hardly move. He glances around him. "This was in the recreational gym at Tracy. Stabbed him up inside his chin. The word is out. We need some get-back with the Bloods."

I've been given my orders.

I'm fitted for clothing and escorted to Dorm One, which is arranged like an army barrack for 150–200 men. I immediately survey the entire room for the enemy. I have two other foot soldiers—U-T and Li'l Harlem—who've gone through reception with me. U-T is light skinned and moves slow as though he considers each gesture and word. Li'l Harlem is short, pops energy like Huckabuck, but talks all the time. We secure two pieces of metal from the mop wringer and begin crafting points. We file them on the cement floor over the next few days and manage to turn them into shanks with three-inch-long points on one end and handles made from tape and underwear elastic on the other. Then, we take turns carrying the knives and staying alert.

Again, appearance is not reality. Each morning, we get up, line up, go to chow, then return to the dorm to clean up. There's a day room with a TV and, outside, a track that goes around the facility in front of all five dorms. At West Yard, we have contact visits and visitors smuggle in drugs, so everyone wants to be sent here. Convicts concentrate on appearing laid back.

Under the gauze of mellowness intensity prowls. Everyone churns inside. The easy sprawl hides a pounding heart and watchful eyes. The man with a towel over his face only pretends sleep. His eyes are open, his ears quickened for the slightest abrupt sound. The population is overcrowded with gang members. There are only a few civilians. Any moment conflict can erupt.

U-T, Li'l Harlem, and I patrol the yard. Five or six Bloods hanging out together could create a little division and suddenly take off on the Crips. We can't let that happen so we check new prisoners as they arrive. They're looking for comrades; we're looking for enemies.

Spider comes off the bus with two other people. He looks like his name— tall, skinny, with arms and legs too long for his short torso. His popeyes give him a surprised but eager appearance. In spite of his disproportioned arms and legs, he's mastered the urban sway. Baggy, drooping pants give the impression his body is longer until I study him. He performs the mad-dog stare— immobile, shining eyes, brows slightly clenched, squinting at the corners. When he shoots it at me, I know he's trying to make me think he's tough. He's trying to ward off the enemy, ward off evil.

I think, *That nigga thinks he's hard. He's telling me, don't fuck with me. I'm a bad nigga. But I'm gonna whup his ass. He ain't tough. He's trying too hard.*

First Spider's friend exits the bus, then Spider with his mad-dog stare and his urban stroll. We ask Spider where he's from, and he says Compton. He's a Blood. Li'l Harlem says, "Blood killer."

"Leave. Leave the yard. Roll it up or we gotta get down," I growl.

"Let them busters come out." U-T's a little older than I am.

They come out into the yard and U-T tries to organize who's going to fight whom.

"I'll take on any of y'all," Spider growls. His mad-dog stare is gone. Instead, the veins pop in his long neck, the veins in his arms fill.

"But I don't have no shoes," Spider whines.

Spider has on gym flex, like flip-flops, that inmates are issued when they go out in the yard.

"Can't fight with no shoes. He'll slip and fall," Spider's friend says.

"What size you wear?" U-T is a OG Crip, not one to play dirty.

"Eleven."

"Here." U-T pulls off his shoes and hands them to Spider. We're real Crips. The kind of soldiers that play by the rules; we're that serious about the war. That serious about our honor. We're going to give you our shoes and still whup your ass just to show you, you can't fuck with us.

Walking through his dorm, I spot some BGF members watching us. The BGFs are Blood sympathizers and may come to his aid or give him a weapon. Not attacking first might cost me my life and would certainly cost me my reputation. I would be labeled buster. I was a Crip on the streets; this is where I fit in and belong in Chino. The feeling that rushes through me is like my first game in the major leagues. I'm at bat; my heart pounds, my fingers cold. I feel the shank we've made in my waistband. It's him or me. I have to attack before he settles in with his allies. "Come on, fool."

As we enter the day room in Dorm Two, Spider's cocky stride is gone. He walks drowsy but his eyes dart. It's too late for him to back down. If he doesn't fight, he can't walk any mainline in the California penal system; he'll become a target for all convicts, including his homies. He won't last two days. We're doomed to fight.

I crouch down. His arms are bent, his reach enormous. This is no game, no kiddy occupation. *This is what I signed up for,* I think as we circle each other. I'm geared on executing my orders effectively. My personal opinion does not make me exempt from my obligation. We're at war. Orders are orders. Period. It's kill or be killed either by the enemy or my own comrades. A bead of sweat trickles down Spider's forehead. I wait for it to reach his eye. My participation means my survival.

The sweat stings his eye and Spider blinks. In one motion, I whip out the shank and take a stab at his face. He jumps back and I miss.

Now, I have not had weapon training and do not know how to position myself or where to aim when attacking with a knife.

"Why'da need a knife?" Spider asks.

"Fool! My homeboy don't need no knife." U-T stretches his

palm and I hand it to him. During this time, Spider takes a swing, but I duck under it. I move in and strike him twice in the face, knock him against the wall. He stumbles to his feet and tries to rush me, but he's too slow. I sidestep him and crack him in the nose with a flush right. Blood covers his lower face and sprays my shirt.

"Put hands on that fool, Cee," Li'l Harlem encourages.

Spider grabs me around the waist and lifts me, then grabs my testicles, but I bite him like an animal, feel his flesh rip away from him.

"Awh." He lets go of my testicles.

I lift him, use my momentum to position him near a window. If I body-slam him here, he'll crash through the window, land head-first on the asphalt.

"Cuz. Don't kill 'em," C-Dog shouts. I don't know where he came from; I'm too busy battling with Spider. C-Dog grabs me and I release Spider.

"The pigs'r comin'," someone yells. The emergency alarm sounds. I bolt from the day room and onto the recreation yard. Jumping over a flower bed, I strip off my bloody state shirt and hurl it into a trash can near the weights. I'm in blue jeans and a tee shirt. Several correction officers run toward Dorm Two. Once they're inside, I return to my dorm, hustle past the day room, shower area, and first set of bunks. At my bunk, I undress, jump to my top bunk, and dive under the sheets. I slow my breathing.

Several officers race up and down the aisles of bunks while I lay inert and imitate sleep.

My escape is short. At 11:30 that night, I'm snatched from my covers, shackled from the waist down, hauled off to Central, and placed in a holding cell. I stay there in shackles for six hours till I'm escorted to the lieutenant's office. "Why'd you go after James Toomy?"

That must be Spider's legal name. I don't answer.

"You think you're tough? We'll show you what tough is." Another officer whacks his baton across my face. Warm blood rolls down my face.

"Who the fuck you get your orders from?"

"Don't know what you're talking about."

"Don't talk back to me, boy." A third officer hits my teeth with his baton. A searing pain shoots from my mouth through my nose to my eye. Another baton strikes my temple. "You motherfuckin' nigger. Tell us what happened."

He slashes my face and I fall to the ground. "You think you hard. You ain't seen hard. You ain't shit." He kicks my head, the other officer kicks my testicles and I lose my wind, the knot goes inward, my head is kicked again and I lose consciousness.

The next day I wake up, my head throbbing, back in my cell. My mouth, nose, and face are covered with scabbed blood. Under the blood are swollen features. I run my fingers over my face and feel the blood caked so stiff I cannot move my lips. My head pulses, a string of pain clusters over my right temple. My forehead and eye are inflated. I have trouble opening my right eye. I feel dizzy and dehydrated. I push myself to stand, and my crotch throbs with a dull ache. I stagger to the small porcelain sink bolted to the wall at the back of the cell. I wash the blood off my face and drink the water as it shoots from the rusty faucet. I have no bedding, no clothes, just boxer shorts and socks. I have no toothbrush. I only own unlimited access to water. I gulp the water and let it spray away the dried blood imbedded in my lips, nostrils, eye. I search the tier and spot an old towel. It's filthy, but better than nothing. I use it to wipe the blood from my face and head and mop the floor.

I step to the front of the cell and toss the towel to the tier. I watch it slice and spin. As it falls in a downward spiral through the gray prison air, droplets of my blood spray. It slams on the concrete floor. Blood and water seep from the towel. Slowly the puddle expands across the floor, stretching to a drain.

I watch my blood ooze across the cement and course down the

hole. Blood as a result of the pigs' beating. I have earned a stripe. I've earned respect the old-fashioned way, the way of the gang.

"Hey. Who's that downstairs that came in last night?"

I hesitate, try to figure out if this is friend or foe. I can't decipher his voice except for the urban rhythm. If I could see his face my memory would click and I'd know him. But now I'm wary. "Who's that?"

"Hank from Seven-four Hoover."

"Whassup? This's Li'l Cee from Harlem." I knew Hank from the Crip Module.

"That was you I saw." A few minutes later, Hank extends his gold-complexioned hand through my bars. He shakes his head when he sees my bruised and swollen face.

After I tell him what happened he asks, "You want me to get at that fool?"

"Wait till I find out what's up."

Footsteps come from the opposite end of the tier and someone shouts, "Man walkin.'"

Hank looks down the tier. "Pig coming."

He leaves and a Black correction officer appears at my cell. "Simpson?"

"Nine. One."

He tells me the lieutenant wants to see me. Someone snitched on me. "Get dressed." He hands clean clothes through the bars. Pain haunts each movement. Lifting my legs reminds me of my swollen testicles. As I dress, he checks me out for tattoos. While in CYA, I tattooed "R 30" on my ring finger, short for Rollin' Thirties Harlem Crip. When he notices my finger, he inquires, "You a Crip?"

"Yeah. Why?"

"I know some Crips. Franklin Thomas. You know him?"

"That's my homeboy Lefty Dog." Immediately I realize that giving his nickname may release critical information.

"He's over on the yard at CRC."

I act like I know this.

"Man, I hope you brothers get outta here. I hate seeing Black folks locked up like slaves."

I meet his eyes. I'm not sure if this is another version of good cop, but I hear genuine compassion and sadness in his voice. He doesn't smile, shakes his head, lips turned down. He's about a decade older than I with a husky build that was once toned and now covered with easy flesh. His eyes with their heavy lids remind me of my grandmother Louise's.

"I just work here," he continues, "I'm not into politics or nothing. Just do my eight hours and go home to my wife and kids. I know how it feels to be trapped in this White man's world. I ain't square. I'm from Compton. I never got caught up, but did my share of shit."

His voice is mellow with slight vibrations with those eyes so like Louise's, he could be her brother. *Trapped in a White man's world.* His words echo in my still throbbing head. Some of his sadness is for me; some is for himself. His eyes tell me he knows me and, surprisingly, I want to tell him my life story. I wonder how I look to him. Here I am young, Black, beaten, and snared in a colorless mass of steel and concrete. He's free to come and go, but stands before me thinking, "Damn. That could be me." His hands are on his hips, his head down, his feet slightly spread, giving me my time to get dressed. No hurry. He and I have all day.

I pull my pants up and stand motionless to let the twinge in my crotch subside.

I look like a battered Black slave held captive in a cage by some White that tried to tame me but now considers me a rebellious nigger. And this Black man talking about his wife and children, talking about doing his job is the White man's servant sent to shackle me and escort me to the grand dragon's office. Betraying his own people.

I zip up my fly and snap the button.

I sense he realizes the plan to rub things in both our faces. Whitey's way to remind both of us, "I'm king. I'm superior. You see how I'm doing your people? Take a good look, 'cause that's how I'll do you if you challenge me. I run this world. You're nothing but my slave, or my servant keeping things smooth. I beat your people to a pulp and then call on you to clean the mess."

I see again my blood dripping down the drain. I slide the state tee shirt over my battered nose and swollen eye. They smart from the slight pressure of fabric. Then I see the other message and understand the White man's tactic. Beat me up and send a Black CO to force me to shackles, hoping I vent my rage on him. A good way to kill two birds with one stone. Both of us could die right here, right now and White America would be rid of two more Black men, easier and quicker than pouring crack cocaine in our neighborhoods.

I smooth the tee shirt over my chest, roll these thoughts round in my head, and compose myself to be respectful, taking the time he's giving me.

"Yeah, brotha'," I say. "I'm gonna do something with my life when I get outta here." And just for that moment, I mean it. Just for that moment, I know I can do it and I'm Grandma Louise's Colton again.

"Hey, man. You can make it," he smiles at me and I feel Smiley's warmth.

At the lieutenant's office, I speak softly, address him as sir, and use the intellectual words I learned from reading books in the Crip Module. His crew cut is so crisp his hair stands from his forehead like soldiers lined up in army regiment. His uniform is pressed and the tips of his fingernails evenly cut and whitened. I stand before him in my shackles and meet his blue eyes. My face is battered, but I hold my head up and breathe slowly. I don't give him the mad-dog stare. He's only a man. His extreme power over me is vanished, and I interpret his strict neatness as armor against his own interior life. His need to control others is a testament to his inability to control himself.

He asks me why I attacked James Toomy, about my gang affili-ation, and zeros in on who gave me my orders. They're the same questions his men asked with their batons and punches. I don't tell him anything. I just say, "Yes, Sir." Or "No, sir." His face turns red as the questioning continues, and I watch a blue vein in his temple enlarge. He personally escorts me back to my cell.

A switch is flipped and his face hardens, his lips tighten, his fists clench. "You little fuckin' nigger," he hisses as we walk the tier, my shackles jingling with each step, his shoes squeaking on the cat-walk. "You think you're smart, huh? I'll show you 'bout fuckin' 'round with me."

I pretend I don't hear him.

He pivots and strides back down the tier.

I maintained my pride, hurting him worse than the beating his men gave me.

The next day, my head is clear. The throbbing has stopped. My balls have returned to their normal size. Hank appears before my cell and slides in a cigarette and his lighter. I pull in the smoke and it fills my lungs. I hold it deep inside. Hank wants to know what happened and I tell him and pass the cigarette back to him.

"This ole buster upstairs probably told on you." He takes a toke of the cigarette. "I'll send a few homies to get at the fool and make him change his story."

I suck on the cigarette.

"Don't trip. I'll let you know what's up wit' him."

A few days later, I'm escorted to my 115 Hearing, which is a minitrial on disciplinary infractions. I'm charged with assault on an inmate and face an additional year tacked on my time and eighteen months in a Security Housing Unit (SHU), which is equivalent to solitary confinement or the hole.

Spider shows up at my 115 Hearing, testifies on my behalf, and the charges are dropped.

Spider stood strong; he wins walking the mainline. He remains without incident before being transferred. He did not involve the establishment. I respect him.

But I realize that those who don't snitch retaliate. He can't give me a pass. I've made an ardent enemy. And it's only a matter of time until we meet again.

When I return from my hearing, the yard is closed so no one knows that I'm back. From the moment I start walking to my new bunk, I feel stares coming from a Hispanic man. As I approach, he turns to speak to his neighbor. When he looks in my direction, I stand directly in front of him in a strategic position I learned from Karate class: feet aligned with my shoulders, arms slightly slanted inward, thigh wide.

Whassup, cuz? You know me?" My eyes watch his hands to prophesy his actions.

"You don't remember me no more, Cokey?"

Who's this cat? I step back and look at him. My brain that usually kicks in a story when I see a face isn't helping me. Must be effects of that beating. He's short, brown skinned. A black teardrop is tattooed high on his cheekbone as though he's forever crying. The tattoo steals my gaze and distracts me. There's something familiar, but I can't place him.

"I'm Crow."

Then it clicks. He and his two brothers played baseball with me in Venice. He was our catcher; for a minute I hear the ball whap into his mitt and see him throw it back to the pitcher in one motion. The mitt was his right hand. I hadn't seen him in a decade. Back then he tried to flirt with my cousin. Back then we were kids. Now we're in the Big House. I extend my hand and we grin.

"Man, I almost didn't recognize you."

He laughs. "How much time you got?"

"Sixteen months."

"Ah, man, you're gonna beat me out. I got two years. Whassup with your cousin, Lisa?"

I reach into my things and hand him a recent photo of her.

"Damn. She got tall, but she's still fine." He examines the picture. "Ask her if I can have a picture of her, Cokey?"

I look around the dorm, trying to locate my bunk. "Where's Twenty-three Lower?"

"Right there." He points across from him.

At least I'm next to a Mexican I can trust. If ordered, the Southside Mexicans would commence war with Blacks. If they're short on shanks, they'll wait until they secure more; they never fight without arms. I walk over to my bunk and take my time unpacking my belongings, scooping out my surroundings as I remove my photographs and letters from Huckabuck and Gina. Two Blacks to my left; one White to my right, and Crow across from me. I pile my letters up on my shelf and line the photos behind them. I'm in good shape.

In the dorm, Crow and I talk about old times. In the yard, he falls in step with the Southside Mexicans and I fall in step with the Crips. We stay away from each other in case something jumps off between the Blacks and Mexicans. An incident could expand to the street and involve our families. We respect each other and are as close as two potential enemies can be.

My first day back on the rec yard is like being embraced after my initiation. I get fives and handshakes from all the Crips. And then suddenly, so quietly I feel the heat of him before I hear him, Big Silky is behind to me. "Gotta commend you for your loyalty." No one hears his comment but me.

I turn to him and smile.

"You won't be called on for awhile. Everyone gets his turn. Now it's someone else's."

"That's how it works?"

"There's no living off the fat of the land. All of us are expected to play our part in the war." He nods at small clusters of Crips scattered across the yard. "Nearly a hundred haven't been called on yet. Each will be chosen for a task, a mission." We stand next to each other surveying the field. Men lifting weights, men talking, men shooting hoops. The sun dazzles their white shirts, warms their brown skin. Our army.

I've been given my next orders. I'm to wait. I turn to say something, but he's gone as silently as he appeared,

A week later, two Bloods are brought from Central and housed in Dorm Four. Li'l Harlem volunteers to deal with them. Because he's from my set, I accompany him, as he had accompanied me. Li'l Harlem and U-T and I put the perfect plan together. I'm still not sure who snitched on me regarding my fight with Spider, but I know the informer could be a Crip among us. Snitches put themselves in a bind. When they're called on for action, their lack of participation attracts scrutiny, and then they pay the price. Their end is always near, a mere incident away. The pigs found our fabricated weapons the day of the fight with Spider. Now we have to fashion new shanks. We hunt for stock to fashion to a point, but, since finding our shanks, staff cut all weapon stock from the mop wringers. I can't tell Big Silky we need weapons. We'd have to admit the pigs found them and that would be like admitting we're idiots.

I turn the problem over and over in my mind. Then, I realize, I know someone I can trust and not worry about it getting back to Big Silky: Crow. It rolls around in my head as I lift weights, lay on my bunk. As a Mexican, he can't repeat our conversation. He'll tip the Southside Mexicans that the Crips are going to stab someone. This earns him a pat on the back for a job well done. He knows I'll tell no one that he led me to the weapon stock. As I consider it, I know we'll be doing each other a favor.

Crow tells me the weight pins on the weight machine in the gym make good "ice picks" and are easy to sharpen. That afternoon, we go to the gym. Li'l Harlem and U-T play basketball while I secure the pins, wrap them in a towel, and place the towel under the trash can. We'll leave it till count time and then divide the pins between us and sneak them back into the dorm.

Li'l Harlem plays basketball with Sporty, a BGF member who is six foot three and has a dragon tattooed on his arm. Now, there's bad blood between the BGF and the Crips since they stabbed Peewee in Tracy Prison. Li'l Harlem is five foot five and is one of those short guys who figure a loud bark is as good as a big bite. Li'l Harlem takes a hard foul from Sporty and threatens to punch him if he does it again. Sporty grabs him by the collar, puts him in a full-Nelson chokehold. I hear Li'l Harlem gasping, his eyes rolling around in desperation.

"Don't touch my homeboy," I yell, but Sporty increases his pressure.

Li'l Harlem claws Sporty's thick arms.

"You ain't no mediator. You don't play no referree," I say. "Nobody has the right to touch your children other than you, so no one has the right to touch my people other than me. Don't touch my people."

He grins, daring me.

I pick up the weight plate, run into the court, and crack Sporty on the head. He releases Li'l Harlem, who falls to the ground. I sling the weight plate out of the area and Li'l Harlem begins kicking Sporty. I'm spotted by the pigs who yell, "Get down. Get down."

I lay on my stomach as the alarm sounds. Fifteen correction officers dressed in full riot gear bolt in the gym, batons in their hands.

"That's him. The one in the blue shirt."

I'm the only prisoner wearing a blue shirt. Everyone else wears tee shirts. I stand out like a sore thumb, like a petunia in an onion patch, like a blue jay among a flock of robins. How stupid. Four pigs surround me. "Don't move," the shortest one demands. I'm handcuffed, pulled to my feet.

The sergeant screams, "You fuckin' idiot. You see that right

there?" He points to a correction officer with a mini-14 assault rifle standing in the tall gun tower outside the gym. "He was gonna
take your head off. You think this is a fuckin' game in here? We'll
kill your ass. We don't give a fuck about you."

I'd heard his speech a million times from the cops in my neighborhood. I figure he's only trying to scare me. It doesn't dawn on
me then that they're killing people in just this fashion in other
prisons. I don't think they're stupid enough to kill someone with a
hundred witnesses around. This is before I'm sent to Folsom.

"Roll 'em up," the sergeant demands.

Once again I'm shackled from the waist down and returned to
the lieutenant's office.

"You wanna gangbang, uh?" He sneers at me. His pink scalp
shows through the close-cut light hair.

I don't respond.

He turns his back on me and shakes his head. I try to imagine
what he's thinking. *Just what I expected. As stupid as the rest. He'll
get what he deserves. These people are animals.*

I'm placed in a holding cell, ordered to strip down to my boxers. Each piece of clothing is searched. About three hours later
the CO from Compton stands before my bars. This time, he's accompanied by a short, scrawny White pig dressed in a green
jumpsuit with a red devil tattooed on his arm. His nose is red, the
tendons and muscles of his arms taut. The CO from Compton
looks at me, his lips together, his eyes slightly lidded, an expression I've seen on my grandmother Louise's face a thousand times.
"You're in trouble again," it says with melancholy, dismay, and fu-
tility rolled into the downcast eyes and lips pressed not so tightly
as to express shock, but sufficiently to show dismay.

"Cuff 'em up. Get his ID and escort him," the White pig orders.

The CO from Compton retrieves my prison ID from the small
pile of clothing, verifies my prison number. He's dressed in a
CDC uniform. I'm bare chested and shoeless, wearing only a pair
of boxer shots. I want to reach out to him. I want him to take me
away. Suddenly I feel like a boy as he trods steadily, silently beside

me. The cold concrete floor is like snow to my bare feet. After moving twenty-five feet, I turn around and look at him. "Where we going?"

He looks me in the face. This time I see disgust and his own loss. "Solitary confinement. The hole."

SEVEN

Solitary

Fanya penye udugu's hapa mi-mi? (Do any brothers hear me?)
        —Big Pup

THE CO FROM COMPTON ESCORTS ME TO A BLACK LIEUTENANT.
I stand there, still in my boxers, still chained.

"Have a seat, Mr. Simpson . . . or would you prefer I call you
Cee Loc?"

As I ease into the wood chair, I wonder how he knows my gang
name. His elbows lean on his wood desk; he's a man in his late forties, medium complexion, hard cheekbones, with broad shoulders
under his uniform.

"Listen, Simpson, do you have any idea what you're getting
yourself into? It's bad enough White folks are scared of you guys,
now you wanna start assaulting the BGF?"

How does this fool know I'm a Crip?

He shakes his head as though to get away from a bad odor.
"Look, I know all about the BGF killing your homeboy Tyrone in
San Quentin. I know about them killing your homeboy Pee Wee
in Tracy."

I didn't know these things. I just knew about the Bloods killing Insane in Tracy.

"You can't bring back the dead. Do you know what you've done?"

"I—"

"Quit while you're ahead. Look. You've only got sixteen months. Do your time, go home, and make a life." He narrows his brows at me. "Look. I know who you are. I know your family. I used to watch your father play ball for the Angels back in 'sixty-five. I remember when your Uncle Albert was police sergeant for the LAPD. Your grandfather used to cut my hair. I used to eat at Fatburgers."

He knows my family, but he won't give me a word in edgewise.

"Look. Why you wanna be the black sheep? Why you wanna be a thug? It ain't worth it, man. I'm telling you, Simpson. Those Crips are gonna use you and mess up your life. Be cool. Or you'll wind up spending the rest of your life here. Right here." He jabs his forefinger to the ground, stops, stares in my face, his eyes wide as though he's waiting for me to explain.

"I didn't—"

He rises, leans on his knuckles, tilted toward me. "Nah. Don't. Don't even open your mouth. I don't want to hear your lies; I've heard all the lies a person can hear. I've worked here thirteen years. What, you think I was born yesterday? I'm not one of those White cops that don't know nothing. Why you think they pay me? They pay me 'cause I know." He jabs his chest, then lets his arms drop. "Look. Take my advice. Be cool. Make it out of here in one piece."

I drop my gaze to the floor. I want to explain, but he's a cop. Black man or not, he's still a pig. But what really trips me out is he knows things I don't—about the assaults on Tyrone and Pee Wee. *Does he think I assaulted Sporty for revenge on Pee Wee? I've landed myself in something I don't even know. I may have brought the war to Chino, a war with no terms. A war so chaotic*

*that spontaneous spats and isolated incidents are defined as retal-
iatory strikes and tallied up for the sake of claiming a point. Two
for the BGF and one for the Crips.*

But he's finished with me and I'm escorted through several
steel gates and iron doors, walking underground until I'm before a
cell that's like a small cave with a cast-iron door sealing it off. I'm
uncuffed and made to strip nude.

A White goon-squad officer, dressed in an army green jumpsuit, commands, "Let me see the palms of your hands." I stretch
out my hands obediently.

"Flip them over."

"Raise your arms above your head so I can see your armpits."

"Drop them and open your mouth wide. Do you wear den-
tures? Stick out your tongue. Lift your lips with your fingers and
expose your gums. Turn around and lift your left foot toward me.
Now wiggle your toes. Now your right foot. Lift your sack. Touch
your toes. Spread the cheeks of your behind. Hold them apart."

His penetration humiliates me.

"Now cough."

I'm directed into the cave cell and locked behind steel bars,
then bolted behind a door made of solid metal plate. Blam. He
shuts and locks the door.

There's no electrical outlet or light switch inside the cell. The
bed is a cement slab no wider than a bus-stop bench. The sink and
toilet are connected and I smell fumes of defecation, vomit.
When the officer covers my window with a steel plate, a clank
echoes in the cave and the darkness is complete.

I see nothing. I can't even see my hand in front of my face. I sit
on the slab until my buttocks begin to numb and then extend my
legs and stretch out on my back. I extend one arm and touch the
coldness of the other wall.

"You don't have to be a thug. Be cool or you'll end up spending
the rest of your life here."

I close my eyes and his words throb in my head. I tell myself,
Trapped in a White man's world. But you can make it. You can

make it. And those words remind me of my mother and the time she blindfolded me and dumped me in a gang-infested neighborhood. Then I curled into a ball on someone's lawn and comforted myself by saying *You can make it. You can make it* over and over. Once again, I curve myself into a tight fist and think about her, her beating me with extension cords, hitting me with skillets. Her forcing hair-straightener into my hair so I'd resemble a bourgeois Negro. Her shame of my darker skin. How she tried to hide me.

I cover myself with a blanket and bend tighter. *You can make it.*

"Chow time!" The lilt is rural southern and accompanied by pounding on the iron door. Half a day gone. The heavy metal covering lifts. I squint and blink to adjust to the light. A tall White goon-squad CO slides a paper plate with a childlike portion of eggs and ham and a half pint of spoiled milk under the door.

Several rats nibble at my food. When I stand, they scamper for cover. I lift the plate, dump the food into the toilet, and flush it. Immediately, the heavy metal covering is closed and I'm in blackness. When the toilet water settles, the rats scurry across the cement floor.

The walls are slightly damp, not smooth. I feel their roughness, exploring my enclosure. I extend my arms and reach both walls. I stand for awhile, my arms outstretched, my fingers on the boundaries of my cage, my life narrowed. Being able to touch both walls is reassuring in the darkness. I'll always know where I am.

I lay back down on my slab. *You can make it.* My mind continues its hunt for sense. My thoughts spiral around as if the walls are talking to me, the walls becoming the Black lieutenant and the Compton CO, my grandmother Louise saying, "You're my sweet, sweet grandson. So sweet. My Colton."

"You're an animal," my father spat at me. "Nothing but an animal." And now in the darkness, I think of my destructive life. My mother's brutality, my brutality. I see the blood oozing from the men I've shot. And the wave of guilt, that sick feeling I had when I was first initiated, returns and twists inside me.

But it was do or die. Kill or be killed.

Don't think of that. I had to. There's no second-guessing. If I didn't get them, they'd get me.

No, you had choices, not just one choice. If you truly wanted to survive, why did you join the gang where Black men die in dog years? You knew. You truly knew.

You can make it.

Maybe I didn't want to survive. Maybe there wasn't much to live for.

No, you lust for that celebrity, that fame, power, admiration. The gang is your clearest vision of stability.

No. It was me. My loyalty and deeds.

A joot ball slides through the door. This one smells vaguely of spaghetti. I slide it out before the rats arrive. The light stabs my eyes and then the window closes and blackness again. *Another part of the day gone. I'm safe in darkness. In my own mind. It's just my own mind.*

I close my eyes and see red and purple spirals gyrating behind my lids. For a while I watch them, fascinated as they metamorphose into paisleys and spinning amoebas. I open my eyes and see nothing, not even coiling blobs. I try to sleep; it's my escape, but I can't. I do push-ups on my slab until I am covered with a blanket of sweat and am warm, but then the sweat cools and I shiver into my tight-fist ball again and cover myself with my limp blankets.

I listen to the rats scamper on the floor. There's no light, it matters not if I open or close my eyes. *I'm blind, locked away from civilization. From everyone. Forgotten. No one even knows I'm here. No one who matters. Not Grandma Louise, or Pops, or Smiley, or Gina, or Huckabuck.* I feel so sorry for myself and my life. I think about my grandmother Louise taking me to church, kneeling beside me and praying. *What I've almost lost. Lost the Colton part. I'm only Cee.* Tears course down my cheeks. When I touch my face, they're still warm, almost hot. When I know I'm crying, I know I still am.

Think about something happy. You can make it. And I replay Smiley and a party we had after a job. *Was it a store we had just robbed, or riding through the jungles?* *I don't remember.* Huckabuck and I go to the roller-skating rink and he hits on some girl with dyed blonde hair and an ass that won't quit. Gina and her warm waterbed. She snuggles next to me. Becomes the wad of blanket and sheets. When she sleeps, she looks like a child. Her hard edge, the always-on-the-hustle-and-defending-herself attitude, so visible in her glinting eyes and quick motions, is erased. In sleep, her lips are open, her eyeballs slowly stir up a dream. Her nostrils quiver with her breath. A lock of her hair sticks up like a crazy curl. She belongs only to herself. And I, I feel proud of being able to protect her when she's being the vulnerable child, and I am the wakeful man watching over her when during the day she is older, wiser, harsher, intimidating.

Food comes again. I slide it back out, wincing in the harsh light. Another day gone.

I play a game of basketball, watch my balls skim through the hoop hardly touching, moving the net. I play it slow, feeling each motion, seeing the other men. It's a game with Li'l Quake and we work as fingers, anticipating each move. We are that united.

More food to shove away. Another part of the day gone. I go back and forth between being Colton, my grandmother's boy, and Cee the gangbanger. My two personalities fight each other. Two different people are in me.

The next day, I think, *You assume you can control your fate by shooting another person, but you don't really know if he'd kill you. Not really. He could give you a pass. But you can't take the chance. You love life too much. You love living.*

I realize I'm talking to myself but don't care. I'm warehousing my thoughts.

I love life. I do. Some may think since I put myself in harm's way, I don't care if I live or die. But it's my love of life that pushes me to danger. Yes, I want to ensure my safety, but it's more than that. It's the excitement when I'm on the verge of possibly dying that reminds me of living. A life that speeds by with excitement. Euphoria, pleasure, brings us closer to death and the fine line between them provokes an awareness we can't otherwise experience.

I shift, my arm numb from being pressed between my body and the slab. *But even the ordinary is sweet. To enjoy a Twix, a cup of water even. To shoot a basketball and hear it whoosh through the hoop. I love being able to do those things. I'm remorseful about the others. They're human beings. But I'm justified.*

It's a twisted thought. Like the Gemini I am. Regrettable but justified.

"What's wrong, Simpson. You okay?" The iron door opens and a medical technical assistant stands there.

Light pierces me. I flinch my eyes closed, and behind my lids suns blare.

"You not eating. You all right?"

"I'm not hungry."

"You aren't having suicidal thoughts, are you?"

"The food's just terrible. Nasty."

A few hours later, the door opens again and a goon-squad CO steps into my cell. "Roll up your stuff. You're going to Palm Hall. The cells are much better in Palm, Simpson."

They can't be worse. I gather my two sheets and a shabby wool blanket, fold them in half, roll them, and back up to the bars. I'm draped with slave chains over my underwear and escorted across the hall to the much better hole.

In Palm Hall, I'm given a shower and a full physical examination. I have difficulty passing the vision test; my eyes still have not adjusted to the overly bright lights. Images of the bulbs burn blue in my eyes and remain blaring even after I look away. Then I'm given clean clothes, a fresh sack lunch, and am rehoused in a single-man cell smelling faintly of ammonia. A welcome fresh scent. The cell has light, a bed with springs, a thin cotton mattress, and a barred iron door. It seems like luxury.

I've been in prison for three and a half weeks, in solitary for ten days. And I am nineteen years old.

That night, I'm handed a letter from my brother, one from my father, who tells me he hopes I've learned my lesson and will change my ways so this is my last time in prison, one from Huckabuck telling me the news about the war with the Black P. Stone Bloods. His arm is better and he's been to see my grandmother, mowed her lawn, took out the trash, and she seems okay. And last, a letter from my grandmother with a twenty-five-dollar money order and a scrawled note in her loopy handwriting.

"Keep praying, Colton. I love you."

I fold it so I see it when I glance at my shelf. I love you, she says.

Late one night, I'm doing push-ups in my cell when the sound of jangling keys echos from the opposite end of the tier. I peak out through the crack in my door and see a White goon-squad CO and a brother. The brother walks a few steps ahead wearing handcuffs, leg shackles. He's tall, in his late twenties; the clunky chains punctuate his bold stride. His nonchalant expression communicates he's beyond this paltry inconvenience. Each motion is necessary; there's no waste as he walks, dragging his shackles, head up, breathing slowly. His hair is twisted in a mane of dreadlocks. When he passes my cell, I feel the heat of him, see the muscles clenched in his forearm, in his calves. All strength and vitality that is ready and untamed. He has figured out a way to be free.

He stops at the cell next to mine. I watch the goon-squad officer uncuff his leg chains and slam the door shut. The convict extends his wrists out the food-tray slot and the binding handcuffs are removed. The CO strolls away, the grill gate slams closed. No one has said a word.

I turn to introduce myself to my neighbor.

But he beats me, "Hey, brother next door, what's your name?" His voice is mellow, welcoming, without a growl to it.

"Cee."

"You a member?"

"Yeah. I'm Harlem Crip."

"Right-right. I'm Big Pup from Eight Tray Gangster. Came down from Folsom to go to court. I just left your homeboys Big BJ, Talib, and Suni."

"I know who they are."

"Send me a kite and tell me what's up."

I write him a note explaining why I'm in the hole, slide it under the cell door, and out into the tier. He reels it in with his towel and then shoves me an answer. It reads, "When I asked what's up, I meant politicwise. Are we at war, and if so, with whom?"

I write what Big Silky told me. Big Pup says, "Righteous homie."

I send him a kite about Pee Wee and Tyrone. Yes, Pee Wee and Tyrone were both killed by BGF, but Tyrone had left the Crips and was part of another war. The Crips had avenged Pee Wee's death. Since Tyrone had left the gang, he was not avenged. When I ask him about CCO (Consolidated Crip Organization) he informs me that's confidential, and if I'm interested in "the movement" I'd have to contact Big BJ.

"You know Kiswahili, the African language?" he writes.

"No."

He sails me a list of words titled, "Lesson One." "This is enough to help you communicate over the tier without our conversation being deciphered by the pigs," he writes.

I begin memorizing.

The vents are the vehicles for communication to the top tiers, he informs me, and hollers into a vent in Kiswahili. "Fanya penye udugu's hapa mi-mi?" (Do any brothers hear me?)

"Who's that?" a familiar voice yells back.

"Right-right. Big Pup from ETG," he says.

"Hey. This is Lunatick Frank from Rollin' Sixties."

I stand on my bunk and place my ear to the vent.

"Who's down there?" Lunatick Frank asks.

"Just me and a little homie name Cee from Harlem," Pup replies.

"Who, Colton?"

"Yeah," I shout into the vent.

"I'm gonna get at the pigs and have them move you up here, Cee."

Then he and Pup talk such rapid Kiswahili it's beyond my level. They holler through the vent while I study my vocabulary words. Then there's silence. A short time after that, another kite skates to the tier in front of my cell.

"Young Cuzin'. You must excuse me for not giving you details about the death of Tyrone and Pee Wee. I did not know much about you. You could have been a spy or snitch. The pigs plant them around us CCOs. Had I said anything, I might have to face trial by the party members of the movement. Secrecy is the major part of security; however, Lunatick Frank says you're stalwart.

"There's a spy working for the pigs that lives in cell fourteen on this tier. Lunatick has told me he's the tier tender. We must get rid of him. How much time do you have?"

"Sixteen months," I write back.

"I don't expect you to fuck off your release date. I'll handle the snitch. But your help will be appreciated. After you eat breakfast, when the tier tender stops by to pick up your tray, knock it on the ground in front of him. Then, back away from the cell bars. Make sure you do it inconspicuously. Make it look like an accident," his next note says.

I use my newly learned Kiswahili to tell him that I will.

The rest of the night, I memorize the Kiswahili and wonder at Pup's plan. After breakfast the next morning, the tier tender stops by my cell to retrieve my food tray. I bump into it with my hip and it falls. The tier tender frowns at me.

"Excuse me, brother." I ice the moment with apology.

"Ah, that's alright." He reaches down to pick it up. As soon as he grabs it and stands again, a long object jolts from Pup's cell, hits him in the chest, then shoots back to Pup's cell. The snitch clutches his chest as blood spews onto his shirt. "Ow . . . I've been speared." He runs toward the end of the tier. "Help me. I've been speared." When he reaches the gate, he rattles the grill to get the goon-squad CO's attention. "They got me. They know who I am. I'm speared," he screams.

All around me, convicts laugh. Pup's laughter is a sad chuckle. Through the vent, I hear Lunatick Frank's boisterous laugh. The snitch's screaming can be heard on the second tier. The laughter is ground out by the noxious sound of metal jingles. The goon-squad CO keys the grill gate, frees the snitch, then proceeds down the tier in the direction of my cell. He glances at me, and then at the puddle of blood in front of my cell.

I'm on my way back to deep seg, I think.

Then, he stops at Pup's cell. "Cuff up," he barks.

Pup extends his wrists out the tray slot. He's handcuffed. His door is opened and he's shackled from the waist down and hauled to deep seg. As he passes my cell, we make eye contact. "Kaa hakika upendo moja" (Stay real, loved one), he says to me.

"Mi-mi fahamu we-we . . . kaa fahamu" (I understand you. Stay strong), I reply.

"Nita" (I will). He raises his head. "I'm off to deal with some more rats," he laughs.

A few days later, I'm told to "roll it up" and am rehoused in second tier. Lunatick Frank is the tier tender and immediately comes to my cell to greet me. He looks like I imagined from his voice. He's a medium-sized man who doesn't smile. He has a scar under his eye slitting straight down into his cheek. The points where the wound was stitched keloided so that an even row of dots march on either side of the slash. He hands me some pruno—prison-made wine—and tells me the story of what happened with Smiley's escape plans. Smiley was not subpoenaed to court, so Lunatick Frank called G to call off the plans. But it was too late, the first part of the plan was already in motion, and I was caught with the weapons and incarcerated. Lunatick Frank cancelled the plan because Smiley couldn't escape with him. With that act of loyalty, my respect for Lunatick Frank mounts.

That night, I'm surrounded by friends. I did not prevent Smiley's and Lunatick Frank's escape and cause them to spend the rest of their lives behind bars. The weight of ten men is off my shoulders. I sleep soundly.

The next morning, Lunatick Frank returns to my cell to educate me about the Crip organization and especially the CCO and BN.

Lunatick tells me the aim of CCO and BN is to unify the entire Crip nation and together fight racism, oppression, police brutality, genocide, and corruption. The Crips' ideology is partly attributed to the Black Panther Party member, Bunchy Carter. Our letters, C-R-I-P-S, stand for Community Revolutionary Innerparty Service.

"I thought we were just our set and the gang." I had no idea what I was joining at age ten when I was initiated. I thought I was running around with Smiley and Big T, fighting for our lives.

"Gotta know our history, cuz," Lunatick says and continues his history lesson. After the Watts rebellion in the 1960s, Black youth moved toward being politically aware. The BPP and the US Organization headed by Ron Karenga offered Black people a way to vent angers, focus energies, and maintain hope.

In 1968, J. Edgar Hoover dispatched a memo calling his agents in the FBI to create dissension within the BPP. The tactics of the FBI's Counter Intelligence Programs (COINTELPRO), an organization designed to curtail national security threats, produced a war between the US and the BPP. The BPP was the target of 233 of the 295 COINTELPRO operations; Hoover's FBI was determined to prevent the rise of a charismatic Black messiah and feared that Huey Newton or Eldridge Cleaver could be it.

"Ah. That's why my picture in 4800 was sent to the FBI."

Lunatick's scar with its points almost looks like a tattoo in his lighter skin. He laughs his bubbly laugh. "Yup. The LAPD set up a special section designed to curtail the Panther's growth, no matter what the cost. See. History." He tells me many of the Panthers had been members of the Slausons, a Eastside club, as had Bunchy Carter, the president of the Los Angeles Chapter of the BPP. His father told him the clubs started as a response to a White club whose members killed Blacks moving into Los Angeles. The US Organization had members from the Westside clubs. The FBI's COINTELPRO wedged the crack of these old hostilities and philosophical differences into a gulf. He says again, "See. History. All this goes back, way back. We just the modern version, a result of so much. The FBI infiltrated both groups, created bogus letters and lies so that the two groups distrusted each other. They were so busy fighting each other they were distracted from spreading their message, and, thus, their effectiveness in the Black community diminished. The lies and manipulations ended with a shootout between the two organizations in which six men were killed. "You knew that, cuz?" Lunatick's voice is gravelly, like an old man's.

I shook my head.

"I'll get you some books to read 'bout it. You know about Raymond Washington? Right, cuz?"

"Some." Truth is, I haven't thought about this before. Didn't think history had any relevance to me. Don't know I'm part of it.

Washington was fifteen and a student at Fremont High School when he started the gang in 1969, emulating the Panther dress and rhetoric, sporting black leather jackets and blue shirts.

I know this from the Crip Module chant.

In three years the gang moved from the Eastside to Inglewood, Compton, and the Westside, grew to eight gangs. The Pirus and several smaller gangs joined together to defend themselves against the Crips and renamed themselves Bloods to establish their pro-Black identity.

The gangs grew from there. In 1980 there were thirty thousand members. In 1998, there are a hundred fifty thousand gang members in Los Angeles County. *Didn't know we had a history stretching to the Black Panthers. Didn't ever think about it. I was too busy safeguarding our territory and winning the war. Didn't know we are so big.*

Lunatick, seeing my expression, says, "Yeah, ya don't know what being a Crip is until you get to prison."

I shift and look out at the stripes of black bars, the monotone walls.

"Don't worry. We have classes, like in the module. First, you gotta learn some languages."

The education of a member of the CCO includes Arabic, Kiswahili, standard English, and Spanish. Kiswahili is needed to connect us to our true ethnicity—African. Recently the goon squad began classes in Kiswahili and we added Arabic to our education in order to speak with each other over the tiers. Standard English enhances chances of employment once released from prison and evades stereotyping in prison. Spanish is taught for security purposes as the enemy—the Southern United Raza and the Mexican Mafia—speak it over tiers and in public, assuming Blacks can't understand.

Within a week, my day is scheduled into physical fitness, informal classes taking place in the cells on topics ranging from the Watergate scandal to slavery to language, a quiet period, and weekly discussions. Military training includes lessons in hand-to-hand combat, how to properly use a knife. I learn that I should drop my arm to my side, move in slowly and, when within arm's length, stab midpoint between the collarbone and waist on my opponent's left side where his liver, stomach, kidney, and heart lay. I'm taught how to use a spear, crossbow, zip gun, poisonous dart, liquid poison, strangulation devices, and explosives. I'm taught how to keester these things in my anus, nose, and throat.

We're trained to believe that survival, morals, and Black pride are first; family means everything. Women, children, and elders are held in the highest regard and are absolutely off limits in a war. The routine and rules are serious. Breaking rules leads to discipline, from loss of television to a browbeating to burpies (a strenuous exercise working all muscles of the body), to being stabbed. Stabbing is inflicted as an example and a message that stagnation is not overlooked or tolerated. Security breaches are dealt with by the severest penalty. That's one of the reasons for the violence in prison.

I am fascinated by all that I'm learning. I absorb the lessons like additions to my armament.

The CCO and BN are only two of the military machines functioning inside prison walls. In California, there are over ten organizations.

Lunatick Frank is a member of CCO, but he doesn't tell me that then. A few weeks later, he leans close and whispers, his gravelly voice surprisingly soft. "Don't get hooked up under paperwork."

"Uh?" I've been lapping up what he's telling me, eager to join such a compelling organization.

"'Cause, homie, you're young and strong. You're your own man and can handle your own, cuz. You don't need to get caught up in prison politics. You're doin' short time."

"Short?" Sixteen months seems forever.

"Sixteen months ain't shit. The majority of people under paperwork have all day. Life sentences, cuz. They ain't never gettin' out." In his earnestness, the scar running from his eyelid to his cheek has darkened, flushed with blood.

Part of me wants the discipline, the power, the celebrity of being part of the CCO.

"Look, Li'l Cee. You're my homie. I wouldn't mislead you or tell you shit. Everything you'll need to know will be taught when you get where you're going. There'll be other Crips like you, Crips that aren't under paperwork but are still respected and solid. Bond with them. Hold your own."

The goon-squad CO yells, "Lock up."

"I gotta roll." Lunatick Frank stands and rotates his shoulders back, as though sitting on the bunk with me has made them stiff. "You stay focused and think about what I told you." He shoves a book he's been holding at me. "This'll prepare you for Folsom." He walks down the tier to his cell.

I turn the book over. *Analytic Psychology.* I lay on my bunk and struggle to understand the contents. I learn how the mind shifts from the logical to the illogical. Before I fall asleep, I hear Lunatick's words. "Everything you'll need to know will be taught when you get where you're going. There're others like you. Hold your own."

Since being in prison, I learned that behavior here is not what it seems. In the free world, people telegraph their emotions and intentions. They show their anger. In prison, people don't show their feelings. The linchpin to survival is secrecy and intelligence.

Words have taken on a different meaning; hidden messages lurk in simple phrases. "What's up?" could mean, "How are you?" or "Do you have a problem?" or "What's the politics as you see them?" "Others like you" could mean young Crips with courage or resisters. My assault on Sporty is deemed retaliation for the murder of Tyrone and Pee Wee. The tier tender is a human rat. The environment is cryptic. Words, if not digested properly, can easily harm. There's no graffiti to post where I am and if I'm safe.

I learn to read earth signs.

At my 115 Hearing for assaulting Sporty, I'm found guilty of battery on an inmate and inciting a riot. I'm given a six-month SHU program and one hundred and eight days are tacked onto my time. I'm transferred to Folsom and immediately taken to the SHU unit—the hole. Over and over, I tell myself, *There are others like you. Everything you'll need to know will be taught. You can make it.*

EIGHT

Soledad

Rapidity is the essence of war.
    —Sun Tzu, *Art of War*

I STAY IN THE SHU PROGRAM FOR SIX MONTHS. I MAINTAIN the classes I had at Chino, especially the physical fitness, as much as possible and practice shadow fights. Then I'm transferred to Soledad Central. Tyrone visits while I'm unpacking. "Hey, turn on the television set to the prison station at seven o'clock. Channel Six." When I tell him I don't have one, he loans me his and I tune the TV to hear my homeboy's voice, "This is dedicated to Li'l Cee Loc from all the Thirties, Sixties, and Five Duces." A familiar Parliament tune roars to life.

I'm impressed with my own welcome. I'm known and recognized. My name has spread throughout the gang world, from the 'hood to the Hall, Camp, Youth Authority, LACJ, Chino, and now Soledad. From the police to the court to Los Angeles County's Sheriff's Operation Safe Street, to prison goon-squad, to the FBI. Li'l Cee Loc has made a mark. Colton is nobody. Cee is a celebrity alright, but not free.

After six days in orientation, I'm housed in B-Wing two cells from the shower. The mainline is mellow; there are no wars raging. However, there's tension between various factions of Crips, primarily between the O-Car—the sets from the Thirties, Sixties, and Five Duces—and the CCO. It's called "car" because it's a complete machine—engine is the OG, wheels are the soldiers—that'll take you somewhere. Big Moncrief and Big Rick, friends of my brother Damon, founded the O-Car. I'm automatically a member. The CCO tries to trick Crips to get under paperwork by claiming that once the constitution is read, the reader has to join. They pressure Crips to share canteen and drugs. Big Buster, a short, buff man, calls the shots for CCO, and Drack is his disciplinary officer. He has a reputation for "putting in work" during the war with the Southside Mexicans for which he received a life sentence. It's rumored he's such a cold-blooded killer he doesn't care about his own life.

Big Rick and Moncrief have already served six years in San Quentin for murder. They work in the kitchen, which allows them access to extra food and weapon stock. I'm instantly employed, arousing envy. Additionally, I'm labeled a resister by CCO. Sensing the undercurrent of hostility, I secure a six-inch-long steel rod from the kitchen and craft it to a point. I keep it with me; it's my insurance, my American Express card. I feel tension in the air. It's thick, hard to breathe. No birds chirp. An eerie quiet settles in the yard. I know the earth signs. The stage is set: my position, their position, our position.

Sure enough, I'm out in the rec yard punching the heavy bag one morning when Drack and his foot soldier, D, approach me from behind and introduce themselves.

I turn to face them, meet Drack's eyes, and say, "Yeah, I know who you are."

"You a 'Rip?"

I can't read if he's approaching me in recognition or in blood. I slide the knife from my waistband, cuff it, and turn sideways as Lunatick Frank taught me. Now, in a striking position, I say, "Yeah. Why?"

"How come you ain't been attending meetings, study classes, and exercise?"

This is confrontational. Not friendly. He's going to make an attempt on my life. I ease a bit closer and tighten the grip on my weapon in case Drack moves first and not his soldier, D. "'Cause I'm a Rollin' O," I explain.

Drack clenches his eyebrows, narrows his eyes. "So? You still have to conform to CCO policy, and I'm CCO."

"Man, I ain't gotta do shit. This is West Side Rollin'." Is the quiver near my eye visible? The victor in this will be the man who doesn't flinch.

"You Rollin', huh?" He touches his baseball cap, which must be a signal, because D lunges for his waistband.

"What you reachin' for, cuz?" I step close, cutting off his motion, and his opportunity departs.

"You from Rollin', huh?" At this point, they realize I'm strapped because of my rebellious attitude. Drack relaxes his eyes.

"Yeah. I'm from Rollin', West Side Rollin' Thirties Harlem Crip!

> "Five two whatever I do,
> "Six-O wherever I go,
> "and Tray-O is all I know.
> "West Side Rollin' O's."

This is the O-Car's cadence, and chanting it is my way to recognize his retreat but stand strong.

"Alright," Drack says out the side of his mouth.

I scan back and forth between Drack and D.

"Chulewa," which is Kiswahili for "later," Drack says to D. They turn and walk away, cursing softly.

My eyes are riveted to them as they drift across the rec yard.

Stuffing the weapon into my waistband, I return to punching the bag. Moncrief, who's a skilled boxer and always won his matches at San Quentin, has the most impressive reputation for fighting in the entire gang community, in and out of prison. I return to practicing a new fighting technique that he's been teaching me.

Drack returns, accompanied by two foot soldiers and Big Buster, the general, the shot caller. They're wearing gloves. My stomach clenches. I pretend I'm so involved in my boxing, I don't notice their approach, but, once again, I secure my weapon. I drop my right arm to my side and operate my peripheral vision to time their arrival. My heart quickens.

Big Buster strides close. "You Cee from Harlem?" His eyes are light brown against darker skin. Shorter than me, his thick neck convinces me of his power.

"I'm Cee. What's up?" I step toward him, close enough I see the pores in his checks.

"My comrade tells me you refuse to conform to CCO."

I'm in striking distance, my weapon tightly grasped. If I'm going to get stabbed; so is he. I'm outnumbered but pumped up. Well armed. I feel like ten men. A one-man army. "Man, I ain't under paperwork." My voice rasps, revealing my anxiety.

Instantly, fifteen people surround me. I didn't see them coming, focused too intently on Buster while pounding the bag. It's as if they materialized from the air. I'll take Big Buster first, then Drack, and if I have any wind left, D. He has a knife in his waistband, arms twitching at his side as he watches me. All these thoughts take place in a second. I know now I'm in my slow-motion thinking mode. The zone. I have control.

"That don't mean nothing," Buster counters. "CCO runs this line. Any Crip on this line that don't respect our rules ain't a Crip. So why're you flaggin' blue?" He points to the bandana hanging from my back pocket.

I don't look in the direction he points. Turn my head and I'd have a piece of metal in my neck. I try to back through a sliver of space in the circle, but it's quickly filled by a man. "I don't care what you consider me. I know where I'm from and who I am." I step toward Buster.

"Fool. I'll have you killed." His breath is hot.

My eyes dart, trying to decipher who's ordered to strike first. I spit, "I ain't no tape recorder. You heard me."

I'm alone. The men pressing me are flushed, necks bulging and so near I smell them. Reminds me of my first day incarcerated, when I was a boy. They're a blur of brawn and fear. My vision narrows. "Do or die. Can't stop. Won't stop. Harlem Crip!"

Big Buster lurches to snatch the Crip rag from my back pocket, but before he reaches it, I grab his wrist with my left hand, spin around, and raise my right arm, aiming midpoint between his waist and chest on his left side. I've cocked my weapon.

"Hold up, Cee." Moncrief grasps my arm.

A man shouts, "Cuz is strapped."

I glide the weapon snug into my front pocket.

"Man, you got something against my little homeboy? Don't be surrounding my li'l homie," Moncrief says each word leisurely as though he's giving it time to sink in. I know he's breathing evenly, trying to decrease the velocity of action, gain control.

"Cuz refuses exercise and study," Buster explains.

"I don't do that shit either. How come you don't get at me like that?" Moncrief asks.

"Man, you trippin'." Buster has a lot of bass in his voice, but his manner is not threatening or aggressive.

"Neither one of y'all gonna do shit to my li'l homie. You got a problem with the way he's doin' his program, take it out on me. I'll beat both you fools down." Moncrief's reputation is his weapon. His huge forearms, eighteen inches round, had once saved his life. In 1978, he strolled through his 'hood and saw Lunatick Frank hangin' out on the corner with a gold watch and decided to rob him. Lunatick Frank never thought twice about shooting someone. He jumped on his bicycle, rode off, returned with a gun, and fired five shots at Moncrief's torso. Moncrief used his forearms as a shield, bobbing and weaving to avoid being killed. His arms caught all five bullets. He's superman. Moncrief doesn't believe in stabbing other Crips. You either fight him, or you're considered a coward.

"And if y'all don't wanna get down with him, you can deal with me." Big Rick enters the circle. Now, Big Rick has a record of 52 and 0. Fifty by knockout in one-on-one prison fights. He uses his rage from the death of his brother on his opponents. His brother's murder sparked a war between the Rollin' Sixties and the Eight Tray Gangsters—a war between two sets of Crips—that is more deadly than the war between the Crips and the Bloods. The soldiers know where each other lives; the two set fires on each other's parents. This inner-Crip war is expanding over South Central. It's called *set tripping* because if you're not from the "set' or an ally, you get tripped on—shot, stabbed, robbed, murdered. This Crip-on-Crip set tripping is responsible for many gangbangers and their innocent friends and family members dying.

Big Rick is the pride and joy of the Sixties. With him and Moncrief on my side, the circle disperses and the CCOs stroll across the field. I fall in step with Moncrief and Big Rick and, for now, that is that.

I form my own schedule and keep vigilant security. Every day, after my work in culinary, I go to the Wing, take a shower, then lock myself in the cell. The radio sets the tone and soothes me. Mail is passed out after five o'clock. I fervently read my mail, then spend the evening writing. Bad news finds its way to my door through the mail, and the slightest unexpected event is magnified when doing time.

In late April 1985, I receive a letter from my cousin telling me her mother, Aunt Deedee, had to have her leg amputated because of gangrene. She sang professionally and then ran the streets when she was a young woman, but by the time I knew her, her roaming was accompanied by her daughter and nephews, and she ran us to Knotts Berry Farm and a lake where we swam. I beat my cell bars until the CO lets me out to the yard and I pound out my anger and sadness on the heavy bag. I've always been hyperactive and, when angry, can't be still. I punch the bag until I exhaust myself, taking out my hostility to keep from "going off" and catching more time. After awhile, the helpless melancholy dissipates. I pace the track, searching for peace. The entire time, I blink away tears.

I drink at the water fountain, letting the water run over my hot eyes. When I raise my head, Drack is in front of me and his soldier, D, to my right. They caught me slippin'. I jump back to reach for my weapon. D grabs me by my shoulders and spins me around. "Cuz, we ain't trippin' on you. If we wanted to book you, you'd be laid out. We've been standing here for sixty-two seconds."

I don't trust a thing he says. I duck under D's grasp and snatch my weapon.

"I just wanted to apologize for coming off the way I did. I never wanted a beef with you. I was following orders. But you're right. You ain't CCO so you shouldn't have to function with us. Do your own thang." Drack extends his hand.

I shake it with my left. I'm taking no chances. "Righteous, apology accepted." I hedge, but allow him the possibility of being sincere.

We shake hands. I go on my way and they go on theirs.

It's late June; summer is in full swing. Hot, humid, no breeze. The prisoners are irritable, thinking of the block parties, nightclubs, and the beaches filled with beautiful women they're missing. Each passing summer brings the realities of life in prison down hard. Me, I'm lucky. I only have a few months left.

News comes via mail that my set has taken the deadly plunge into set-trippin' civil war. We gave guns and stolen cars to one side, Rollin' Sixties, assuming they were doing robberies and fighting the Bloods. Then, Big T's little brother, Li'l T, is arrested for the murder of a Crip from Eight Tray Hoover. Li'l T had been a rider. With this charge of murder, he's climbed another notch. Each level of participation brings points, an upgrade in rank and status. Now, he'll have to pass a series of other tests in the Crip Module and, then, in prison. When he passes, he'll have climbed further.

My friend, Steve, is from the other set. I fret that my homies might kill him. He fears that his homies will kill me. My friends are now my enemies. On the street, I could prevent it. In prison, I'm unable to keep track of things as they unfold. I can only wait to hear outcomes.

I try to call Big T to make sure that Steve is sheltered and off limits. He's not at home so I call G. He tells me Smiley was convicted of the bank robbery and sentenced to fifteen years and twenty-two years for the murder of the ice-cream man, each sentence to run consecutively.

Thirty-seven years to life.

Smiley's last look at the 'hood will be from a Los Angeles County Sheriff's bus en route to prison. His love, camaraderie, bravery sequestered by cages. I remember the expression on his face as they pulled him through those steel doors in LACJ. His downturned eyes, straight lips, his sadness at seeing me. But that image of sorrow is erased by his welcoming smile. Now he's essentially forever behind bars and his unquenchable, spontaneous, surprising spirit chained, his actions controlled by the pigs.

I slowly walk the corridor to my wing and enter my cell. I turn on the radio looking for comfort but the music scratches my ears; the beat is furious and increases my anxiety. Mail arrives and with it a letter from Pops. "You only have a few more months now. I'm looking forward to you coming home. That and staying out of jail."

"Stay out of jail." *How am I going to do this?* In jail, my focus is surviving and getting out. But that's as far as my thinking goes. I never think about staying out. I always come back. *Come back and come back. Jail's my second home. When I'm not in the streets, people know where to find me.*

"Man. Y'all seen Cee?"

"Nah, he must be in jail."

How can I stay out of jail, but not ruin my reputation as a banger? As a child, I wanted to follow my father's footsteps and become a professional athlete. I had the genes to fulfill my dream, but the lure of the streets seduced me. Fast cars, money, celebrity, status, jewelry, glitz, drugs, attention, women chasing me, men giving me praise. My environment channels my vast ambition. Like my father who hit and caught balls, fighting to scale the baseball ladder till he made the major leagues, I lust and work for my celebrity. In the streets, I'm a star, a super-star. I crave the praise my father got.

Now, as my time closes, I wonder, *What has to happen so I can stay out? Is it in my control?*

A few days later, a transfer to CRC (California Rehabilitation Center) comes through and I'm told to "roll it up." I don't know why I'm transferred. California Prison System doesn't let prisoners stay in one place too long; the system doesn't want us to amass friendships, loyalty, or power. So we're constantly moved. As I place my letters on my blanket, I hear the strangest sounds coming from the showers. I peek in. Tyrone, a sergeant for CCO and Chevy, a BGF, are under the same showerhead. Mists of steam and hot water surround them. Chevy is bent over, moaning and groaning, and Tyrone is deep in his ass, stroking away with his eyes fully closed, his head back, and his lips open.

I back away and compress my eyes. I've heard stories of men who fall in love with other men. I replay how strong Tyrone seemed when he greeted me and loaned me his TV the first day in Soledad. He had the posture and attitude of "rider" written on his face, his dialect, his stroll, his firm handshake. "Cripism is about staying strong, controlling your emotions, and being disciplined. As long as we're true to Cripism, Cripism will be true to us. And be true to yourselves. Don't be messin' with no boys," Tyrone said at a meeting. Now, seeing him in the middle of a steamy shower, having sex with another man, I wonder, did I misjudge?

"Wait a minute. Look. Somebody's watching," Chevy says.

I dash to my cell and lock the door. I turn the water on in the sink and wash my hands. *So this is what Cripism is about? Fucking another man. An enemy at that.* I'm relieved I won't have to take a shower in that same room, under that same showerhead. I resent their sex being in my face.

I consider reporting him to Drack and Big Buster, but that would be snitching. I tell Moncrief, who takes it with a grain of salt, like it's no big deal. I almost ask him if he has done it but decide against it. I'm afraid he'll say yes. I guess sex with Chevy was about the feeling; he felt like a woman and Tyrone was nympho enough it didn't matter that he was a man.

Later, I find out that Chevy changed his name to Mother and moved into the cell with Tyrone. Ain't love grand?

I'm transferred to Soledad North. My new cell window provides me with a view of the entire yard. I gaze out the window and try to get a feel of the politics. The races are clustered together. Everyone is dressed in Levis and state shirts with blue flags and red flags hanging from their pockets or tied around their heads. They jog the track, play cards, talk. A few are wearing shorts and sling-shot tee shirts, lifting weights and playing basketball. Two hundred prisoners dressed alike.

After I unpack, I go to the rec yard to check in with the O-Car. While strolling past the baseball diamond, I spot a familiar face dressed in a burgundy robe and red pajama pants. "Web?" I call out.

"Cee? That you? Man. Look at you. Six feet tall, two hundred pounds, seventeen-inch biceps." We haven't seen each other for eight years.

"What's up wit' the burgundy robe? And those dead pants?"

"You know I don't bang." This was the same cat who had me

break into a house and steal drugs because the dealer wasn't from the set.

I search his face for signs of a grin, but he's serious or at least trying to convince me.

"What happened?" I ask.

Boom.

Out of the corner of my eye, a man slashes the face of another. A seam of blood oozes down his cheek. Another man runs into a group, arms wild, a knife in each hand. The keened edge of knife flickers and a man doubles over.

The Hispanic population erupts into an all-out war.

Boom. Boom. Two more bullets ring out.

Around me are the glint of weapons, the spurting of blood, the whack of landed punches. Building-and-yard alarms reverberate their echoing screech. Emergency lights whirl. The yard that thirty seconds before was peaceful has churned into chaos.

"Look out," Web shouts.

I look to my left and see the gun-tower CO chamber another round and turn the gun toward us.

Boom.

"I said get down. Get down! Get down! Get down!" the tower officer yells.

I dive for pavement. As soon as I land, he fires two more shots. They graze the cement, ping, and ricochet across the yard helter-skelter.

"Get your fuckin' asses down."

Silence. I look to my right. Flashes from emergency lights illuminate a gunshot wound on the leg of a Southside Mexican. He lies on his side with a knife in his chest. Blood seeps from his wound to the grass. It stretches across the green, claiming territory. His body looks limp. Then he goes into convulsions.

Boom. Another shot rings out.

"I said get down. Get down!"

Everyone in the entire yard is face down except for the Southside Mexican still twitching. Several COs run past. Two of them lift him from the ground, put him on a stretcher, and carry him out.

We're searched. We're escorted to our cells. The incident makes the Top Story on the Channel 46 News. Fifteen people were stabbed. One was shot. The shooting victim was eighteen years old.

The battle started after an argument between the Southern and Northern Mexicans over twenty feet of grass. Each claimed it was their space. Both lost. The grass belongs to the establishment. They win.

The institution is placed on lockdown. There's no movement. During the lockdown, I'm told to "roll it up" and am herded into a transportation bus and driven to California Rehabilitation Center. I never finish my conversation with Web.

NINE

Chess Games

We have become convinced that certain offenders...are no longer "members of the public" and cease to be deserving of the kinds of consideration we typically afford to each other. Perhaps because we already assume a social and cultural divide between "us," the innocent, long-suffering middle-class victims, and "them," the dangerous undeserving poor. By engaging in violence, or drug abuse, or recidivism, they reveal themselves for what they are: "the dangerous other," the underclass. "Our" security depends upon "their" control....We allow ourselves to forget...that offenders are citizens too and their liberty interests are our liberty interests. The growth of a social and cultural divide between "us" and "them," together with new levels of fear and insecurity, has made many complacent about the emergence of a more repressive state power.
   —David Garland, *The Culture of Control: Crime and Social Order in Contemporary Society*

THERE'S NO WAR GOING ON AT CALIFORNIA REHABILITATION Center and I breathe the air easy, enjoy the sun. Birds fly over the yard. I pay attention to the earth signs, but this is a place of relative harmony. The honor yard resembles a college campus with dorms. Along the fence, a group of men play chess. A White cat in Juvenile Hall taught me how to move the pieces. I walk toward two men crouched over the board to watch. A man in his thirties with a carefully trimmed mustached captures his opponent's queen, looks up at me, and says, "Now I got his broad." He points a forefinger to the sky. "You see, he should've never put his broad there, he coulda used his horse instead." He points to a knight.

Then he rises. Because of his broad shoulders and arms, I assume he's a tall man, but his height is only average. I hold out my hand and introduce myself.

"Lafayette Rainey." His hand is surprisingly warm.

I have heard of him as a Black revolutionary. Now, Lafayette is head of the Slauson Village, which is an organization in South

Central Los Angeles dedicated to eradicating gangs. I nod at Lafayette.

"Your game." He moves aside so I can play his vanquished challenger. He leans against the fence, smoking a cigarette, one thumb hooked in his pants. "If you understand prison politics, and politics period for that matter, then you know the importance of security and thus will understand chess," Lafayette says.

I move my knight.

Lafayette nods. "You see, Cee, in prison, war never ceases. It simply fluctuates from seethe to subsidence, but there's always plotting and, with every action and reaction, intrigue thickens. You're required to maintain a visual on everything relevant. Not only from your point of view, but the opposition's. So, Cee, you have to have vision and foresight."

My adversary slides his pawn two spaces.

"So too in chess," Lafayette continues. "Recognizing plots will keep you moves ahead of your opponent and help you read his game. Once you're able to read your opponent, you create ploys to counteract his strategy." He looks away, sucks on his cigarette, blows smoke into the sky.

My bishop captures the pawn. Lafayette watches.

The next day, he plays me without his queen. I swap all my pieces for his and am left with my king and queen. All he has is his king naked in the corner of the board. He chuckles during the entire match.

"Why're you laughing?"

"Cee, brotha. You're the first youngster that realized how to beat me without my broad. I can tell a lot about a person by the way he plays. Right off the bat, you knew what to do and weren't thrown by my plot. You concentrated on swapping pieces, knowing you'd have your broad and I wouldn't."

He got my strategy, all right. I scratch an itch in my chin.

He leans back, hooks his thumb in his pants pocket. "You see, people like you think big. I bet you're very ambitious."

He read my burning lust, my obsession with celebrity.

"People who think small tend to devote a lot of time to capturing pawns, but they're the least important pieces on the board and are one dimensional. Those people aren't playing to win. They focus on the immediate forefront and not the peripheral. They steal money but don't realize that people are watching. There are consequences." His eyes lock on mine. He repeats the word. "Consequences." His eyes narrow. "Even if they get away, there are consequences, serious consequences, for every move you make in life. So, too, in chess." His forefinger points at me as he leans closer. It's as if he reads me and knows my life. "Never make a move before weighing the potential consequences." Now he wags his finger. "If you do, you'll make deadly mistakes, mistakes that can cost your life. More than likely, you'll lose the war, not because you're weaker, but because you played into their plot."

Back in my cell, I lie on my bunk and think about his words. He's right. I have played into the establishment's hands. I joined the gang and became employed as a thief without realizing the plot was thickening and I was moving further into it. The consequences for those actions are still on my periphery.

A chill courses through me and I pull up the blanket. Pretty soon, if I don't take heed and look at the big picture, I'll end up right where Whitey wants me. Dead. Or in prison the rest of my life. I'm running full speed toward a wall with no way to brace my impact. On a collision course, digging my own hole, chasing death.

"Keep thinking as far down the line as you can. Think ten moves ahead. The person who wins the game is the person who thinks the farthest," Lafayette tells me. "Consequences."

A few weeks later, in the middle of the game, as though suddenly bored by it, Lafayette leans back and forks that thumb into his pants pocket. He scans the yard, the clusters of prisoners shooting hoops, lifting weights, walking in circles on the track. The fog hasn't burned off yet and the sky is white. "Cee." I meet his eyes.

"These brothas are prime examples of cats who don't weigh consequences. They walk 'round talking about Comrade George and don't even know who he is."

"I know who Comrade George was. A Black revolutionary who fought against racism. When he was eighteen he was convicted of stealing seventy bucks from a gas station and given one of those indeterminate sentences—one year to life. He served eleven years, seven in solitary. Transformed himself into an activist, political theoretician, and revolutionary before he was killed by the pigs in 1971 allegedly trying to escape."

Lafayette stretches his lips down, nodding his head. I've impressed him. I learned this in the classes held by Crips in Chino. "George says that young brothas in prison believe they don't need tactics. Being a brave warrior is enough. But without direction, they'll be unclaimed bodies in the morgue."

He stands up, asks me to wait, and strolls to his locker. When he returns, he carries a manila envelope. He reaches in and pulls out a Polaroid and offers me a picture of George Jackson. Then, he extracts a newspaper clipping, soft from age and folded so long and so often the ink has worn off along the creases. Carefully, I unfold it to see prisoners laying face down on the ground, naked at San Quentin. They lay in rows, hands behind their heads, elbows pointing to each other.

He points to one figure in the center of the group. "You know who that is?"

"George Jackson."

"Right. You recognize any of the other brothas?"

I shake my head.

"That's me on the ground." He points to a figure. "I was with him that day." He slides the photo into the envelope, tenderly refolds the newspaper clipping, smoothing it slowly and replacing it. Then, he steps back from me. "What do you feel when you read about a White man killing a Black man?"

"Angry."

"Why?"

If anyone else pushed me like this, I'd bristle, my heart quickening, my hair rising, but I know Lafayette, so I give him his lead. "Cause it ain't right."

"You're a gangbanger, right? And your set is Harlem Crips, right?"

"Yeah." Where's he going with his rhetoric?

"As a Crip, your job is to kill Bloods, right?"

I shrug one shoulder and nod.

"You feel killing a Black man isn't right. Then answer my question, why do you gangbang?"

I'm angry at Whites who kill Blacks, but I'm dedicated to killing Bloods who're Black. How can I say killing a Black man is wrong, when I shoot Black men? Doesn't matter who kills him,—White or Black—he's still dead. "Man, cuz, what're you tryin' to say? You disrespectin' me, cuz? Man, we're at war, what am I supposed to do?"

Lafayette holds his palm toward me. "Hey, brotha, don't get angry. All I did was ask a few questions. If you wanna get mad at someone, get mad at yourself." He nods his head, his eyes even. "It's not in your heart to kill another Black man. If killing a Black man is wrong, you realize being a gangbanger is wrong. You don't believe in what the Crips are doing. What you've done. You just told me that."

"I like what I'm doin'." The sun has burned away the fog and heats my head. I step close to see stray gray in his mustache. "Them slobs been shooting at me and my homies. Do you know how many of 'em have died? I know what I'm doin'."

"Think how your family would feel if you got killed. Think how you feel when you learn one of your homies got killed."

Just last week, Huckabuck wrote one of the homies—a Crip I had initiated—had been shot in a drive-by. Now his leg was shattered and he'll need a brace to walk.

"The way you feel is the same as they feel. It ain't you, Cee. I see it in your face, brotha."

We stare at each other. I swallow to stiffen my mouth. I purposely flex my bicep. Lafayette's eyes remain soft, no anger, only blackness and behind that melancholy. He's open with his sorrow, which he doesn't limit to himself or me, or all of us trapped in prison, but it encompasses everyone.

"Just think about it."

I do think about it, recalling his words. Our discussion about killing Black men plants a seed that slowly takes root. *They feel the same as you feel. It's wrong. Consequences, consequences. You have choices.* I add his words to the pile of others gifted to me in good faith and strong hope.

It's mid-August, 1985, and I make early parole for good behavior. The bus zooms down Santa Barbara taking me to the 'hood. First thing I'll do is walk to Huckabuck's, then go to Louise's. Unfortunately, seeing her is dangerous as she has moved to a Blood neighborhood. I'll be living with my Aunt Deedee, now wheelchair bound, and her daughter, Cezanne, who takes care of her. Aunt Deedee is on the edge of a Blood neighborhood. I know I'll need to move out as soon as I can.

I sit twisted on the edge of my seat to gaze out the sliding window at my neighborhood. The sparse White people I saw walking the streets are gone. More Hispanics are in South Central, but my 'hood is totally Black. My 'hood, familiar and safe. Home. I note the changes with dismay; I want it to be waiting for me just as I left it. But Ralph's Market has been torn down and replaced with a Boy's Market. Freeway Records is now a 7-Eleven and Popeye's Fried Chicken. A park has been built on Western between Thirty-ninth and Santa Barbara. I see a few boarded-up buildings, empty storefronts. Chipped paint. More faded signs. Reagan's recession and his trickle-down economics haven't trickled down, I note. Or at least not *this* far down. The windows and doors on the houses are crossed with bars. No children play in the street. The 'hood has a funereal silence; I don't even hear music.

Cars zoom past the bus, impatient drivers cursing and flipping off the driver. I look out the other window and see a hovering sheriff's helicopter. When we reach Van Ness, I stand and press the buzzer. The bus halts; I jump onto the sidewalk near a gas station. I note the faint aroma of gunpowder. The 'hood smells just the same.

I walk to the end of the block and look at the street sign. What was Santa Barbara is now Martin Luther King Boulevard. The laundry is owned by Spike, across the street from his liquor store. Two businesses. Good for him. He at least is doing better.

Everything seems smaller and I realize how much I've grown. I've reached my full height of six feet two, two hundred and fourteen pounds. Muscles bulge. I have a sense of ownership of the streets because of the work I've put in for the set, but the 'hood looks like a ghost town. There are no people. No cars. Nothing moves but me and a cluster of kids huddling home from school. Not even the wind stirs the palms. Not even the birds chirp. Then, *We Are the World* drifts faintly.

I spot a crew of homies hangin' out on Smiley's old street. When they see me, their vigilance begins.

"Cuz, who tha' fuck is that?"

"Man, I ain't knowin', but he comin' this way."

"Yeah. No shit."

"Well, don't just stand there, fool. Get the strap."

"Hold up. You trippin'. That Wino, homie." They stare at me.

"Man, that ain't Wino. Cuz too big to be the homie."

Now, I'm only half a block away. "Cee, is that you?" The shortest one calls out.

To keep them on their toes, I don't respond.

"Man," the tallest one says, "That's Cee."

Now, only a few feet away, I break into a grin and say, "What that Crip like?"

G is in the middle of the pack. Black Kev claps me on the shoulder. "Check this fool out, G. He's swoll like a mutha' fucka.'"

"What was they feedin' yo' ass in there, Cee, steel?" Amp asks.

"Man, this ain't shit but seventeen and three quarters. As soon as I get some weights I'm gonna blow up to some nineteens." I flex my bicep.

G steps toward me and we hug. I haven't seen him since I was at his house after he left us in the parking lot holding the loot. He looks just the same. His cornrows a little longer, that's all. Still skinny and quick, but now his motions are smooth. As he embraces me, I realize my anger at him is done and the love resumed. And now, I know his limits. Like Smiley told me, "Cuz ain't like us."

There's an awkward silence as eyes stare at the ground.

"What's up, Kev?" I ask.

"The little homie, Teekey, got killed. The Eight Tray Hoovers killed cuz. They got in a shootout with the Sixties and Teekey just happened to be wit' 'em."

We don't even know the Hoovers, but we're gunning each other down because we hang out on different street corners. In prison, we stuck together, one nation under Crip. But here, we're killing each other on sight over trivialities.

"We dropped a few bodies, but you know how that goes. They bodies ain't gonna bring cuz back. His moms took it hard," Amp says.

I remember Lafayette's words. *That killin' ain't you, Cee. I see it in your face.*

"Huckabuck went straight-up gung ho. He's drivin' around wit' a Uzi, shooting niggas in broad daylight and shit, right in front of the police. Cuz seems to be loosin' his mind," G says. "He's moving too fast. Maybe he might listen to you 'cause y'all's dogs." G shakes his head. "That nigga's a nut now, Cee."

I open my mouth to say something and hear screeching tires off to my right.

"Twinkies," Amp shouts.

Tat-tat-tat-tat-tat. I'm blinded by flashes of automatic gunfire. Bullets vomit from the mouth of the barrel.

I dive for cover.

Tat-tat-tat-tat-tat.

Behind Amp's car, I protect my face and head with my arms and curl into a fetal position. I lay surrounding myself while shots chink the car, buildings, cement, trees. My ears ring from the piercing blasts. Tat-tat-tat-tat-tat. I twist tighter as metal sprays. Seconds slow to eternity as I lay there listening to the tat-tat-tat-tat-tat, wondering if I'll get hit. Finally, silence.

Then the car squeals away.

I unfold and stand. I look around to see if any of us have been shot. Only Amp's car and neighborhood houses. Drive-by. You never know who or what gets hit. This time, everyone is spared.

I bolt to Spike's Liquor and call D'Andre. He and Steve beat the gun-theft charges. While in CRC, I told him to tell the judge the guns were mine. I'd already been sentenced to sixteen months. What else could they do to me? I didn't want Steve and D'Andre messing up their lives with a criminal record and prison term. They both got off on probation.

I say to D'Andre, "Come get me."

He starts to say something, but I hang up. Who's to say the shooters aren't returning? Or the police. They're both a threat to me, to my 'hood, the city, and my freedom. Just my luck, if I stay on the phone, I'll get a bullet in my head. Or an old fashioned beat-down by Southwest police.

D'Andre pulls up and I jump in his car, slam the door, and bark, "Drive off."

I've been home thirty minutes.

TEN

Short Freedom

Let me have war, say I; it exceeds peace as far as day does night; it's spritely, waking, audible, and full of vent. Peace is a very apoplexy, lethargy; mull'd, deaf, sleepy, insensible; a getter of more bastard children than war's a destroyer of men...and it makes men hate one another. Reason; because they then less need one another.
—William Shakespeare, *Coriolanus*

A DRIVE-BY OR A DEATH OF A FRIEND ENCOURAGES A NORMAL individual to avoid the same fate and drop out of the gang. For me, for other bangers, it increases participation. Teekey's murder and the drive-by reinforce my belief that the more enemies I eliminate, the more stores I rob, the bigger my reputation, the greater the proof of my invincibility and, thus, the odds of my continued existence. If I have a hundred enemies and knock out fifty, then I've doubled my odds of living. I buy my own life with the death of others. In other words, I walk into the tornado to achieve the eye of the storm and safety.

Now, drug and alcohol free, I see how distorted this thinking is. Drugs—the cocaine, alcohol, and marijuana I used as a teenager— allowed me to misconstrue logic and twist my decision making. In my 'hood, those who perfect robbing, selling drugs, and killing rise to celebrity status and have supreme power that keeps them from becoming victim to someone else's violence. We believe this

so wholeheartedly, when a friend is killed, we figure it's a fluke—
he's in the wrong place at the wrong time. Or we blame him—he
was caught slippin'. So when Teekey is killed, and I'm exposed to
a drive-by, instead of saying to myself, *This shit is dangerous, I'll
quit the gang,* I think, *I knew the job was hazardous when I took
it; I better wipe out my enemy so he can't kill me.* I don't consider
the fact that I'm making more enemies. The more enemies I
wipe out, the better my chances for life. I can't let my death occur. I attempt to defeat my death by killing others. I buy time, I
buy life.

It isn't simply the drugs and alcohol that distort thinking. The
'hood itself plants the seed of joining a gang in your mind. Over-
worked, broken families don't have the ability to fight streets that
hold out the lure of belonging, thrills, fame, money, the American
dream. We have our own heroes. And because of the segregation
imposed by the combination of White racism and the housing
industry—the real estate agents who made money by blockbust-
ing and the banks that made money by redlining and charging
Blacks higher interest rates and thus creating the ghettos—we
have developed our own culture. Some of it you know about—the
charged energy in African rhythm and complex rhymes of rap.
Our unique twist in clothing, walk, and talk. Whites come into our
lives via TV, mostly in commercials, or as cops, or teachers. Unemployment for Black men in South Central L.A. is 30 percent; the
national average is 5 percent. And as hopes for jobs diminish,
other alternatives—the underground economy—become a way of
life. The gangs organize the underground economy. The gangs
provide heroes. The gangs teach skills. The gangs provide love
and protection. The gangs fill in where America has failed. Just
like the Pledge of Allegiance to the American flag plants the seed
to join the armed forces and die for your country, attend the
streets of South Central Los Angeles and you're likely to die for
your set. When you don't have power, space becomes important.
So we fight over our territory. We fight to protect our neighbor-

hoods. We fight to prove our invincibility and stay alive. If we enlarge our space, we're safer, we have more power.

Yet, the words of Lafayette turn in my head, pumping up the Colton aspect of my personality. My family—my father's professional athletic career, my uncle's law practice, my mother's businesses—has shown me there are other ways of fulfilling ambition. I've passed my GED, enrolled in Santa Monica College, and set out to find a legitimate job, even though I know I'll make significantly less than I made as a jewel thief. I have no luck finding a job. No one wants to hire a high school drop out/ex-con/parolee.

Pride and hate put aside, I start working for my mother, who has opened up a maintenance business and appointed Damon as manager. I wash department store windows, buff floors, and paint walls. For awhile, the money is decent, we designate our own hours, and I'm away from the 'hood and the temptation of street hustles. But then Damon decides to start a used-car business. My transportation to and from work is gone. I haven't saved enough money to buy a car. I can't ask my mom for a handout; she wouldn't give it to me. She'd use the excuse of not having the cash, since she has no speck of generosity when it comes to me. I try buses and walking, but it's too difficult in L.A. Once again, I fill out job applications. While waiting responses, I visit family and friends.

My friends—D'Andre, Steve, and practically everyone else I know—try to solve my job problem by pulling me into the drug trade. Crack has tightened its chokehold on the ghetto. The crack is cheap, not like the cocaine I freebased in the late seventies, and it can be bought a hit at a time. It's the perfect drug manufactured and marketed to meet the needs for a quick, inexpensive high to poor people with sad and often frightening life situations. Cocaine is usually sold in hundred-dollar lots, whether it's snorted or freebased; now it's sold in twenty-five-dollar rocks—guaranteeing an economical, fast euphoria. There're several Crip dealers operating at this time in South Central. Freeway Rick Ross undercuts all competitors and his crack is cheap. But he's a Hoover Crip—the set responsible for Teekey's death and Li'l T's incarceration—and we're at war with them. Harry-O, the Cocaine Cowboy, supplies the Avenues, my 'hood. Also operating is the Bennet-Villabona drug organization. Waterhead Bo Bennet and Michael Flarvis, known as "Harry-O," buy their cocaine from the Columbian drug cartel fronted by Villabona.

I remember when Beauty said that the government imported the drugs to obliterate Black people. Now, I hear rumors that the crack destroying some of us and making some of us rich is being flown in by CIA operatives who're flying guns down to Latin America and returning with planes filled with cocaine. Two Nicaraguan dealers—Danilo Blandon and Norwin Meneses—supply it to Freeway Rick, which is how he undercuts competitors. A genius of marketing, he floods cities across the country with the inexpensive ghetto-designed drug. There's still controversy over whether he's responsible for the nationwide crack epidemic, but the dispute is over details regarding the extent of his empire and if he, with Blandon's cocaine, is the first to mass-market crack. Even the United States government concedes that at least some of the cocaine hitting South Central streets as crack is from Blandon and the drug profits used to supply weapons to the Contras. Ross sells cocaine by the ounce until he meets Blandon and suddenly he starts buying it by the kilo. He buys one hundred kilos a week from Blandon in 1984. It is estimated that Freeway Ross earns two hundred million dollars in 1985, the year I'm released to South Central. He sells at least three tons of cocaine from 1982 to 1989. Three tons. Imagine that amount. It is about five semitrailers full of powder.

There is no controversy about where he gets his cocaine. Blandon is a wealthy Nicaraguan with a master's in marketing, determined to help oust the Sandinistas and reestablish the Somoza government. Blandon funnels the money from the sale of cocaine to finance the war through the Contras. CIA operatives fly down guns and return with cocaine from Colombia. It's not till 1996 that the facts behind these rumors are broadly published. The government Department of Justice in 1997 admitted "there is also undeniable evidence that certain groups associated with the Contras engaged in drug trafficking." The government allows crack to sweep South Central, and some of their own operatives fly it into the United States, giving voice to the war on drugs while really waging a war on Blacks.

Freeway Ricky Ross uses his profits to expand his empire to Cincinnati, Tyler and Dallas, Texas, Seattle, Louisiana, Kansas City, St. Louis, Oklahoma, Indiana, and New York. He had been a low-budget car thief who stripped stolen vehicles near the Harbor Freeway. Now, he buys up property and builds malls and office buildings alongside the freeway, amplifying his nickname, "Freeway Rick."

But because he's a Hoover we don't buy from him.

Michael Harris, known as Harry-O or the Cocaine Cowboy, is the dealer we buy from. He invests some of his profits to start Death Row Records and negotiates deals with Time Warner, Polygram, Sony, and Viacom. He works with Bo Waterhead Bennett, and they receive their cocaine from Villabona and other Colombian drug cartels. All the cocaine comes from Colombia. Some is brought by the cartels; some is brought by CIA operatives. Some of the profits go back to Colombia: some of the profits go to the Contras Contrast to fight in Nicaragua with guns flown down by the CIA.

In 1989, the U.S. Attorney General describes the Bloods and Crips as the nation's most powerful crack-trafficking ring, urban terrorists who have achieved dominance in at least forty-seven cities, "due in part to their steady recourse to murderous violence." By the midnineties the Black dealers—Harry-O Harris, Bo Waterhead Bennett, Freeway Ricky Ross—are in prison.

Danilo Blandon is a well-paid and highly trusted operative for the U.S. Drug Enforcement Administration, described by federal officials as one of the top informants in Latin America collecting intelligence on Colombian and Mexican drug lords. I know this now. I only understood part of what was happening as it occured.

Crack changes the atmosphere of the 'hood, and I'm released into the height of the epidemic. Crack has become the largest neighborhood business. I turn away all suggestions to be a dealer. I'm trying to live straight. If I get back into the life, I won't be a dealer. Dealers are not seen as serious bangers, but as drug dealers. We rob dealers, unless they're from our set.

So I'm in limbo, rejected from one underpaid job or another, staying with Aunt Deedee, and trying not to get spotted by the Bloods in her neighborhood.

When I see Huckabuck, he tells me he has fallen in love with a girl named Tina and they're thinking about having a child. His easy manner and gleaming happiness don't jive with the rumor of him as a crazed shooter. We laugh and joke about times when we were both "wannabees," and how I beat up Moe when he caught me crying about Huckabuck's bullet in the arm.

"Cee," he looks straight in my face, "it's still 'Do or die,' cuz. Man, I love you. I wish Smiley was here. We could tear shit up."

I grin back at him. "It's good to see you, cuz. Good to see you so happy."

"You need a coming-home party. Think I'll throw one for you at World on Wheels Skating Rink." It's the latest gang hangout where all the Thirties, Forties, Sixties, Nineties, and Hundreds go.

With Smiley's incarceration, Big T is running the set. G, Big T, and I drive to Big Mel's and catch him in the backyard lifting an engine out of a stolen car.

"Fat Boy," Big T calls out to him, "Look who's back."

Big Mel squints his eyes and bursts out in a huge grin. His belly has gotten soft and his face is rounder. "Li'l Cee. What's up, nigga . . . when you get out?"

"A few weeks ago."

"Ah, hold on . . . I got something I've been savin' for your crazy ass."

He reaches into the trunk of the stolen car and pulls out a big box with a blue ribbon wrapped around it. "Here, go ahead."

I open it while the fellas watch. It's a ten-pound sledgehammer. When we see it, we fall out laughing.

I go to the party with Li'l Dog, Smiley's cousin and member of the set. He's a dark-skinned, short guy, but with none of the easy grin and generosity that flits through Smiley's family. He's slow to laugh, his laughter blurts, and he walks as though he's on a boat, from side to side, seasick. G and Big T are with us. When I enter the skating rink, I see more than a hundred men Cripped down. They turn to face me and start throwing up their sets, flashing gang signs. There are a few women, but the crowd is men, men here to see me. I walk toward one of the tables with my fist balled, thumb in the air representing Harlem Crip. "La di Da di" by Slick Rick and Doug E Fresh plays on the loudspeakers. I scan the room, recognizing nearly every elite soldier from my set, that is those who are not dead or in jail. Huckabuck, grinning and stirring with his energy, F-Bone, Vincent Lovett, Magic, the Cocaine Cowboy, Big Mel, Hawk, Ray Dog, Amp, BJ, Li'l Jimbo. All the crew. They crowd around me, shining me with grins. "Hey, cuz. Welcome home." Sleep Rock hugs me.

"Whassup?" Hawk claps me on the back, his grin as wide as his face.

"You cool, cuz?" V-Dog says.

Money and large quantities of cocaine are offered by the "ballers"—cats who're successful robbers and dealers. I accept the money and pass on the drugs. They're eager to help me start in the neighborhood business.

"What're gonna do now that you're out?" Ray Dog asks.

I shrug. "Don't know. Haven't figured that out yet." I've already enrolled in school and dropped out. Had a job and quit.

"Did you fuck any guys in the ass while you were in prison?" Sleep Rock asks.

"Hell no. I didn't fuck no man in the ass."

"How'd you and Smiley manage to make so much money? Back when you were on the streets? Take me on a lick," Amp requests.

As I move across the lobby, a group of thirty men follows. I halt and they surround me. Off in the corner a group of men dance the Crip walk to *Thirty Days* by Whodini. A few zoom around the rink on skates and throw up signs as they pass.

"Cuz, you want some?" Li'l Jimbo passes me some Hennessy.

I tell them about solitary and about Big Silky and about CCO and about the Hispanic war in Soledad. As soon as I finish, they bombard me with more questions. I tell them about Crip history, how we were founded with the philosophy of the Black Panthers, about Lafayette and chess and consequences. I tell them about Pup.

I play the expert witness, clarifying twisted rumors about prison. The cats sit or stand, attending every word, encouraging me to tell more. These men would cover my back, as I cover theirs. We're together, fighting the pigs, the Bloods, the Whites. Struggles breed camaraderie when you go through them as a whole. White guys enjoy an activity together, but Black men know that the shit can fly at any minute and we'll be fighting together, rescuing each other. All of America is our war zone. In such a threatening situation, the need to rely on each other creates bonding. Being a Black man means—when you're in public— you're on alert, keen to the possibility of war exploding. This blatant love is the result of that war, the palpable spirit between Black men. A positive consequence of America's racism.

Now, sitting on the table of the roller rink, I'm loved. I'm home. Here with these men, my set, my Crips, in my 'hood. The camaraderie is sweet syrup between us. I trust them with my life. There's no quicker way to earn someone's trust than give them mine. That's how our bond grows. The death-defying events create that bond. *No one loves us like we love us. I belong with my set. I'm someone here. A celebrity.* I have become what I always longed to be.

When the night is over, I realize this is my first party since my fifth grade birthday party. It's been ten years.

The next afternoon D'Andre and I get drunk and decide to visit G. G has blown one hundred sixty thousand dollars in six months, so I figure he's smoking crack. But D'Andre tells me he lost the money betting on horses at Hollywood Park Racetrack. Pissy drunk, we drive to the 'hood to recruit soldiers for a mission that we hope will solve all our money problems on Monday. Our first stop is Big T's house. His mother tells us that Li'l T is facing life in prison for murder. Her hair has turned gray, deep creases drag from her nose to the corner of her downturned lips. When I left for prison, she was vibrant and young; now she's old. When I see her, I think of my grandmother and understand the pain my time in prison caused her.

Big T enters the house, sees me. "Ah, man, the old crew is back. We're back together. We goin' get paid out here now."

G tells Big Mel we need a stolen car. A buddy of his has recently been fired from Boy's Market and knows the security system. They make thirty thousand dollars a week and we're robbing them Monday at five A.M.

The rest of the weekend I think about our mission, rehearsing it over and over in my mind, visualizing each move. Women hit on me, but my mind is on the operation. On Monday, at 4 A.M., I leave Aunt Deedee's house and climb into the waiting car. The streetlights illuminate the sleeping neighborhood; shifting, distant lights quicken my heart. I welcome the adrenaline priming me for my task, getting me into my zone. Li'l Dog drives behind us. We arrive at Boy's Market and I sit reclined in the front seat and scan the store through binoculars G loaned me just for this lick. There's nothing out of the ordinary—no guards, no circling patrol car. We drive to the entrance of the store. Li'l Dog and I get out, walk inside.

Boom. Li'l Dog shoots a round into the air. And just like that the store employees remove the money from the safe. They hand it to me with solemn faces and timid motions. I grab it and we're out the door.

So easy.

Good intelligence, a good plan, perfect timing, a solid crew.

I've made more money in a night than most people make in months. I'm empowered. Invincible.

It's addicting.

I move into my own apartment in a Crip neighborhood. Huckabuck and I party at the skating ring every Tuesday and Sunday. Sometimes Tina comes with us. Sometimes she brings a friend for me, but I'm too busy thinking how to solve my money problem to focus on a woman.

In the weeks that follow, I form a small crew of my own and embark on a robbing spree. Back into hustles and hanging out with the cats from the set, I resume heavy drinking and smoking weed. I'm in the thick—shooting Bloods, getting high, robbing, acting crazy. Even though there's a war with the Hoover Crips, I never fight them; I don't believe in Crip-on-Crip violence. Me and Huckabuck concentrate on the Bloods—the Rollin' Twenties and Black P. Stones. We still look for B. K. It's like prison never happened. The 'hood and my life here are all that exist. My sex life slumps. I'm so focused on destroying the Bloods and hustling that I've no time for the women who want a little vicarious celebrity by having a little bit of me for a little bit of time. The only woman I spend time with is Gina, who is pregnant again. Marcus, now about two, is usually with us. She and Marcus still live with G and so when I'm on business, she's there. Marcus is a cute kid with Smiley's grin and Gina's fierce independence, so he either wears her stern concentration or a grin. He loves pretending to drive my car. But, sometimes I resent the time I spend with her because I forfeit hustles. The pregnancy takes the bitterness away from her face. Mostly, when I'm with her, just like before, I'm on Crip business.

Then one night Huckabuck and I are at the Skate City when we find out K. B. is in the jungles. "We gotta finish our business, cuz. Santa Claus is cooled out. Now we gotta get our get-back for that drive-by," Huckabuck says, "Let's go, cuz. Let's go now."

We pick up two stolen cars and Goofy V and J-Dog ride with us. Huckabuck is ahead of me and he parks his car in the middle of the street, while I stop mine by the alley. Before I can get out of the car, Huckabuck jumps in the middle of the street and starts shouting, "Nigga, it's Huckabuck. Yeah. K. B. I know you hidin' in there."

Ten cats jump out from behind cars, run out of houses with guns pointed. It's an ambush. Huckabuck stands in the middle of the street by himself, upright, chest exposed, arms and legs spread, yelling for K. B., a gun in each hand.

Bloods all around him start shooting 12 gauges, .38s. Poppop. Boom. Ta-ta-tat. Guns set up a war-zone racket. Huckabuck is stranded in the middle of the street, in the middle of the ambush, exposed and vulnerable. They don't see me. Goofy V is flat against a building, J-Dog still in the car with me. I could drive my car through the alley and get away, but I can't leave Huckabuck, my Huckabuck.

I jump out of the car and crouch by it, the poppoppopopop all around me. Windshields hit, windows hit, glass sprays the road, the sidewalk, falls in my hair, shoulders. Huckabuck fires back. I shoot as I run, providing Huckabuck cover and protection, time to do some damage and get to my car. A pellet hits my calf as I run toward him. Getting Huckabuck into my car and us away is all that's important.

A Blood falls, I don't know whose bullet hit him.

Huckabuck fires from both guns, runs, dips, turns, dances toward me. I reach him and we race through the alley and J-Dog drives the car to us. When I'm beside the car, a shot takes the window.

Finally, we get in the car, zoom through the alley, and we're in traffic.

"Man, you got hit," Huckabuck says. He looks so sad. "You bleedin' from every pore."

Blood trickles down my face. Shards of glass gleam like diamonds in the streetlight. I didn't even feel the punctures of my face.

"What you doin' standing in the fuckin' street exposed like that, cuz? Get yourself killed."

"I got so mad, I wasn't thinkin'. It was do or die."

"Yeah, but not do and die."

We all laugh, his laughter in gobbles of joy.

"You saved my life, cuz." Huckabuck hugs me. "But I knew you would. I knew we'd be cool."

I'm still charged from the sixty seconds of absolute peril, terror for Huckabuck, barrage of bullets, shooting, excitement. I feel most alive when I'm with him or Smiley. "Gotta get some soft-white, cuz. And get Gina to get this shit outta me. I got some lead in my leg, too."

We get to our 'hood, pick up my legit car, and Huckabuck gives me some powder cocaine. Then Huckabuck drives me to Gina's.

I wake her up and when she sees me, her eyes widen, her mouth opens, her hand flies to her mouth.

"Colton," is all she says as she shakes her head. "Colton. My God."

"I need you to help me get this shit outta my face."

So first I snort the soft-white and rub it on my calf. She heats up tweezers and fishes in my leg for the pellet.

"Got it," she says as she twists it out. I don't feel the alcohol she pours on the wound. She blows on it so it'll dry, adds antibiotic cream, and wraps it up with gauze and tape.

"Get on the floor," she orders. "The bed be too wavy."

She moves her lamp so she has good light and kneels beside me. She shakes her head. "You niggas coulda been killed. Lucky it was glass that got your face. And not no bullet."

I snort some more powder. And she starts pulling out the splinters of glass with the tweezers. Her face is concentrated as she picks up a sliver and wipes it on a tissue, folding it carefully so Marcus doesn't step on it.

"Close your eyes. Don't like you watchin'."

Obediently, I close my eyes.

"Besides. Don't you trust me?"

"I'm here, ain't I?" I wait for her to be finished. It takes an hour for her to pull all the glass out. I'm up all night listening to her sleep beside me.

A few months later, wounds healed, J-Dog, Goofy V, D'Andre, and I rob a jewelry store of one hundred and fifty thousand dollars worth of Rolex watches. I'm the smasher and the leader, so I always get a large percent of the split. The smasher and gunman get the most; the driver and fence get less. The split is agreed beforehand. When I fence the watches, I discover that several are missing. I pull a gun on the crew and force them to strip nude. I search every inch of their clothes and recover the missing watches in J-Dog's and Goofy's clothes. I knew D'Andre wouldn't have them. Because they're from the set, I spare them but cut all ties. I haven't seen either since. The crew I glued together has fallen apart.

Big T starts sweating me to take him along on a lick. I keep shaking him because of his inexperience and my lack of patience to teach him. Now, with Goofy- V and J-Dog off the crew, and Li'l Dog disappeared, I need someone. Huckabuck is too busy dealing drugs for the Cocaine Cowboy. So I agree to use Big T. Now that I'm grown, we look like brothers. We're the same size, the same color, same beaked nose. My arms are as big as his.

So we hit a jewelry store in a strip mall. I smash the jewelry case; the glass shudders but doesn't break. I whack it harder, but it stays solid.

"Cee. It ain't workin', man. Come on. Let's get outta here before we get busted." Big T's brow is wet. The gun in his hand shakes.

I ignore him and swing the sledgehammer. One of the store employees takes advantage of T's fear and shouts, "The police are coming."

I jog to the entrance and glance down the plaza walkway. There're no pigs. I lift the sledgehammer, turn to the employee, hiss, "Shut the fuck up," and hit the glass with all my might. The glass vibrates. I grab the case and heave it to the floor. Glass and jewelry fly. Glass cubes lie like diamonds. Big T and I grab the loot and race from the store.

Hours later, when I fence the goods, I discover that there's a gold watch missing. I have to lower the price. After the exchange, I drive to Big T's to give him his cut. "T. We missin' a watch. What happen'?"

His brow is still damp. "Cuz. You know me, on the set, cuz. I don't know where the watch is. Maybe that shit fell on the way out the store."

I stand there listening. His mom is in kitchen, taking pots out of a cabinet.

"I swear on my Moms, cuz."

I nod.

"You've always known me. I'm a loyalist."

Silence. I chalk up the missing watch as a loss.

A week later, I call him. His mother answers and she tells me he's won two thousand dollars in the lottery. Ghetto folks don't win the lottery, so I check it out with G. He says the lottery talk is bullshit. He had fenced a watch for Big T and gave him two thousand dollars. The disappeared watch has reappeared. Big T always had mixed feelings about me, undermining me because of his insecurities and lack of courage, and jealous of my relationship with Smiley. But now, I question his loyalty to others as well.

With Goofy V, J-Dog, and Big T out of the picture, I'm left with Li'l Dog and G. After being gone for a month, Li'l Dog has reappeared with a serious thirst for money. Every day he presents me a new idea for some lucrative hustle that will allow us to retire from robbing. We've made over a hundred thousand dollars, so I don't understand his desperation. He has some nice clothes and a car, but why's he so broke? He tells me he bought himself a condo in the Valley, but I find out he's living in the projects with his girl-friend. He stays clean and decked out with fine clothes. Perplexed, I let my concern wither away.

I use my money to fix Aunt Deedee's car. With her leg amputated, she drives around the streets, her old excited-by-life self, instead of watching TV. I buy myself a white 280Z with custom rims and a nice sound system. I listen to the soothing tapes I brought with me from prison as I roam around L.A.

Besides hanging at Skate City with Huckabuck, I hang around with Steve, who races his 911 Porsche with custom rims at the street races or visits clubs with other "ballers." Steve is from Hoover and we're still at war with them. One Sunday night, Steve and I go to the Carolina West for a social gathering with some of South Central's best-known hustlers, dealers, gamblers, and gang-sters. Standing in line near the club's entrance, we bump into G, Crazy Keith, and Big T. Big T recognizes Steve, knows he's from Hoover, and wants to extinguish him.

"Yeah, cuz from Hoover. But he's my cousin. Family. There'll be no extinguishing." I smell the onions Big T ate for dinner. Big T introduces himself. G passes Steve a joint, his way of saying hello.

"Put it out," orders a security guard.

"You stupid ho', who you bitch for?" G shouts back.

The security guard blows his whistle for backup, pulls his ba-ton, and attempts to physically remove G from the area.

G snatches the baton, lifts the guard off the ground, and body-slams him through the windshield of a parked car. Other security guards come running. Fists and clubs fly. All of us fight except Crazy Keith, who's high on PCP and stands, hands at his side, as though we're a scene from a movie. Big T is drop-kicked into the middle of the street and lies there, not even trying to get up.

After the brawl, Big T covers his embarrassment. "Fuck that. Let's blast 'em."

We follow Big T to his car to get the guns. His respect and power are still intact as a result of his connection to Big Tookie and Smiley. "Come on, man. Get in. I'm gonna blast 'em."

We pile into his mother's Vega and sputter to the club entrance. "Man," Big T says, "Maybe we should come back later. This Vega is slow. We might get busted."

He's committed himself. The cardinal rule is—once you commit yourself, you have to follow through.

"Cuz, you scared?" I ask. "It's do or die."

"Yeah," G pushes him to prove his metal, "Mr. Big T, alias super-Crip, are you scared or somethin'?"

"Man, fuck y'all." Rivulets of sweat trickle from under his bandana. His eyes look light, almost blue.

"Y'all trippin'," Crazy Keith points out the window. "Look. Police."

A black-and-white police car enters the club parking lot.

"Nigga, you're scared," G tells Big T. He's stopped goading him; he says it as a statement, as though he's just realized who Big T is.

'Bout time.

"Man, I ain't gonna get busted tryin' to prove somethin' to you fools," Big T retorts.

"Man, you know it ain't got nothing to do wit' provin' yourself. You're just scared."

I let G say it. I let this scene play out. Suddenly, to make my point, I snatch the gun from Big T's hand, jump out the passenger side, grip the handle for impact, and fire. Boom. Boom.

Screams ricochet around the street. Partygoers dive for cover. People run every which way. I dash to Steve's car, dive into the passenger seat, and we speed away.

Later that night, I meet up with Big T and the others at his house. "We should discipline Crazy Keith." Big T drinks Hennessy; his words slur. "Man, we should do this nigga! He didn't do shit."

"You know Crazy Keith was high on PCP. You know he's not a fighter, he's a shooter," I say.

"Man, cuz didn't get down, he needs some discipline." Big T stands, bounces to demonstrate eagerness, his fists clenched, his thick brows shading his eyes.

I realize exactly what he's trying to do. I've seen him do it a hundred times—keep the attention off himself by diverting to someone else. I feel stupid for ever admiring him. I rise and touch Steve on the shoulder. "Let's roll. This fool, Big T, is on one."

The excitement of being the girlfriend of a known thug is the equivalent of winning a trophy. Your "man" is a member of the gang—robbing, stealing, selling drugs, and gangbanging. They're part of the exciting whirl of money, parties, drugs, danger. But often, once your man is captured and jailed, he's forgotten. The search for another man begins, usually another gangbanger. And the pattern repeats itself. It's as addicting to be the sideline woman as it is to be the banger. If it happens repeatedly, the woman is labeled a "hood rat" which explains the life of jumping from bed to bed, set to set, sleeping even with enemies.

Gina is not like this. Her man, Earl, the father of her son and her growing fetus, is a square. A bus driver. Having Marcus has turned her into full-fledged woman, sometimes almost soft, all traces of tomboy erased. She spends most of her time at home, out of harm's way. But although she's energized by the money and the stories, she says, "Colton, I trust the homeboys. But you need to stop hangin' wit' them, cause they gonna get y'all in some shit."

I'm not going to let a woman dictate my life. Anyway, I don't believe her. Maybe she says this so I'll spend more time with her. Maybe that wouldn't be such a bad thing, if we were having sex. But even after the seven years of dating off and on, we've not had sex. We kissed maybe four times, two of those times between bars.

And then one night, tired after a job, I come to bring G the loot, but he's out. Gina is alone watching *The Cosby Show*. Her hand rests on her swollen stomach; her face looks soft. The house is quiet, Marcus's Legos and action sets put away. His playpen stands in the corner of the living room. He must be asleep. I sit beside her and she says, "You want somethin' to drink? Eat, maybe?"

I'm working on a bottle so I shake my head no and we watch *The Cosby Show* side by side on the sofa, not touching, not paying attention to each other. I focus on fencing some jewelry, putting the money in my safe at Aunt Deedee's, considering my next job. A commercial comes on and, as if she's been thinking about it the whole time Dr. Huxtable was giving a charming lecture to his son, she asks, "Colton, you never tol' me, when you was at CYA and I told you I found another man, how you feel?" She says it to the TV.

I turn to her, her face still straight ahead, my elbows on my knees, the bottle dangling between them. "How'd I feel? Shit. I was mad. Wouldn't you be?" My voice is slightly raised.

"I only did that 'cause I was trying to replace you. I don't care about Earl, Colton. It's you. As I sit here, I think 'bout you. Even when you're not here, you in my mind. But I get mad 'cause you never listen to me."

I've heard this spiel before, but I'm not in the mood. It feels like she's nagging me, or wants to own me. I light a joint and pull in a toke. I need something to help me cope.

"Put that out. You crazy? You can't smoke that in my father's house." She snatches it from my hand and stabs it out in an ashtray. I ignore her disrespect and light an unfiltered Camel, making a show of tapping the tobacco down before I light it.

The Cosby program is over and an advertisement plays. Gina changes the channel, looking for *Cagney and Lacey*.

"Ain't you tired of running the streets?" She asks when she sits back down.

I suck on my cigarette, trying to figure out my response. "I don't wanna watch no cop show. Even if it's girl cops." I turn off the set, but I know that I'm distracting her to avoid the subject. After I sit back down, it's quiet. "Let's play Pac-Man," I suggest.

"I already lost my brother to the streets. I don't wanna lose you, too."

Gina isn't big on expressing her feelings; this is her way of telling me she loves me. I pause a minute, then pull her to me. I hold her close. My eyes get watery, the tears welling inside me. I think about all I've been through with the fellas, with the set. I'm frustrated with what's going on, the petty betrayals, the puffing and bragging. I've distanced myself from most of them. *None of it is what it seems. I think I know the players, but even here, in my own 'hood, there are layers of gauze. Love and dismay seem inextricable from the 'hood.*

But the street life is my life. I think about Marcus, asleep. Her getting knocked up when she was supposed to be my woman. But I can't seem to get her out of me. No question her leaving me still affects me. I don't tell her any of this. Instead, I hold her.

"Promise me you ain't goin' to go to jail again," she whispers into my shoulder. Tears clog her words and wet my shirt.

How could I promise her that? "Gina . . ."

"No, Colton. Promise me. Promise me we'll always be together."

I look into her eyes and wipe her tears with my shirt. "You know what I'm about. You know what I do for a living." My hands are on her shoulders so she faces me. "I'm out here taking risks. This is what I know. Look around the neighborhood, Gina. Just think about the ones who avoid this shit. Think about where they are. Unemployed, broke, aimless. Anyway, enemies don't wanna hear my sob story. What am I supposed to do when some fool catches me in traffic, huh? Tell him I don't bang no more?" I stab the butt of my cigarette out.

Gina just looks at me.

"I'd rather be judged by twelve than carried by six. You hear the shots. You know how these fools are doin' it out here. Your past is who you are. That's what they see when they see me. They see me and Smiley gunnin' for their asses. I'm a Crip. I don't know how to be square. I tried it. It ain't me." I'm telling her my truth, the truth as I see it.

"You don't have to steal, though. Colton, your family has money. Everyone respects you. You have everything you need. How come you can't just slow down?"

I wipe her tears a second time. What she's saying is true. I have nothing to say. *How can I justify something I don't know how to explain? Something I don't even understand myself? I'm engulfed in crime as if it's some contagious disease that no one knows how to cure. I've caught it. Become it.*

"Colton," Gina continues, looking straight into my eyes with the innocent, concerned look she's mastered, "You gotta stop runnin' the street. What do you be thinkin' about when you're out there ridin' around wit' guns, acting crazy? What do you guys see in that shit? I just don't understand." Gina shakes her head. Then the innocent look is erased. Her eyes are wide open, her words firm. "Stop hangin' with your homies, or something bad's gonna happen. Last time you didn't listen to me and look what happened. Smiley didn't listen and look what happened. I get this feeling. This crazy feeling. This twisting-inside sick feeling that something bad's coming."

I pull her back into my arms and kiss her forehead.

"Nothing is gonna happen. I'm cool. Don't be negative." My fingers weave through her hair, massage her scalp. I press her near to me. She's warm.

That night we sleep wrapped in each other's arms. We kiss

again. We don't need to have sex to feel secure. We feel close, fused already. I think about making love, but she falls asleep and while she's sleeping in my arms, her words run around my head.

Bad things are happening. Right now. Maybe not the ones Gina predicts, but still bad. I can't trace them back to their origins because I'm searching in the actions of other people—Big T, J-Dog, Goofy. Now, I know it's my own drug use that creates the gauze, the crazy things that happen lickety-split, crashing like dominoes, that seem so confusing. Marijuana and, especially, alcohol make my mind shift from logic to illogic. One minute I'm focused, the next indecisive and disillusioned. A sad skepticism about me, about life, keeps me in the hustles, keeps me insecure and unstable. I tell myself I don't have any choices. It becomes a spiral. When I'm adversely affected by events, I use more drugs to cope, to put me in a different state of mind. Then I make choices that lead to negative consequences. But I don't realize any of that.

Instead, the next morning, Gina and Marcus still asleep, I smoke a joint before breakfast to put myself in my nighttime mood. My tunnel vision returns. All I see is reputation, power, respect. And so I start the daylong chase for more as I kiss Gina good morning and good-bye. And the dominoes of my life start crashing into each other.

Li'l Dog and I are on the way to fence some jewelry in downtown L.A., so I am unarmed, stoned on marijuana, when he convinces me to stop off at Michelle's house. "She's a strawberry," he tells me.

"Cuz?"

"You know, a rock star, a woman hooked on crack who'll do sexual favors for drugs. And she's beautiful."

When we arrive at her apartment building, a bunch of shysty cats loll outside. Because I'm not armed, I stuff the bag of jewelry into Li'l Dog's glove compartment. Michelle lets us in and she *is* beautiful. So are her two friends. All three of them are high.

"I gotta gram. Whassup?" Li'l Dog holds up the tied plastic wrap filled with the pale yellow rock. When they see it, their eyes light up like it's the Fourth of July.

"Who going first? You or your friend?" Michelle asks, moving close to him.

I know her from somewhere. And it's not a good place. I start shuffling through my memory. *Damn. Where do I know her from? I can't remember. She's known by another name, not Michelle. She's an enemy; I feel it.*

"Hey. Where's your bathroom?" I buy myself time.

"Go down the hall and make a right," Michelle tells me.

As I stroll past her bedroom, I enter and look around, hoping to see a picture that'll jog my memory. And then there it is. T-Bone. She was T-Bone's girlfriend. Enemy. I knew it. And I'm not strapped. Shit.

I make my way to the bathroom and see myself in the mirror. My face is purple with rage, my eyes wide. I wash my hands and put some cool water on my eyes, return to the living room to get Li'l Dog and leave.

He's gone. I dash to the parking lot in search of his car. It's gone.

"Did you see a cat in a white Ninety-eight?" I ask one of the sleazy looking cats.

"Ya mean homeboy you was wit'?"

"Yeah."

"Him and three chicks jumped in that car and left like they was in a rush."

Li'l Dog has played me. I run to Spike's Liquor Store and call D'Andre. He picks me up and drives me to my car, I go home, re-trieve my strap, then search the hood for Li'l Dog. I drive around the avenues the entire night. As dawn breaks, I go to G's and tell him what happened.

"Man, Cee, Li'l Dog's on crack, homie. He's fucking wit' a bitch from Denver Lane. T-Bone's girl is probably her friend."

I light a joint, trying to dampen down my rage.

"Trip. While you were in the pen, he stole one of my Rolex watches and traded it for dope. Why you think he's always broke? In spite of all those robberies you do? The boy's on dope, Cee."

How could I have been so blind? "That fool better give me back my shit!"

"Don't kill him, Cee," G whispers. He doesn't want Gina to hear him. "That's my cousin. And you know he's sick. The dope done fucked him up. Beat him up a little, but don't hurt him."

I don't even say hello to Gina. I get back in my car and roll a joint. Every one of my homies—except Huckabuck, G, and Smiley—has crossed me. *They have no sense of loyalty.* I bolt down a bottle of Hennessy. *I've treated them all fairly, looked out for them, but it's not enough. I'd risked my life for my set, embraced each of them like family. Tears well in my eyes as I pass the alley where I was initiated. This is how they repay me, by stealing from me?*

I roll another joint and search South Central streets. They are preternaturally still. Only my restlessness haunts the 'hood. I stop and buy more liquor. I drive to Hazel's, a friend, and sit on her sofa, smothering my anger and disillusionment with weed and the bottle of liquor, and finally find relief through sleep on her living room floor.

I wake with a migraine and a vast hunger. Hazel and two girlfriends sit at the table, talking.

"Let's go get something to eat, Colton," Hazel suggests.

"Don't you have work today?"

"Nah. I'm off."

"I thought you're off on Saturday."

"It is Saturday." She's matter-of-fact.

"No. It's Friday."

All three of the women start laughing.

"What's so funny?"

"You slept for two days, Colton. Check the TV."

The morning news announces its Saturday, November 15, 1985. A death toll of twenty-three thousand from a volcano erupting in Colombia. Two mail bombs exploded in Salt Lake City. I've just come out of a drug-induced sleep. I was out for forty-eight hours straight.

I spend the next few months doing my jewelry licks, hanging out with Huckabuck Tuesday and Sundays at Skate City. The war with the Hoovers continues, but I'm not hurting another Crip, so Huckabuck and I ride through the Blood jungles still looking for K B., fueled by Hennessy.

The licks come fast and furious. One after another. The money is spent on more cars, more booze, more clothes, and gold jewelry. I'm decked out like a candy store, shining even in the night. One of my fences, BJ, tells me that Lewis's has a bunch of rings. "One ring in there waiting to be picked up by a baseball player who had it made for his girl."

Baseball player, uh, I think, but I just nod at him.

It's a cool day and I dress nondescript, wearing a blue Fila casual outfit. Even though it's midday, the mall bustles with the traffic of people shopping till they drop. Housewives with shoulder pads and big hair amusing themselves, men on lunch breaks, teens wearing hightop basketball shoes and parachute pants, Calvin Klein jeans. It's a small mall. As usual, the cheap skinny chains are in the front of the jewelry store with a sign screaming 30% OFF. I spend a half hour wandering the mall, checking security cameras, personnel, cop tours, noting the exits and the parking lot. I buy a new pair of Nike Airs at Foot Locker, put them on, and throw away the dirty ones.

My preliminary work is complete. I enter the store. A young couple examines diamond rings, holding hands as they crouch over the case. Buying an engagement ring, I surmise. I stroll to the rear, alert for earth signs, but this is all easy. Everything is clear. A woman with blonde fluffy hair and iridescent blue eye shadow waits behind the counter. I ask to see a diamond ring, pick up the jeweler's glass to examine it.

The young couple tries on engagement rings from a tray. "I like this one, with the baby diamonds on each side," she says.

"It has a flaw. In the corner." I return the ring to the clerk. And then, as though seeing the ruby for the first time, I say, "Let me see that one." The red is bright as fresh blood.

"This one is custom made and is already sold," she replies.

I grab it, clutch it in my hand, spin, and run.

"Help, Help. He stole the ring," she screams.

But I'm already racing in the mall as she screams. I slide the ring into my pocket, pump my arms. My new shoes are light, traction perfect.

Footsteps pound behind me. With an abrupt smack the weight of a man is on my back.

"I got him. Help. Police, here he is." he yells.

I try to shake this burden away. *Fuck you.* "Let me go." I try to run.

He grasps me tighter. I slam him with my elbow. His arms choke me. I grab his white arm, but he holds fast. "Let me go, muthafucka." I warn.

"Police. Here he is," he shouts.

I can't get him off me. I can't run. *Man is going to get me arrested; the fucking pigs'll get me.*

I reach under my jacket into my shoulder holster and grab my strap like the ones plainclothes police wear. I've never practiced drawing my .32 revolver from my shoulder holster. Never practiced a day in my life. Now, I just draw it from desperation to get away. The handle is warm from my body. The man's breath is hot on my neck; his arms strangle me. I reach over my shoulder and shoot.

He flinches, but his arms tighten. "Help. Help."

I stretch under my arm and fire again, this time into his side.

He releases me. I don't look back. I run out of the mall as people rush past me to his aid.

That was too close. That man playing superhero. Always worried about coming across some superhero. Well, I'm okay. I got away. Too close. I breathe slowly, but anxiety pounds my heart, I'm cold from sweat. I get rid of the stolen car, get in my own, and buy a bottle of Hennessy and cocaine. *Something bad's coming.* I hear Gina's voice in my ears. I snort some of the cocaine, drink the Hennessy, and watch TV. I throw the ring in the back of a drawer. Drink some more till I sleep, then go meet Huckabuck at Skate City.

A few days later, I visit G and show him the ring. "You'll get some paper for that," he nods. "Twenty-five, maybe even thirty."

I know he wants to get in on the action. "BJ told me about it." And I tell him about the man trying to hold me for the cops.

"You did what you had to," he comments.

"I know. Fucka was trying to hold me for the police and I didn't even rob him. He was on some superhero bullshit trip," I shake my head. "Man, muthafuckas are stupid." *Why would you play superhero and risk your life to protect some shit that don't belong to you?*

"You hungry? Im'a get us some Chinese food." G leaves and I move into the living room. Gina is doing her nails. As though they're the reward for giving up her scrapping and fighting when she quit being a tomboy, she grew long, curved nails, and this night, she strokes each nail with polish. The TV is on, but she concentrates on a blood-red caress down the center, then a curved swipe on each side. She tilts back to study her work, slithers the brush into the bright bottle, lifts it against the lip, and starts the next nail. I've seen her do this before, but tonight I see her pleasure and perceive how sensuously she paints.

"You in love with those nails," I comment.

She drops the brush in its bottle and her face, when she turns to me, has the soft-lipped look she wears when she's sleeping. "No. I'm in love with you."

"Me?" I laugh and jerk my thumb to her growing belly, "and you pregnant with another man."

"I didn't plan to get pregnant. I don't love him. I've always wanted you. I keep tellin' you this, but you don't hear."

"How can I be your man? How can I be your man now?" But I know as I say it, I love her. I turn my attention to the TV and light one of my Camels. She watches me and then resumes stroking, but the smooth expression is gone and her brows are clenched.

I cruise through the 'hood on my way to bring BJ the ruby ring when my car runs out of gas and jolts to a stop on Arlington Avenue. I push it to the curb and walk the rest of the way, the ring in my back pocket. As I cross Thirty-ninth Street, I spot Big T's car with its custom wheels cruising up the block.

"What's up, cuz? You need a ride?"

"Yeah. My car ran outta gas."

"Where you goin'?"

"BJ's."

I climb in the passenger seat. Once we get to BJ's house, I enter, hand him the ring, and he hands me back thirty thousand dollars. "See. Knew you'd get it," he smiles. We high-five and I return to T's car.

"How much did you get?" Big T asks as he pulls away from the curb.

Why's he worried about that? I wonder. "Make a right here at the gas station so I can get some gas."

As he pulls into the station, he says, "Can I get a few dollars? I'm broke."

"Yeah. Don't trip." I don't think I should pay him for driving me four blocks, but I'm feeling generous, so I give him a half ounce of cocaine, worth about fourteen hundred dollars.

When we get back to my car, he asks, "how much you get for that ring?"

"Thirty," I tell him.

"Can't you give me more?"

I pull out the wad of money and count off three hundred dollars and hand it to him. "Here."

"Man, this ain't shit."

"I don't owe you shit."

"You got all that money and all you're giving me is three hundred lousy dollars?"

"Five minutes ago you was broke. Now you got three hundred." I stand up and lean back. "And the cocaine. You don't appreciate what I gave you."

He gets out of his car. "You treating me like I'm a buster. When G came up, he gave me five. I'm the one who initiated you." He stabs himself in the chest with his thumb then slams his palms on the car hood.

"Hold up, cuz, I don't owe you shit. Matter of fact, fuck what you talkin' about." I say.

"What did you say, little nigga?"

"Fool. You heard. You don't pump no fear here."

He blasts his vicious stare. I return it, though I know my mad-dog stare is weaker than my fists and his face is a convincing mask of hate and rage.

"I'll catch your ass later." He climbs in his car.

"Yeah. You do that," I shout as he zooms off.

I drive to G's house. Gina plays Nintendo. G and I move to his basement where I relay the events.

"His bark is bigger than his bite," he says.

"I know."

Just then Big T walks in.

"Man, what you doin' kicking it wit' this nigga?"

"Who you talkin' about?" G says.

"Fool." Big T points at me.

I rise from G's couch. "I'll beat your ass right now. In front of the house, right now." I run up the flight of stairs, stomp through the living room, and hop over the railing of the porch. Waiting.

G is right behind me. "Don't kill this fool in front of my house, cuz. Take 'em round the corner."

Big T appears in the doorway.

I pull off my jacket and toss it on the car's hood. "I'm gonna show you how tough you are," I tell him.

"Why you need a gun?" he asks.

"I don't." I hadn't planned to use it. Now, I pull the clip out of the strap and place both on the hood of G's car. "It's just me. Let's go." My knees are bent; my arms spread wide, my adrenaline surges. I'm ready.

G puts up his hand. "Hold on, Cee. Let me talk with Big T." He tries to defuse the situation as they whisper to each other. Then G's voice rises. "What? I ain't givin' you no gun. Cee is like my little brother. Get your punk ass outta my house, T."

G grabs him by the arm, forces him from the doorway and off the porch. Big T bolts to his car. I chase him, but can't catch him. He jumps behind the wheel, ignites the engine, and speeds away.

I'm in my car and zoom after him for a mile or so and then my car sputters out of gas. In all the turmoil, I had not filled it and the little gallon was gone. A friend rides me to his house where I call G, who tells me that Big T is riding around the 'hood with an AR-15 assault rifle looking for me.

I can't sit and wait for him to shoot me. I know Big T counts on his reputation as an elite soldier, his standing bolstered by his huge arms, gangster cars, and gun collection. I'm not one to submit to a bully. I'm more likely to retaliate.

So D'Andre and I start searching. We check all the known hangouts—Second Avenue and Jefferson, Thirty-ninth Street and Western, Denker Park, Thirty-sixth Street and Western. No Big T. I decide to go to his house.

When his mom sees me, a big smile plays across her face. "Hi, Colton."

"T here?" I hold a 9 mm behind my back.

She notices my expression; her smile evaporates as her brows come together. The pleading look painted on her face says, "Please don't shoot my son."

Big T pops up behind her, huffing like he'd just run a 10 k.

"You ridin' 'round tellin' the homies you're lookin' for me. Here I am," I say.

He pretends to pass his mom. "Look out, Moms."

I stare directly in his eyes but witness only fear. He's done nothing to impress me since the day we met except have big biceps.

"Colton," his Mom says, "Why you guys looking at each other like that?"

I continue staring.

D'Andre tugs my shoulder. "Come on, Cee. This fool don't want no problems, homie."

"Man, if I ever hear 'bout you runnin' round with a gun lookin' for me, I'm gonna pay your ass a visit and it won't be as friendly as this."

I stuff the strap in my waistband before I leave.

The very next day, Gina calls. She and Marcus are visiting Earl's mother when her car battery dies. Will I pick her up? As I drive down Main Street, my heart pounds. I break out into a sweat. The earth signs warn me of danger, but everything looks normal. I search the traffic, memorize the cars behind me, and make a right turn. I pass some graffiti that brags of Harlem Crips. *I'm safe.* Then, I inhale slowly to decelerate my heart and check the rearview mirror. About a block away, a black car trails. The hair rises on my neck. The driver is Black. I make a quick left and drive down an alley. When I hit the street again, there's no black sedan. Maybe it's getting to me; maybe I'm getting paranoid, I think. Maybe I'm having an anxiety attack.

I arrive at my destination, park my car, trot up the long flight of stairs, look back and forth over my shoulders. *No black car. I'm okay.*

When I ring the bell, Gina answers and lets me in.

"Let's go get the new battery," I say.

"Colton. Nah. I just want this one charged."

I know when she starts a sentence with my name she's stern in her idea, but I'm wearing new clothes and don't want battery grease on them.

"I don't want to waste money on a new battery," she adds.

"I'll buy it."

"Don't need no new one. I just need this one charged." The independence that remains from her tomboyishness is nonnegotiable. She's wearing jeans and one of those maternity tops that drape over her belly in such a way that she looks like she's about ready to pop, even though she's only seven months. When she places her hand on the small of her back, I sense how tired she is, so I acquiesce.

I take out her battery, put it in my trunk.

Gina carries a yellow diaper bag with her things, Marcus's legs wrap around her. One arm supports him as she sways toward the car. I grab the bag out of her hand while she buckles Marcus in his car seat. "Whassup, Mister Colton?" He grins.

"Whassup, li'l champ?" I say as Gina gets in the passenger seat.

I walk to the back of the car to slam the trunk closed, wiping my hands on a rag.

An abrupt whine, a whirl, comes from out of nowhere. I flinch and look up. A helicopter hovers ten feet above me, blowing my jacket with its wind.

Tires squeal as undercover cars zoom from all directions.

Click-click. I hear the round chambered in a rifle.

This is like in the movies. Just like you see on TV.

I turn around to see the gunman's face, but a voice shouts, "Get down on the ground." *They're here for me. They've come to get me.*

Click-click. Black-and-white cars screech to a stop. Uniformed pigs jump out of the cars, guns drawn.

My heart pounds. *They're going to shoot me. Fucking cops. I shoulda blown up the Southwest Police Station. That's what I should have done.*

I lay face down on the ground. Car engines growl.

Click-click. Click-click.

They'll kill me. I raise my head. Keep my eyes open. *If death comes, I want to see it coming. I want to witness it, see how it happens.*

Plainclothes cops and now uniformed cops surround me, guns drawn and pointed. They tighten their circle.

Maybe I should run. Maybe I should try to grab one of the rifles, go down fighting. Fucking pigs will kill me anyway.

"Put your hands on top of your head and lace your fingers."

The helicopter rises to the treetops, its spotlight highlights me. Several plainclothed pigs bend over car trunks, weapons aimed, ready to blow my brains out.

I shouldn't have ignored my anxiety. My heart thumps in my neck, in my ears. I lay motionless, guns pointed, light blaring on me, my pulse pounding the cement, my sweat wetting it. They'll look for any excuse to kill me. Gina warned me. *This is the bad thing.*

"Jewelry man, jewelry man," a cop says.

"Mama, Mama," Marcus wails.

A cop orders Gina out of the car and makes her lay face down on the street.

Marcus screams as the cops remove him from my car and push him next to his mother, on the cement, between us. "Mama, Mama."

"Jewelry man. What's your name?"

Marcus's cries escalate. He can't even say Mama now, he's shrieking that furiously, he's that scared. His head thrashes from side to side.

"Colton Simpson."

When Marcus twists toward me, I muster a smile to decrease his fear, but his eyes are squeezed closed as though he can't bear to watch and he shrieks so persistently, he gasps for air.

Maybe I should run now. Let them shoot me in the back. Fuck them. Be responsible for my own death.

"Jewelry man. Jewelry man. Where's all that jewelry from all those stores?"

No. I don't want Marcus to witness that.

A cop ruffles through Marcus's hair, his pockets.

A cop claps cuffs on me.

"I don't know what you're talking about." I'm still on my stomach, my hands now cuffed. Too late to run. A cop kicks me in the ribs. Surrounding us are cops with guns.

They'll beat me to death. Muthafuckin' pigs.

Suddenly, Marcus is quiet. He passed out. And then his eyes open, and his wails begin again. Two pigs pat down Gina, search through her pockets. They're rough with her, pushing her belly. She doesn't protest. The cops find nothing. "You two are free," a cop says. Gina stumbles to the sidewalk quivering, crying. Marcus clutches her leg.

Several neighbors have come out to the street. They stare and shake their heads, whispering behind their hands. I hate them seeing me. Gina and Marcus stand together, apart from the crowd, apart from me.

"Where's all the jewelry from Austin's and Perry's and Gems?" A cop barks.

"I don't know what you're talking about." *I'm not going to tell them a fuckin' thing.*

He bashes my head with a club. My ears ring. I see lights flash.

Gina screams, "Why you hitting him? I see you hitting him. You got 'im in cuffs. Leave him alone." Marcus cries as loud as his mother yells.

"Where'd you get that ring?" A pig kicks my hand.

"Stop hitting him."

"I bought it."

"With what money?"

"Jewelry man, jewelry man. Where's the money from Crown and Lewis's?"

"Money I got from working at Office Maintenance." I name my mother's company.

They pull me to my feet and shove me into the backseat of a cop car. "Motherfucker. Jewelry man. We know all about you. We got a witness."

I'm hit again in the head with the billy club and pushed to the floor of their car. They pound my back, my kidneys with their clubs.

I'm right. They're going to beat me to death.

"Leave him alone. I see what you're doing." Gina shouts. "Why you keep hitting him?"

"Where's all that jewelry? You're under arrest for robbery," a Black pig spits.

Which one?

"We've been following you for three days. We know all about you, jewelry man. Mr. Colton Simpson, alias Damon Johnson."

Three days. After I fenced the ring. While Huckabuck and I hung out at Skate City on Tuesday night. Good. They don't know about BJ. They were running after me while I was running around after Big T.

My right shoulder is clubbed again.

"You got him cuffed and in your car. Why you keep hitting him?"

I glance out the window at Gina's wet face looking so much like Marcus's smaller one, both with mouths open. The onlookers stare, now their arms are crossed as they scowl at the cops.

I'm lucky. Without them watching, I would be murdered. Now the pigs can't use the he-was-trying-to-escape excuse for gunfire. I'm not shot.

The cop shifts the car into gear. I'm alone in the backseat. I shoot a smile at Gina and Marcus. I send my gratitude to the nosey neighbors as I'm bashed in the arm.

The pigs start driving and I know they're taking me to Parker Center. *Good. They're not going to pull in some field and finish me.* As we go through the 'hood I see a familiar figure with familiar seasick sway to his short legs and bulge in the forearm. It's Li'l Dog walking out of a drug house.

He glances back at the car, sees me. Our eyes meet. There's a flash of recognition, and then his expression changes from shock to guilt to fear. In this moment, the air is electric with my stirred anger and his scared shame sparking between us. But I don't quite understand the guilt-shame part of his expression. Maybe because I've seen him exit the crack house. But for this split second we're connected, the next part of my life determined as sure as the crack in his pocket determines his.

I know the necessity that drives him. But there's no forgiveness.

Our eyes lock while all that knowledge passes from him to me, from me to him. Then, he wrenches his head from me, puts his hand in his pocket, reassuring himself of his rocks, and sways forward. We drive away.

At Parker Center, I'm taken to Robbery Homicide Division and beaten again. I find out that the pigs are part of the Rampart Division Special Surveillance Team and they have followed me for three days. I'd been in the free world for six months. Just six months.

Seventy-two hours after my arrest, after my bruises have faded to pale yellow, I'm taken to Torrance Court for arraignment. Iron-

ically, the robbery for which I'm arrested is one I didn't commit.
I've never heard of the store.

After my initial arraignment, I'm charged with two more
counts of robbery, four counts of assault with a deadly weapon,
and attempted murder. Some of those are mine.

Then I'm taken down to the holding tank awaiting transport to
LACJ. There's the same routine of happy-go-lucky faces joking
amidst the stink of urine, feces, vomit, sweat, fear.

Once again, I pull my blue Fila jacket over my nose and discover a decent place to stand. When the bus arrives, I volunteer to
be handcuffed first. The other prisoners think I'm crazy, but I've
never been so happy to be in cuffs because it means escort onto
the bus where I can breathe.

Actually, the handcuffs don't bother me. We've embarked on a
loyal relationship. Extending my arms early in the morning has
become second nature to brushing my teeth and getting dressed.

ELEVEN

Discipline

Men are not gentle creatures who want to be loved...they are, on the contrary, creatures among whose instinctual endowments is to be reckoned a powerful share of aggressiveness....[W]hen the mental counter-forces which ordinarily inhibit it are out of action it...reveals man as a savage beast to whom consideration towards his own kind is something alien.
—Sigmund Freud, *Civilization and Its Discontents*

AS SOON AS I ENTER THE MODULE, I RECOGNIZE THE DANGER signs. It's too quiet. Not enough music. More men are crowded in each cell. The air feels thicker and more treacherous than when I was here a few years ago. I'm housed in cell Baker Three. My cellmates are Keitarock from Rollin' Sixties and Al Capone from my set. They warn me the entire module is on the verge of set-trippin'. That accounts for the peculiar texture; everyone is at a standoff waiting a frivolous issue to justify tribalism.

At the center of the tension are the Rollin' Sixties and the Eight Trays. On the street they've been locked in war since 1978. The recent murder of Mumbles from the Rollin' Sixties by Joker from Eight Tray and the retaliatory deaths of Joker's mother and little brother have raised the decibels of violence. Notables— Peddie Wack, Big Fee, Keitarock, Big Cat, Big U and Li'l Eddie Boy from the Rollin' Sixties, and Monster Kody, Fish Bone, and Big Football from the Eight Trays—are in the module. Because of the tension, the deputies segregate the module according to set. The two tiers are stacked on top of each other. All the Eight Trays are housed on Able and Charlie rows and all the Rollin' Sixties are housed on Baker and Denver rows. There are fifteen members of my set spread among the different rows. Those living in Charlie and Able bond with the Eight Trays. But for me, the Eight Trays are affiliated with Hoovers who killed Teekey and robbed me.

Of the men in my cell, Keitarock becomes my road dog. We are both in for attempted murder, we're both light skinned, we're both dedicated to the O-Car. We are our only supports through the trauma of captivity, absence of family, possible stiff prison sentence, which threatens the likelihood of ever seeing the 'hood again. When the harsh reality of my charges, the stretch of prison ahead hammers in, Keitarock and Al Capone assure me that things will work out. For some strange reason, which I still don't understand, I believe them. Maybe because I sense they'll be with me.

The violence within the module has escalated. The police house inmates here according to address so that men who've never been Crips, but happen to live in a Crip neighborhood, are housed here. Each tier competes to discover and discipline busters. When we find one, we shout out the number of our catch and our discipline. Our revenge on the fraud evolves into a routine.

Within our cells, we prepare each other for combat by accustomizing ourselves to pain. Or perhaps physical pain distracts us from the other agony in our lives. We play a game called pluck. The loser has to bend over and take a swat on the behind with a plastic shower shoe, or drink three cups of water and receive two blows to the chest. By enduring pain we prove over and over again we're fit as Crips. We're not busters. Most nights, we go to sleep with sore butts and chests, waking up throughout the night to piss. Sometimes, we play "going body"—throwing toe-to-toe punches to the torso. We buff and polish our macho attitudes, staying harsh and standing strong, perpetually preparing for the next fight. Over and over again we prove our valor, our ability to withstand pain. We vent our rage where we're safe.

I'm transported for a lineup. My lawyer, Ray Carter, hired by my mother, greets me. He's a light-brown-skinned guy with a purposely serious expression.

"That's the man who got shot in the robbery. The Good Samaritan who tried to hold the robber for the authorities. Twenty-three years old." Ray jerks his thumb toward a thin White man slumped in an electric wheelchair, leaning to his left, threatening to spill. Almost frail, his hair brushes his bowed forehead. Carter chews the inside of his lip. "He was in the store buying an engagement ring with his fiancée."

That's the superhero who tried to hold me for the pigs.

In the lineup, I'm in number-four position flanked by tall light-skinned Black men. The twenty-three-year-old hero can't identify me. He only saw the back of my head when he grabbed me. And me, I would never have recognized him if Carter hadn't pointed him out.

I figure I might beat this case and hope sparkles.

Driving back to the Crip Module, I think, *superhero is in that wheelchair, maybe forever, but me, I still walk. That's what most people would think. Why you got the right to walk when he's in that chair?* Then, I brush feeling bad away with another set of thoughts. *I told him to let me go, but he didn't. That's good for your ass, you trying to hold me for the pigs when it had nothing to do with you. You turned a simple theft into an armed robbery with attempted-murder charge. Me facing these charges and yourself in that wheelchair.* The Cee side of me is glossed, brushed to a metallic sheen. The Colton part, my grandmother's churchgoing son, is almost extinguished.

But that night, as I lay down to sleep, I see him slanting like a child in the wheelchair and Colton flares for a moment. Funny how you view yourself from various layers. Depending on the layer you're in at the moment, you judge a different self, the self itself shifting from your own view. In the Colton layer, I have an ember of regret. It's my grandmother's voice, the view that society has of me. But then, in my reality, in the Crip layer, Cee shrugs. *Casualties of war,* I tell myself. *You tried to hold me for the pigs. Fuck you. You had nothing to do with it. Why you get involved with my business?* I go back and forth in how I see it. Back and forth, shifting through the layers, the guises within my own self.

I turn over to sleep. I'm in the module, in the mix. *I'm here. Gotta stay in the Cee layer. I don't have time to think about this shit.*

And sure enough, a few days later, the pigs bring in a cat named Loco to our cell. As he stands at the cell door, Keitarock and Al Capone shoot him mad-dog stares. I'm sitting on my bunk writing Gina a letter. The pigs let him in and leave.

"What's up, cuz?" Loco says to Al Capone as he hoists his bedding to the top bunk above Keitarock.

"Harlem Crip, that's what's up."

"I'm Loco from Cat Walk." Loco seems average in every way. Medium-brown skin, average height, a face you'd see on a thousand streets and pay no attention. No show of anger, but no apparent timidity.

"Cat Walk is over. So what you doin' here? You think we soft?" Al Capone steps toward him, fists clenched, ready to test him. We have no beef with Cat Walk Crips, but they're no longer in existence and since Loco is only twenty, we don't believe he's an ex-member.

"Even though Cat Walk played out, I still claim Crip." As he stands across from Al Capone I notice they're the same height, same hard, muscular build. Al Capone has a broad face, while Loco's is long and narrow. Al Capone has a full beard and mustache. His hair is braided and hangs past his earlobes. He flexes his biceps and slightly shifts to the side, staring out the corners of his eyes.

"Fuck you and Cat Walk, nigga. This is Harlem Crip." Capone bounces his thumb off his chest.

"I ain't trippin' that." Loco starts putting his property away, ignoring the challenge.

What's wrong with this cat? He's gotta know he needs to fight. Looks like we got us a coward and Capone's been aching for the prestige of finding and disciplining a buster.

"Hey, muthafucka, don't turn yo' back on me," Capone pushes.

Loco backs up to the gate, facing us. His arms are at his sides; his face is frozen, his lips open, eyes staring at the wall behind Capone. "Hey, cuz. I ain't got no beef wit' you."

"Shut up, bitch-ass nigga. Why'd you say you was a 'Rip, huh?" Al Capone slaps him across the face like a pimp would do one of his whores.

"Aw, Harlem. I just don't bang no more." His limp hands hang to his thighs.

"Hey, Bomb." Loco doesn't turn his head when he calls out to the tier-tender. His eyes are still frozen on Capone. He should know not to stare; he should have learned to sense, rather than confront like that. "Get wit' yo' homie, cuz."

"Nigga, I'ma get wit' you." Al Capone grabs Loco's boxer shorts by the elastic waistband and yanks them up the crack of his ass.

I know Loco will fight now. I get ready to come to Capone's aid if need be.

"You a bitch. Bitches wear they draws in they ass," Al Capone taunts.

Loco blinks. He's a bug caught in Al Capone's web. "Man, I ain't got nothin' against you."

Al Capone connects his fist to Loco's face. "You ain't nothin' but a bitch."

Loco hits the cement. "Ahhh," he moans. He doesn't rise to defend himself. He lies on the floor.

Keitarock kicks him away from his bed.

"You in my cell. You gonna do what I say." Capone inhales, his shoulders and neck expanding. He's trying to figure out how to amplify his control. Loco still rests on the floor. "Kiss my shoes, nigga."

"Why you doin' me like this?"

"Shut up, bitch-ass nigga. You know you ain't got no business here wit' the riders." Al Capone is bangin' full speed ahead, with no brakes. He only respects violence. Everything else is for "bitches." Violence and more violence.

Loco looks spineless as he lays there the same size as Al Capone with no aggressive drive, not even for self-defense. Instead, he curls into himself, announcing weakness and timidity. Loco must know the score. *How could he be so passive? How did he survive Crip initiation? Hadn't he been tested for weakness?*

"You heard me, bitch. You heard me, 'ho." Capone kicks his shoulder. "Kiss my shoes."

And then, Loco crawls to his shoes and kisses them.

Keitarock meets my eyes and we shake our heads, not believing what we're seeing.

"You know you like this," Al Capone says.

Al Capone starts undressing. Now, he's unable to defend himself. I won't let Capone rape Loco if that's what he has in mind. This is my cell and I don't want to see that where I sleep. I wait to see if it gets to that point.

Loco struggles to his feet.

Al Capone stands in boxer shorts, muscles bulging. "Suck my dick."

Loco turns away.

"You goin' to do what I tell you?" Al Capone pulls out his dick and promenades toward Loco. Al Capone is not into boys, but he's into putting on a show of his supremacy.

"Please, Harlem—"

Al Capone punches him hard in the torso. "I tol' you what to do."

I want to see how far Capone can push him.

Doubled in pain, Loco whispers, "Oooh."

"Now what you gonna do? You goin' suck this shit?" Al Capone maneuvers his way past me and behind Loco and shoves him to the rear of the cell where they're not visible to the pigs.

"I'ma do this, man. But I ain't no fag or nothin'".

That is it. Me and Keitarock jump off the bunk and grab Al Capone.

"Cuz," I say, "Fuck this bitch. Let's beat this fool down, 'cause he give ex-'Rips a bad name."

Al Capone pounds everywhere at once like Sugar Ray Leonard on Thomas "The Hitman" Hearns in their middleweight boxing match. The irony is that Al Capone knows if Loco fights, they're evenly matched. Capone's flurry of punches assures Loco's inability to beat him, and Loco's passivity increases Capone's fury.

Loco lies, unconscious. His mouth is open, blood seeps from a split lip to the floor.

Al Capone jumps with adrenaline, eyes racing around the cell, looking for what to do next. He strips Loco's bed and grabs the mattress cover that we call a fart sack and tears it open. He stuffs Loco inside and ties the top. Still bursting with aggression and arrogance, Capone ties a blue rag around his head and stomps to the bars. "Crip!" he trumpets. "Crip." It echoes throughout the silent module, almost forever.

"Crip," Al Capone yells. "I got me a buster."

Loco, still unconscious inside the fart sack, is motionless.

Someone down the tier shouts, "That's five for Baker."

"We still got seven," replies someone from Charlie Row. "We still beat you niggas."

"Wha's his name? I'm keepin' a list on my wall," shouts F-Dog.

"Loco. His name is Loco," shouts back Capone.

Loco regains consciousness and pushes against his fabric cage. Bomb shouts, "Lock it up," to the tier.

"Cuz is straight-up soft," I muse. If you claim Crip, you have to represent well, follow the rules, and be serious. Loco isn't serious.

Capone looks down with disgust at Loco, now reduced to pitiful lumps in the white sheet.

"Deputy, deputy," Loco shouts.

Al Capone kicks Loco. "Shut the fuck up."

"Ahh, Harlem. Please, man, please—"

Al Capone kicks Loco hard where his head should be. "Don't ever tell no-body you used to be a 'Rip. You a disgrace to the Crip C." Capone spits.

"Man," Keitarock says, "let's tie this fool up on the bars and play darts on this nigga's ass."

Al Capone lifts Loco off the ground and drags him toward the bars. Keitarock and I tie Loco eight feet high, upside down. We tear a hole out of the fart sack to reveal his ass. He's sheeted mounds with brown flesh sticking out. He's reduced to merely an ass that hardly seems to be part of a person.

The three of us back to the rear of the cell, wet strips of toilet paper, twist them up into spitballs, and throw them at Loco. They land with faint thuds, stick, and then gradually slide down his brown flesh, leaving shiny trails. Finally, they fall to the floor. With the smack of each spitball, Loco flinches from the humiliation, from the furthering of Capone's domination.

The person whose ball lands closest to the crack in Loco's ass earns the right to make others do push-ups, drink cups of water, or take a swat on the ass with a plastic shower shoe.

After an hour, the fart sack quits moving. He no longer cringes, he doesn't jerk. Soon his ass becomes merely two half circles. The darker line between them, a bull's-eye. It's like he's fallen asleep, or has died.

We do this version of pluck for three or four hours. My arms and shoulders throb from the push-ups, my stomach bloated from water. Then it becomes deep night and we tire. Al Capone cuts Loco down and slides him under the bunk. I lay on my bunk waiting for sleep to help me escape. Busters have been caught in other cells and I've heard the fights and humiliation, but this is the first time I've witnessed the punishment. The first time I've been part of the absolute power and retribution that is part of discipline.

I get up throughout the night to piss. Our cell is quiet, except for the noises of the sleepless men in the tier.

The next morning, Capone prances around the cell, laughing loudly, as though the world is his. "It works. It's just like I read in that book."

"What book you talking about?"

"That book on slavery they got in the module. You ain't read it yet, cuz? You gotta read this book. It tells all about what the slave master did to us. Trip. The first thing you do is make the slave feel your power, your control." He zips up his pants and places his hands on his waist. "Then you degrade him. That's why you jerk his shorts in his ass. He feels like a bitch then. Less than a man. Wit' threats and show of aggression fool ready to do anything. You saw, he woulda sucked my dick. Then, you tie his ass up to let him know you the master."

"Where's that book?"

"Bomb has it. Tha's how the masters did us. Tha's how to discipline busters."

"You on one now, Capone," Keitarock says.

"You tellin' me that's what the slave owners did to us?" I muse. "Tha's how they broke us?"

"You think I'm bullshittin'? You should read this book. Where'd you think we learned how to do busters? Tells ya' all ways to break a man and get him to do what you want. Look at that fool." He nudges Loco's body with his shoe. Loco doesn't struggle, just lies there. "He broke. He'll do anything. He's my slave," Capone chuckles.

"Shit." And now we did it to one of our own. *We handled one of our own like a slave, aimed to despirit him. How much did we learn from our slave master?* Loco's arm pushes at the sack, his fingers outlined by the fabric. *For a while, we become the slave master.*

This is how it must feel to have absolute power, to do with another as we wish. Humiliate him, sexually abuse him, torture him, watch all pride ebb away. Each pleading, each sorrowful abased look and moan, increases our sense of authority, strength, invulnerability. And yes, he hardly seemed human. Just an ass in a sack to be used as a target for our perverted game. It's a feeding frenzy, where the violence and the lust for power and meanness and demented desire merge to torture another person who then is rationalized—a buster, a slave, a criminal—as deserving. I have an inkling of what it must be like to have absolute control over others. I can't imagine what it must be like to see that as your birthright. Looking at Loco, I can only guess at what it did to him.

It's what I've fought against all my life.

Loco punked out on the first level of combat and then was treated like a slave, like we, Black Americans, were all treated. I look at the light skin on my arm and see the reminder of my ancestors' slave days, of the abuse they endured as a result of another's ultimate power.

"Cee," Capone says to me, "let's kill this nigga and set an example. He's a disgrace."

"I can't let you do cuz like that, homie. You done vented enough anger on cuz already. Untie him and let 'em go."

"He's a mark now, cuz," Keitarock agrees.

Al Capone swings his legs off the side of the bunk, puts on his shoes, and retrieves his knife from under the mattress.

"You already broke him down to bitch status. He can't go nowhere. Everybody's gonna find out what happen. Release the fool," I insist. "Cuz not an enemy. Not a threat," I add.

Capone unties the sack, pulls out Loco, breaks his nose with a hard kick to his face, drags him out of the cell. He lays naked outside the cell and then pushes himself up and limps away.

I suck in the air, slightly sweet now with the smell of Loco's blood mixed with smoke and sweat.

Catching and disciplining busters by tying them and humiliating them is routine in the module. Sometimes sheets are torn into strips and the buster hog-tied and stored under the bunk. Sometimes the buster is stripped and tied to a chair and the other guys debase him by sticking fingers up his butt. Occasionally, a buster is beat to death. In just this way, one man came into the module with a traffic ticket and got a murder rap.

The slave book was brought in to teach us Crips history, but we turned it around. Started doing what the White guys did to us. Instead of "Do unto others as you'd do unto you," we do unto others as has been done unto us.

We try to get rid of frustration and rage. If you don't have a White guy, what's the next best thing? A buster.

We keep our adrenaline, our rage, our fear on the edge. We keep ourselves perpetually alert and ready to explode. So much rage.

And almost immediately, another domino falls. That morning, I'm called over the PA system, escorted to the first floor to see my lawyer, who gives me a copy of the police report that I read in silence. It reports that a confidential informant gave them information about the robbery of the ring and the shooting.

Who?

"This looks bad. All these charges," he slaps the papers in his hand. "Taylor was shot in the liver, colon, and lung. He's been applauded by the media and police as a hero for his spontaneous desire to help. And you're portrayed as the crazed armed robber."

Only four people knew about the robbery and shooting: G, D'Andre, Li'l Dog, and Big T.

Carter gives me a wrinkled-chin look as though he's waiting for what I think about this case, but I'm thinking about who ratted me out. Both Li'l Dog and Big T have motive. Big T thought I was going to kill him and resented me; Li'l Dog had run off with my jewelry and was addicted to crack. I remember the guilty look Li'l Dog gave me when I was arrested. I think about the craziness, the continual price of split seconds. *Amazing, isn't it, how one act done on the spur of the moment has so many consequences.* I just grabbed a ring, didn't hardly think about it. He just tried to capture a thief. *Now look. Both lives changed, tattered.*

"If he were a brother they wouldn't bother." They wouldn't have bothered following me for three days, putting the squeeze on some informer, doing the movie-scene arrest scene. *It would have been just another nigga hurt. So what.*

Carter nods at me. "Maybe. Maybe I can get you a plea bargain. Might be able to get a sentence of twelve years. But with this witness, there's no reason to go to trial."

Maybe I'll insist on one just to see who ratted me out. "Well, see what they'll give me," I tell him. *Shit. I'm not yet twenty-one years old. I'll spend more than half my life in prison.*

That night, I call G and tell him someone snitched on me. "Probably Li'l Dog or Big T."

"Big T and Big Mel caught a case together and Big Mel told me that T was trying to put a gun beef on him. They got busted with a gat in the car up at Denker Park. I don't know what happen', but Mel got a warrant for his arrest and T beat the case."

Could be I'm wrong. It's not Li'l Dog. Maybe that guilty look was his shame. And just then the phone clicks off; my time is up.

A few weeks later, my name is called for a visit. It's my first visit in the two months I've been in jail and as I go through the procedures, I imagine it's my grandmother, or maybe Huckabuck. But it's Gina. Her promises to visit have been vague, so I didn't imagine it would be her. Her face, sufficiently rounded with the end of her pregnancy, makes her appear like the girl she was when I first met her. She spreads her fingers on the glass between us. My right wrist is cuffed and chained to the table, which is standard procedure for module inmates. I place my free hand over hers. Her fingers come up to my second knuckles, and the sight of her small hand and skinny splayed fingers reminds me of her fragility.

I pick up the phone. "Hey." My voice is softer than I mean it to be and echoes in the phone.

"Earl asked to marry me."

So that's why she's come. To say good-bye. I'll watch her play this out. I lean back.

"He's pressurin' me . . . went and bought me a diamond ring."

I nod. "You wanna marry him wit' the baby coming?"

"Tha's what he says. Wit' the two children, we should make it right."

"You here asking my permission?"

"Nah." She looks down and then swallows. "I did somethin'." Her voice is whispery. "I tol' him it's yours, your baby."

"Huh?" I can't see her eyes as she examines her nails, I see instead her smooth brown forehead and the part that slices through her hair ruler-straight, both predetermined, revealing none of her emotion. "But it can't be."

"He don't know shit." She notes the confusion on my face. "I tol' him to back him off. Get 'im to quit bugging me."

"Can't he add? I was in Soledad."

She shrugs one shoulder in a dismissive jerk, "He don't know when you got out."

"You told him this? Even though I'm here?" Now she's got herself hanging on a cliff, me and her and this baby, when I can't give her anything but letters. *Maybe she wants it to be my baby. Maybe this is her bitter way of proving she loves me.*

She gazes at me with her liquid eyes and a somber expression tugging her lips, waiting for me to make a statement. But I don't know what to say. *Maybe she's changed. Maybe she can be loyal now, even if I'm locked away.* I'm still working on figuring out how much she cares. I've known her almost my whole life, but she's full of surprises. I lean toward her, my mind twisting around the situation, knowing we don't have much time. I pretend it isn't about me, but her solution to solve her uncomfortable situation. I'm a convenient excuse. Maybe, after all, that's all I am.

"Did it work?"

"Yeah. He just comes to visit Marcus. Doesn't even talk to me."

I guess I'm right. I'm her defense; this isn't an expression of love.

Then she meets me right in my eyes, doesn't smile and doesn't flinch, and says with all her bravery and the risk-taking tomboy she used to be. "But tha's not the only reason why I tol' him."

"Time's up," the guard commands.

"Hey. You didn't say, 'Colton. What did I tell you? You never listen to me. I told you somethin' bad was gonna happen.'" But she doesn't laugh. She puts her hand back on the glass and watches me back out of the visitors' room.

That night, I tattoo her name on my left hand, watch the trickle of blood ooze from the curve in the G, the dot over the eye. The letters flow across my hand. Then, I write and tell her so she knows that I received both her messages. I know she isn't just getting rid of him; she's claiming me. And now I've claimed her.

Meanwhile the set trippin' heats up. The Rollin' Sixties start fighting the Eight Trays in the visiting room. That night, Monster Kody beat a Rollin' Sixty unconscious. Both sets start fashioning weapons, holding strategy sessions to organize an attack. Keitarock, a Sixties notable, is one of Eight Tray's targets. Because of the alliance between the Hoovers and the Eight Trays, the tensions between us and Hoover, already taut because of Teekey's murder, escalate. I put security on Keitarock—watch his back.

Then, I catch J'Bone, one of our homies, revealing our military preparation to one of the Hoovers. I question him about his actions and he tells me the Hoover is his first cousin. I investigate this and find out he's lying. His discipline is assured and I connect my fist to face. "That nigga ain't your cousin."

J'Bone collapses to the floor, then jumps to his feet and races down the tier. He hurdles a flight of stairs and bolts to the OSS office, running out of his shoes, which are scooped up. Bomb is called to the OSS office and J'Bone tells him that I stole his shoes. Robbing another homeboy is a violation taken more seriously than tribalism.

Bomb informs me I'm being disciplined for fifteen days. I have to give him my letters, writing paper, do two thousand burpies, and can't use the telephone. I have to return J'Bone's shoes.

"I don't have the buster's shoes, cuz. Never did."

"This is Bomb, cuz." Bomb's thumb points at his chest. "I know you and Keitarock and Capone. Y'all niggas ain't nothin' nice."

"On the real, on Harlem Crip, I ain't got his shoes."

He knows I won't swear a lie on my set. "Well, who has 'em?"

"I'll try to find out."

Bomb steps closer to the cell bars and whispers, "Do that, cuz. The homies on Charlie Row are makin' a big deal about this shit. And Monster Ken got love for J'Bone.

I get word that T-Dog from Compton has the shoes. I ask T-Dog to give them to me, but he refuses. So I go public and holler over the tier, "Cuz, T-Dog, don't play no games wit' me. Give me the shoes."

"Aw, Cee. I found 'em first," he yells back.

"Fuck that. I was checkin' that fool. Not robbing him. Give me the shoes, Dog.

He passes the shoes through the bars. They are standard Nikes, the heel squashed down, the shoelaces dirty, important only because they aren't state issue. A promise, reminder of the 'hood. I call Bomb. "Here. Take these tore-up-ass shoes."

Bomb holds the shoes, but doesn't leave my cell. "The homies want me to get your property. They say you gotta be disciplined for beatin' ole boy up.

"How they gonna discipline me for beatin' down a buster?"

Keitarock gets off his bunk, slides his hand under his mattress. I know he's strapped now.

"Yeah. J'Bone's a buster who ain't put in work. Just fake like you're givin' me your shit. Hand me a balled sheet, so I can play it off, cause Monster Ken is lookin' through the catwalk." He walks close to me. "I don't trust 'em, when them fools killed Teekey."

I hand him the balled sheet.

"Just watch 'em," Bomb advises.

"I'm on point," I tell him. And I assume that that incident is over.

So many people are being beat up and stabbed that the jail doesn't have sufficient medical staff to treat the wounds. Cats are going to court with black eyes and busted lips, begging judges for court orders for medical attention, phone calls, medication to help them deal with the pain.

One night, at about eight o'clock, the pigs swamp the module. They call out, "Awright. Listen up. All Rollin' Sixties report to the Baker Row showers. All the Eight Trays report to Charlie Row showers."

The gates are racked.

Men file out of their cells like urban troops, with a hip South Central sway. Keitarock walks out on the tier; I fall in step behind him. Even though I'm not from the Sixties, I'm not going to let Keitarock go alone. Keitarock is family; our bond stands. Irrespective of the situations he faces, I'll be right at his side. I know he'll have homeboys with him. But I'm his road dog. His enemies are my enemies; my enemies are his enemies. I'm with Keitarock, win, loose, or draw. He's not alone.

If it's going down, I'm going to be there.

As I stride down the tier with the company, I get smirks and mad-dog stares from the other Crip sets, especially the Hoovers who know I'm not a Rollin' Sixty. But I believe in the Sixties-and-Thirties Crip alliance. Besides, if the Eight Trays destroy the Sixties, they'll start on us.

I shake off the sneers and move to the showers. A Nazi deputy begins calling off the nicknames of the Sixties set members. "Keitarock, Big Fee, Big U, Cousin Karry, K' Dog . . ."

Each name is met with a loud, "Yeah."

The deputy turns to me.

"Who're you? You're not from Rollin' Sixties."

"I'm Keitarock's cousin."

The pig scans me, walks away mumbling something under his breath.

We've been invited to a gladiator contest. They plan to allow three members from each set to battle one-on-one in hand-to-hand combat. The battle will be in Able Row shower area. Once a winner is declared, the violence between the two sets will cease. Sheriff's deputies are going to referee the fights.

Big U from the Sixties, who looks like a serious nerd, agrees to fight Youngster and Jimbo from the Eight Trays at the same time. That battle is swift and decisive. Big U lays both of them out.

Monster Kody is supposed to be next, but he's so much larger than his opponent, another man is chosen in his place. That fight is won by the Eight Trays. But from my point of view, the "loser" has minor scrapes and bruises to his knuckles and looks like a pretty boy. The Eight Tray cat's eye is black and his lip split.

During the fights, the officers line up to watch. They have money riding on each contest. The cheering is loud as the men go at each other.

The pigs bet the Eight Trays will win. It's a draw, and the pigs lose money.

The shower gates are opened and we stroll to our cells. The gladiator contest is finished. We have served our purpose for entertainment. But the fighting between the Sixties and the Eight Trays decreases.

My allegiance to Keitarock earns me hostility, and my loyalty to my own set is questioned. Monster Ken, still angry that I beat up J'Bone, makes negative comments behind my back but never confronts me. After watching him, I decide he's a chaos agent, but there's something familiar about him. As I think about it, I realize he reminds me of Big T. Maybe he's not as hard as he would like everyone to think. I'm alert for anything implying a threat and stay strapped with a six-inch piece of steel. I widen my personal space.

Keitarock and I have our sets tattooed on our faces. Mine is under my left eye, sitting on my cheekbone. "30's," it says.

"Harlem Crips" is tattoed on my forearm. Up until now, faces have been off-limits for tattoos. We have tagged ourselves, turning our faces into graffitied warnings of danger to intensify our safety.

One morning, during my exercise routine, the cell door is racked.

"Simpson. Baker Three. Report to the OSS office."

I wonder why the pigs want me. I secure the piece of steel to be safe and stroll to the OSS office.

When I open the door, Smiley stands shackled from the waist down. He smiles at me as the pigs remove his chains. A sun shaft shoots from the window and surrounds him as he stands in the beam, the dull chains reflecting random sparks.

"Ah, cuz, my nigga. What up, loved one." Last time I saw him, two and a half years ago, was through a thick Plexiglas window in the jail's visiting room. Then, I was on the street and he was in jail. Now, we're both in jail.

Arms free, he extends his hand with the crescent scar on his knuckle. I shake it, and then we embrace. It's the first time we hug since my initiation in 1975. He looks the same, bulked out a little in the thighs, but not taller. His hair is braided. He's clean shaven. The slash from running through the plate-glass window has faded on his face but bulges thickly on his neck. I'm taller than he is now, but in spite of the years between us, I'm brought back to the day I met him and he was the Crip shot-caller, powerful and beneficent, and I was the scrawny boy.

"Man, what's up wit' you and Big T?" He doesn't spread his smile.

"I don't know what's up wit' him. But I know he's a coward."

"It ain't cool puttin' a snitch jacket out on cuz if you ain't got no paperwork to back it up."

"Snitch jacket? Check this out. I don't know who told you that, but they full of shit. All I did was tell G and BJ that someone snitched on me and read them my police report. I figured it was T or Li'l Dog. They assumed that cuz is the one who snitched. I can't say he did, and I can't say he didn't, but I ain't puttin' it past him."

Smiley's mouth is motionless. His eyes watch me. I don't mind him staring at me, but there's something in his stillness that is unsettling.

"You ain't been out in a while. You don't know T no more. Cuz is soft."

"I knew him before I met you. He's always been straight." He steps back.

"Look man, there's a first time for everything. If you try to tell my grandmother half the shit I've done, she ain't gonna believe you 'cause she has a predetermined opinion. I'm tellin' you, Smiley, the boy is soft."

"Yeah. Well. When you get back to the module the homics'r gonna holler at you. I was just brought over here so I could see you, but they're sending me to High Power." High Power is maximum security, for the most dangerous and disruptive inmates in the county jail.

"Ah. I'd hoped you'd be on the module."

"Gina's gonna be up here in a few days, so I'll see you again, then."

"See you in the visiting room." We shake hands a second time.

Later that day, a trustee informs me that Don Don and other homies on Charlie Row want me to come to their cell to tell me something important. The gate is racked and I walk to Charlie Row.

When I enter, seven homies are playing cards, including Monster Ken and Don Don, shooting the breeze. I shake everyone's hand and sit down on Don Don's bunk and start playing pluck with him and Black Boy. The gate is closed behind me.

As I deal the cards, Don Don says, "You know how to play, Li'l Cee?" "Yeah. I know what's up."

I gather my cards. There are no aces in my hand.

"Your play," Black Boy says.

I reach to play a card and—

Bam.

Don Don strikes first, smashing my face.

"This is from Smiley and Big T, nigga." Don Don punches me in the nose.

I rise to my feet, grab him by the armpits, ram him into the bars, and throw toe-to-toe blows on his face and head. There's no way he can recover now I've connected.

Black Boy jumps off his bunk and whacks me in the back of the head.

I fall against the bars; the world spins.

Bam.

Monster Ken has joined in, hitting me in the torso. Now, it's three-on-one. The wavering world stills. I twist around and throw furious punches. I'm midpoint between the cell bars and the sink, surrounded. Three men hit me from all directions. I fight back, hoping to knock a few of them out and decrease the numbers. Then, Eddie Dee, Watt Nifty, Li'l Nut, Sinbad jump in and it's se-men men against me.

I fall to the floor.

I swim up from the dark and am kicked in the head. A foot stomps my face, and I'm out again.

As I wake, I hear Don Don say, "Naw, Black Boy, Cee is a homie, cuz. We can't stab 'em. Give me the knife."

I blank out, dead to the world.

The rasping clank of opening cages wakes me. Blinking my eyes, I see the cement floor, the legs of the bunks, the cell. I'm alone. A sharp pain in my lower back doubles me. Blood, my blood, fills my nose, mouth. Splotches of irregular patterns splay across my shirt and pants. It spews out of my nose and mouth, a wound on my side.

I crawl out of the cell. *God, please help me to stand.* I rise to my feet. I'm ready to fight again for my life.

I stagger to the end of the tier, but my assailants have run out of the cell and locked themselves in the shower. I look directly into Black Boy's eyes as he stands sheltered.

"Do or die, muthafucka," I shout. I raise my fist high and roar, "Harlem Crip, West Side Rollin' O's. Do or die, nigga."

The pigs spot me, put me on a stretcher, rush me out of the module and into the infirmary. I'm placed on a bed and examined by a nurse who injects a needle into my arm. Warmth floods me. Pain subsides. I float in the bed.

"What happened to him?" the nurse asks the deputy. Her voice strobes in and out, rocks in my ears.

"Crips," he replies. *Criiiips, criiiippps,* the word echoes.

"Is he a Blood?"

"No, he's a Crip."

I feel myself floating over myself. And I wonder for moment if I'm dying; my mind seems separated from my body as my body shrinks, increasingly weak. "A Crip did this to another Crip?" the nurse asks.

"Yeah."

"Why?"

My eyes flutter open and I see the officer looking at her. "There's a thin line between love and hate." His words are muted, throbbing. I struggle to understand them. I think I've heard them before somewhere. But maybe it's just because they echo.

My eyes shut, my body seems to disappear, disengage from my mind as I drift in the spaces of the sounds. I'm lost.

TWELVE

Betrayal

Let us treat men and women well: treat them as if they were real: perhaps they are.
   —Ralph Waldo Emerson, *Experience*

I BOLT FROM THE STORE, CLENCHING JEWELRY. MY HEART throbs in my ears as my legs pump. A diamond digs into my palm, a gold chain wraps around my thumb. I hurdle a short fence and race, gasping. Then, from around the corner, comes a cop running at me. Heart pounding, I look for an alley, but the pig leaps at me. As he nears, I see his face. It's Big T. He draws an AR-15 and fires several rounds.

Boom. Boom. Boom. Boom.

Like shards of glass, bullets puncture my cheeks, my forehead, my nose, my chin, my shoulder, my chest. I feel each shot pierce my skin, enter me, course through my body. The blast throbs. The bullets travel through me and I fade and shrink.

I'm dazed, confused from drugs. Straining for clarity, I rise from the bed and look around.

I open my hand and it's empty. No chains. No ring. No robbery. No Big T. I'm in the infirmary. Before this, my dreams have been crammed with fun—me on a baseball field, me riding with Huckabuck. I never had one filled with violence. I pull the blanket up. *I must retaliate. I must protect myself. Stay loyal to the gang. To myself. I close my eyes. Big T's face looms on the back of my lids.*

Can't trust anyone. I'll shield myself from those around me. My heart pounds again, my fists clench. I'll never drop my guard. Everyone will be pushed away as I widen my space. Every thought will be survival. I'll train harder in military combat, remain in constant preparation for the war with the Bloods. War with the Crips. War with the pigs. War with myself. It's up to me not to let this nightmare become my reality.

I don't know why I was beaten. I'm the staunchest member of the set. All I've done has been overlooked and unappreciated. Maybe it was Monster Ken who had me beaten because of J'Bone and those muthafuckin' shoes.

I have no control over the circumstances of those homies. I can only control myself and develop further into a superior weapon, a potent fighting machine.

The explosion from Big T's gun ricochets.

I'm taken from the hospital to the Operation Safe Street office. A captain from the general population comes to see me. He takes pictures of my disfigured head and face.

"What happened?"

I don't answer. I touch my split lower lip with the tip of my tongue. My cheeks are swollen. My nose broken. Each motion results in pain.

He switches to another topic. "You're being rehoused in protective custody."

"Protective custody?" Li'l Cee Loc in protective custody?

Never. I think of the vows I just made. I think of the vengeance I must conclude.

"We can't return you to the Crip Module," he says. "It's LACJ policy to rehouse all victims of attempted murder."

I'm no coward. Homies, enemies—whatever they really are— will have to kill me, or try. Returning to the module will force their hand. I can't live with myself unless I strike back. As a banger, to be victimized and not get revenge is an occupational hazard. Have you ever seen a war without retaliation? War is re- taliation. Without it, there're no victims. As a banger, survival con- tinues only with retaliation.

"There's only the strong and the weak. Nothing in between. No midpoint," my father told me when I was a child. I took his advice to fear nothing, not even death. In South Central, the strong strike back and live; the weak die. The victimized usually strike with vi- olence more lethal, escalated from their suffering. Thus, you learn from your affliction, from your tormentors. You return greater than you received and become fortified. Once you show signs of vulnerability, you allow room for the predators. Look at Loco and Al Capone. Perfect example.

I must return to the module to get my revenge, to protect my- self, to live as myself. I must maintain invincibility. My enemies are weak.

"I want to return to the module," I insist.

The captain and I debate the matter. Each word is accompa- nied with a twinge from my lip. My voice has a peculiar murkiness to it, slurred because of my swollen mouth and busted nose.

"Well, you'll have to sign a waiver acknowledging your choice to be housed in forty-eight hundred and diverge from policy."

"Fine."

"The waiver also removes responsibility for your welfare from the LACJ and the sheriff's office."

"Good."

I hold the pen, tap its hilt against the desk. The point shoots from its sheath. I sign the waiver. I'm so strung out on retaliation, I sign it again.

I'll take my respect. They'll feel my wrath. My pressed double signatures indent the paper. Reaffirming my commitment to endurance, to principle, and to Crip makes me feel secure. I know what I must do. I'll climb the merit ladder, notch after notch. I'll rise to even greater ghetto celebrity status.

I don't know who orchestrated my beating. Monster Ken? Smiley? Can't be him. We love each other. We're brothers.

I'm placed in the day room and Big Cat from the Sixties enters. "Cuz." He studies my disfigured head, "What happened?"

"The homies rat-paced me yesterday."

"Yesterday? You was in the cell yesterday, Cee."

"What's today?"

"Friday, homie."

"Damn." Being unconscious and in pain, I thought an entire day had passed. But it was only eight hours. "I gotta get to my cell."

"Don't trip." He walks toward the booth where the pigs are. A few seconds later, my name is called over the PA.

"Simpson. Go to Baker Three."

Home. I stroll down the tier. Keitarock stands at the bars talking to Bomb. "Cuz, tell him what's up."

Bomb explains the entire incident revolved around the dispute between me and Big T. *My nightmare knew. My nightmare read the earth signs.* Smiley received a letter from Big T, complaining I labeled him a snitch. Smiley was called to the county as a witness to Kato's crime. Kato's lawyer subpoenaed Smiley to court. The prison transported him to LACJ, and because he's a Crip, the OSS interviewed him in the OSS office, which happens to be directly across from 4800. Crip trustees move back and forth from there, so Smiley had them manipulate the pigs to bring me to the OSS at the same time he was there. Smiley told Bomb to set up a fight between Don Don and me. This order was given prior to my seeing Smiley in the OSS office. He made his decision before he spoke with me. He didn't care what I had to say. He didn't trust that I would act on honor and wasn't forthright with me. Instead, he lied and pretended something positive would soon occur. What did he say? "The homies are gonna holler at you."

He was supposed to be my road dog. My brother.

Smiley had not seen me for four years. He assumed I was the same old Li'l Cee Loc. But I had grown. He had no idea that I was taller, quicker, stronger than Don Don. Don Don did not feel secure winning a "heads up" fight against me after hearing how I'd dismantled the man in the basement kitchen during my first trip to the county. He recruited others and turned what was supposed to be a one-on-one fight into a seven-on-one beat-down. He formed a group of homies who had animosity toward me: Monster Ken was angry I beat up J'Bone, Watt Nitty was irate I accompanied Keitarock and the Sixties to the showers, Black Boy and Li'l Nut were initiated by Big T, and Eddie Dee and Sinbad wanted in on the excitement.

After Bomb leaves, I focus on plans for my get-back. I push Smiley out of my mind. Within hours, Bomb returns. I'm not to worry. Those involved in my stomping will be dealt with, Bomb tells me. The men are with you. I take this information to Lefty Dog, Big Cat, and Big Fee, and we begin preparations for a lethal attack.

The next day, I hear a familiar laugh, like corn popping, in the module. It comes from a cell down my tier.

"Hey, who's that?" I call out. "Is that Huckabuck?"

"Cuz, Cee, you know it's me," he shouts back and his laughter bounces in short bursts.

"Ah, nigga. Let me get at you." I let him know I love him.

Huckabuck. Just when I need him. When he sees me, his brows come together and he starts his angry jumping. "Smiley? Homie did this?" He darkens, his face filling with his rage. He pounds his fist against the bed. "We can't let that shit ride, cuz. We ain't gonna let those muthafuckas do us like that. Crips or not."

I tell him about Big T and that I've been snitched on by either Big T or Li'l Dog.

"Big T be trippin' sometimes, cuz. Always been like that. Cuz uses his size to intimidate and manipulate homies. Punk-ass nigga." His energy pops through his arms, his fists, as they flash in the air with each word. "Let's go. What we waitin' on?"

"It's gonna happen, cuz. We kill the head and the body will follow." I fill him in on our plans.

"What're you in for, Huck?" I ask.

"Robbing Way-out." Way-out is a small-time dealer working for Freeway Rick and paying the set rent to use our 'hood as his territory. "Homie missed his rent payment, so I took it."

"Is that right?" I start to tell him how Way-out tried to hire me to break a man's legs, but Huckabuck's face lights up, "Hey. Tina had my baby, cuz. A boy. I got me a son." His antagonism is gone like windshield wipers rub away raindrops as his brows lift, his lips spread in a wide smile, flashing white teeth.

"Li'l Huck." I slap him on the back.

"Last week. I was wit' her when he came out, screamin', hands all balled up ready to fight. Look." He reaches in his pocket and pulls out a photo, examines it before he hands it to me as though he's reluctant to relinquish it even for a minute, even to me. I hold it by the corner, careful not to fingerprint it.

"Li'l cuz got some hair. More 'n you already," I tease. "Where's his flag? Li'l homie needs a C-rag."

"Named him after me."

"Hope he's as strong as his pop," I tell him.

That weekend I'm called to the visitors' room. My nose is swollen, the slit in my lip has crusted to a slivery scab, the bruise on my cheek has faded from purple to brown. The black "30's" under my eye is unblemished. I sit, cuffed to the table, waiting.

Huckabuck is a few booths away and Tina enters, holding blue blankets.

"Hey, Cee. Looka my li'l man," Huckabuck shouts at me while Tina uncovers the baby's face, holds him up so I can see him through the glass. He has heavy brows for a baby, giving him the same helmeted appearance as his father.

"Damn. He looks jus' like you, cuz," I shout to Huckabuck.

He picks up the phone and turns to Tina and his son.

My visitors are Gina and G. They heard about me being rat-packed and knew Smiley had given the order. When Gina sees my face she clicks her tongue in the roof of her mouth.

Then G moves away and I know he's visiting Smiley. Since he's housed in High Power, he doesn't use the same visiting row as the Crips from 4800. When I realize Smiley is in the room with me a clot fills my chest; a churning mixture of rage and love twists. I don't know what to feel, how to deal with the roil of eagerness to meet my old friend, frustration at not being able to, and swift rage, immeasurable disappointment for what he did to me. I know him so well, his face as familiar as my own, our ability to anticipate each other in the clutch, flawless. I envision him clasping the phone, the keloided scar echoing the phone's curve and talking with his brother. I know the wide smile that will greet G. Smiley is smaller than me now. His forearm is narrower than mine. His back curves, still broad and powerful. *But he's not even aware of me. My road dog.*

Then Gina glimpses him at the far end of the room and starts shouting, "You muthafucka. Smiley, why you gotta beat him? He family. And you the one call it, fool." She stands, shaking her fist at him. The Plexiglas blunts her words, but I hear Gina twice, once through the phone still pressed to my ear, and once in spite of the barrier.

She sits down and picks up the phone and says to me, "I'm gonna fuck their bitches up." She can't get the men so she'll take her anger out on their women. "Find out who those ho's are. G and me gonna lurk round the county. They ass is mine." As her eyes flash, the bitter angry girl is reborn in spite of her pearly nails.

I laugh at her signing on to be part of my army. Her choosing me over Smiley vindicates me, and I feel suddenly the bonding that happens with the fellas when we're united for the same purpose, our spirit and reliance on each other heightened by life-and-death danger. That's the thing about Gina; she's like one of the cats with a woman's body. Strong and scrappy, all muscle for a petite woman who just had her second baby.

She sees then her name tattooed on my hand. Her fingertips reach for my hand as though to transmorph through the glass and touch me. She whispers into the phone, "Never saw my name so pretty." Her lips part, her eyes shining from her anger.

"You never look so fine," I tell her.

She tilts her head, smiles, and tells me about Marcus trying to feed the baby and that she visited Grandma Louise.

Then, Big T enters to visit Don Don and Watt Nitty. I learn later that Big T gives Don Don and Watt Nitty as well as Black Boy and Li'l Nut twenty dollars a-piece. Their payoff for rushing me. I see his black goatee, broad shoulders, and glinting eyes, and my chest heats.

When Big T sees Gina, he orders her to tell me that there's no love lost.

I want to jump through the wooden booths and kill him. My hands twitch to surround his throat. I shoot him my most evil stare, stand as tall as I can in spite of being bolted to the table, and shout at the top of my lungs, "Nigga, if I ever see you again, I'ma kill yo' bitch ass." I want him dead. I want to see his sightless eyes open, his mouth drooling blood. I want him to feel my pain. More, he doesn't deserve to be free and laughing after what he did to me. I never wanted anyone dead, I just wanted to stop the war, protect myself, and shelter my neighborhood. My fury burns hotter than it ever did at the Bloods, the pigs. I've been a soldier. Big T makes me a killer.

Every Crip in the visiting room looks at me like I'm crazy. I am. Rage obliterates rationality. My threat ends my visit.

Back in my cell, I plot revenge. My support comes from surprising forces. Even the CCO, set against tribalism, the Eight Trays, and the Hoovers back me. No one approves of the seven-on-one beat-down.

On an overcast Wednesday morning, Baker Row is called to the roof for recreation. While there, Keitarock, Huckabuck, and I secure a six-foot metal slab that bolts down the telephones and holds the wires in place. We break it into six pieces and smuggle them to the module in our jumpsuits. My court hearing is a few days away. On the night I return, Huckabuck, Keitarock, and I plan to take off on Don Don, Black Boy, and Monster Ken. The head of the group will be destroyed; we'll deal with the rest later. As I plot my revenge, I remember to think of the consequences as though playing a chess game. I increase my combat training. I maintain a low profile with the pigs.

I'm turning myself into a silent killer, I think as I watch myself from one of the layers inside me, remembering my fiery fury at the sight of Big T. *A silent killer.*

I'm transported to Torrance for my preliminary hearing. I distract myself from the humiliation of being shackled from the waist down by envisioning my retaliation that night. I'm prepared for Torrance. I refuse to go through another episode where I'm beaten by the Bloods and the pigs for wearing a gray jumpsuit. A handcuff key, made from a thick staple, is in my pocket and a knife is secreted in my anus. The 30's tattoo under my eye acts as my clearest vision of stability. When I see it, I know I'm safe and prepared. Like graffiti, it warns of danger and brags of confident aggression. Through all the changes, my set remains the same. Harlem Crip is constant. To ensure its continuance and my belonging, I play a vicious part.

After walking into the holding tank at Torrance court, I strain the steel from my anus and secure it in my hand. I scan the tank. There're no enemies. I slide the knife in my left pocket and sit, my hand over the knife. There'll be no mishaps.

I'm escorted to the third floor to see Carter, and he gives me a copy of the police report, which is not much different than the first one and clearly mentions that an anonymous informant gave facts leading to my arrest. The additional proof is that the rat knew where my mother lives and my brother's real name. It confirms what I suspected: only Big T or Li'l Dog could be the snitch. But it doesn't reveal which one. During the drive back to county, I gaze out of the window. One day, I'll be back in South Central. I'll pay Li'l Dog and Big T a visit.

When I return to jail, it's near count time, so the pigs rush me to the showers. Then, twenty pigs bust into the module. I wait in a spooky silence. When the shower gate is opened, I walk toward my cell. Lefty Dog waves a blue flag, so I stop. He enlightens me to the presence of CCO. All the central figures are down from Folsom and are housed in the module: Askari, Imara, Nasau, and Suma. Rumor is that they came to put a stop to the set-trippin' and tribalism. Lefty, who'd done time in Folsom, knows them. "They some no-nonsense cats, cuz. Intelligent, disciplined. All in for murder."

Their presence explains the excess pigs and silence.

I continue down the tier to my cell and, when I enter, a brown-skinned brother about five foot eight stands and extends his hand. "Whassup, brotha. I'm Imara from Compton Crip."

"I'm Li'l Cee from Harlem." I grab his outstretched hand.

"I know who you are, li'l homie."

I'm unsure how to talk to him when I find out who he is. I wonder if he has wind of my plans to retaliate that night. *Is he here to prevent it? Is that why he's here? Maybe my plans are exposed and I'm now targeted for discipline.*

"What happen to your face, Li'l Cee?" He looks at me with such concern and seriousness, my reaction is not to become defensive. I stand back and watch him for a minute, trying to capture a sense of him. He's bald and his skull is round, his nose long and pointed. The light bounces off his head as he stands there, weight evenly distributed on his feet, chest open. He has no fear of impending attack, but no attitude of victim either. He is who he is. He's got all the time in the world for me.

I explain the situation. Start to finish. I tell him what happened on the street, my capture, and my stomping. I am completely open with him.

As I talk, he sits on the end of his bunk listening. When I finish, he says, "Let me see your paperwork."

I hand over everything relevant to my case and he reads it piece by piece, page by page. When he finishes he looks me directly in the eyes and asks, "What're you gonna do about this?"

I don't know if it's a trick question. I turn away from his steady waiting eyes and fingertips gently holding my court documents. It's night now, the lights blaring, Doug E Fresh plays on my radio. A homie raps and slaps a beat. I look beyond my bars to the bars of the tier across the catwalk. *If I tell him the truth—that we're retaliating tonight—he might put a hit on me for conspiracy. If I tell him I'm taking it in stride, he might label me a buster. Cee, a buster? Never.*

I waver there in my indecisiveness, walking my mind through the various scenarios to their consequences. I draw in some air and tell him of my plans for revenge.

Imara listens quietly with his patient ears and mind. When I finish he looks at me and nods. "You one of the most forthright Crips I've met, Cee." He sorts and stacks my file of papers. "Anyone else might have been scared to tell me the truth. Might have been scared of being disciplined for tribalism."

I don't tell him that I am scared. I'm sure he senses it.

"Here's your solution. Inform Talib. All those involved, including Smiley, will be thoroughly investigated." Talib is CCO, an OG Crip and one of the founders of the Harlem Crips. "If what you say is true, all will be dealt with accordingly. But tribalism in the Crip Module is not the place to deal with this."

My lust for retaliation burns. I've been geared on tonight and the cleansing of my revenge, the washing away of my victimization.

He senses my reluctance and says, "I must lead by example. I promote peace among Crips."

I'll get my chance to retaliate in prison.

I sleep that night with one eye open. Imara might set me up as an example.

The next day, me, Keitarock, and Al Capone are called to roll it up for transfer.

"Capone, what you done got us into?" I ask. "I bet that fool Loco tol' on us."

"Damn." We roll up our property, walk to the booth to face the pigs.

We receive kicks to our testicles and batons to our arms and legs, which we can do nothing about as we're handcuffed. They send me to the hole for twenty days. Back to joot balls.

In the hole, I learn the CCO takes control of the module. They reorient the Crips and set out to establish the Crip name as positive and productive rather than malicious and destructive. For those who resist, there's a price. Monster Kody is told that he's done too much destruction and he must either join CCO or face Crip Court. The latter would probably find him guilty of tribalism and sentence him to death.

I'm called to my court date during my stay in the hole. Carter informs me that Taylor's been given a citation as citizen of the year.

I snort. Yeah, some good citizen. Turned a simple theft into an armed robbery with attempted-murder charges. Gonna cost the citizens of the state a pile of money. Got himself put in a wheelchair. Stupid people, complicating my life. Taylor. Big T. Li'l Dog.

I agree to a deal, or plea bargain for ten years, but when I walk into the court, damn if Cecil J. Mills isn't my judge. I'm chained from the waist down, jingling with each motion while he sits in his black robes up on his dais just like he did three years before. A file is in his hand as he shakes his head. "What did I tell you, Simpson?" He doesn't look at me but at the papers on his table.

I jerk at the chain between my cuffs to force a link open, but merely achieve aching wrists.

"I told you last time you were in Youth Authority that if I saw you I was going to be hard on you." Now he raises his head and narrows his eyes at me, shakes his head in annoyance. "You need to get your act together." He raises his voice. "You have a great family background. You don't have to steal. You don't have to rob. You don't have to be a gangbanger. You don't have to do any of this and you're out here doing it anyway. You've turned yourself into society's nightmare."

I'm tired of people telling me how great my family is. They think poverty is the only legitimate reason for crime, but crime occurs at all levels. They don't know. They think being financially middle class, getting degrees, or owning businesses make a family good. They don't know shit about my family. Love is what makes a good family. Love and kindness.

"You have no remorse. You have no remorse." Mills rattles the file in his hand and then shakes his head, but now he's looking down as though I am useless, worthless.

I'm furious. I jerk my chains. The resounding pain in my wrists is comforting.

"You put a man in a wheelchair. You've burnt up L.A. with your thievery. I warned you I'd be hard on you. I'm going to be."

He wants to be a man of his word and not show any sign of weakness. I feel the same way he feels. *He's going to be cruel to me, so why would I show signs of weakness and kiss his ass?* So, I act just as hard as he does. "Can I go? Can I leave?"

"I'm going to make an example out of you." He pushes his glasses up to his forehead where they glint like sharpened steel.

"Can I go? Can I leave?"

"Twenty-four years. I'm sentencing you to twenty-four years."

Twenty-four years. Almost a quarter of a century. More time than I've lived.

"Can I leave now?"

"You are dismissed." Judge Mills waves me away like a mote of dust trapped in a sunbeam.

Once again, I'm sent to Chino to be classified. On a Tuesday, as I'm coming in from the yard, I run into Kincaide who tells me I have an enemy housed in Cell Fifteen on the third tier of A-Side. I rush to the cell and there's Black Boy asleep on the bunk. He breathes deeply, his eyeballs shifting under his lids, one hand protecting himself, the other palm open to heaven. As I watch his chest slowly expand and deflate, images return of a shoe kicking me in the nose, my cheek, my ribs. The bridge of my nose is still hooked from one kick. Once again, the screeching rasp of the opening gate wakes me. Once again, I stumble to my feet and stagger down the tier.

I sling his cell open and hit his head with my fist. His eyes open, widen when he sees it's me. I punch him three times in his face before he sits.

"Help," he screams.

I pull the piece from my waistband and plunge it into his side. His skin is a flimsy membrane. My blade, the precisely filed point of a straightened bed-spring, inserts without resistance. It just slides in, enters him easy. When I withdraw it, blood oozes, coating the metal and my fingers.

"Aw, cuz. We homies, Cee," he pleads.

"We homies now, uh?" Another blow to his face.

"Help."

"Shut up, bitch-ass nigga. You know what this is. Get-back for that punk shit you did to me in the module."

He tumbles off his cot and runs out of the cell and down the tier, yelling, his voice squealing like a woman's.

I pursue him, stab at his head, miss him. My awl is jarred from my hand and hits the wall. I pick it up and race after him, following his splatters of red.

At the end of the tier, a distance of one hundred feet, I lunge toward him. He loses his footing, tumbles down the stairs, and lands on his side with a thud that echoes in the stairwell.

He doesn't rise. I surmise he's unconscious, but I wish him death. Still amped from the battle, I stand motionless in the adjacent stairway looking down at him. He doesn't move.

"Cuz. Cuz," Kincaide hustles toward me, pulls me by the arm. "Go flush the knife, cuz."

I hear him clearly, but I don't know what he's talking about. I don't comprehend his words; they're like discrete bird calls with no meaning.

He shakes me by the shoulders. "Cee. Go flush the piece."

I have never stabbed anyone. I had been trained to stab enemies, I had attempted to stab enemies, but I had never connected. Now, here I am dumbfounded, stupid, standing stiff with a knife in plain view. Black Boy's body still warms the point of my forefinger. His blood smears my piece. A stabbing is so much more intimate than a shooting. Much closer than I want it to be. I want his blood off me. I don't want this connection.

"Cee." Kincaide jerks my arm.

"Whassup?" I snap out of my stupor.

"Go flush the strap."

Still staring at my stained hand, his words and my action unite. "Yeah. I knew that." I run to my cell and flush the knife. Toilets in the prison are very strong when it comes to flushing. The wire whirls away, the water pink for a moment and then clear. As I watch the foam cascade into the bowl, I remember Lafayette Rainey's words. "You're not a killer. I can see it in your face."

That night, I write Keitarock and Huckabuck to tell them I obtained revenge on Black Boy. Huckabuck is free, so I write him back in his home in South Central. The knife is gone; my hand cleansed, the bottoms of my shoes clean. I got some revenge. Not as sweet as I had planned, as I am only able to hit the body not the head, but at least no one can label me a buster and my sense of vulnerability and defenselessness diminishes. I'm safe.

Because I'm a second-termer with a twenty-four year bid and a gang member, my counselor recommends that I be transferred to Folsom and notes that I require close supervision. Folsom is the closest maximum-security facility and considered the toughest prison.

By the time I'm paroled, I will be forgotten. It'll be the twenty-first century. I will be in my late thirties, middle-aged, the power of my youth depleted by prison. My lengthy conviction threatens to overshadow my reputation as a ghetto celebrity. Things aren't looking too good for Li'l Cee Loc.

At least going to Folsom will allow me to catch up with Smiley, I comfort myself. I still need to hear what he has to say. We're brothers, road dogs. We're united by our crimes, by my attempt to help him escape and my subsequent arrest. We were together in death-threatening, electric circumstances. Then, adrenaline heaved us close as we relied on each other for our very lives. Life-uniting actions. The excitement of shared women, various drug-induced states revealed new parts, new layers of ourselves to each other, but, always, with Smiley, acceptance and security. I still can't reconcile that love and the bond forged by our life together with his order for me to be stomped. They're two different sets of facts that I try to hold together simultaneously, try to fit in one picture. But fail.

How could our love and brotherhood exist and his betrayal occur? One has to be wrong.

In June 1986, I'm jolted from a deep sleep by the harsh blast of the PA announcing my name. Twenty-eight of us are forced to strip nude and go through the degrading body-cavity search in a room the size of a doctor's office. Twenty-eight naked men spread ass cheeks and endure rectal searches. It's sexual abuse. I can barely breathe. The air smells like underarms and ass. Then I'm fitted into a red jumpsuit two sizes too small and shackled from the waist down like a runaway slave being shipped to his slave master. Sweating from the heated room, we're led into surprising chilled air.

"Simpson?" A fat forty-something pig calls out.

"Nine one." Once again my name is Nine One. I'm ushered to the gray goose, the transportation bus, and snatch a window seat in the back. It'll be my last view of the world for a quarter century.

Folsom is located ten miles from Sacramento in a small community named Represa, six hundred miles from Chino. I'll see the free world for ten hours.

The world looks so exquisite. The green trees, bright flowers, blue blue sky, mountains. Before it seemed only a battlefield. I pass forests and cars and houses and strip malls and even, once, achieve a glimpse of ocean. It's the world of Colton, the world Grandmother Louise tried to open for me, but I shrugged away her dreams as old-fashioned attempts to prepare me for peace, which I thought made me weak. I remember how she made me kneel and pray, get a paper route and save my money. She tried with me. I wonder if I could have had a life as a basketball player. I had the genes and body for it. I loved it. Then, I imagine being a lawyer like my uncle. I did well in school until the streets blurred my concentration. I envision my other lives and fall asleep, as tough to avoid these thoughts.

"Cee, Cee. Wake up, homie. We here."

I look out the window and see a small cemetery so jammed with headstones it appears the bodies are buried on top of each other. The cemetery is two feet from the prison's granite wall, shadowed by oak trees, the wedged-together headstones pallid in the dense shade. I shudder at the Transylvania castle and the eery prophesy of falling asleep thinking about my grandmother and waking to this foreboding vista, as though this juxtaposition is a judgment on me and a prediction about the remainder of my life.

The gray goose stops, a cast-iron gate creaks open. The bus chugs up a steep driveway and through the recreation yard. A high school-sized baseball diamond, a small track, a full-court basketball court, boxing rink, small weight pile are surrounded by four gun towers occupied by a corrections officer armed with a mini-14 assault rifle and a .38 revolver. We jolt to a stop at the administration building encircled by the mad-dog stares of five hundred prisoners in the yard. Men press against the bus, searching for friends and enemies, for "new booties." I scan faces for Smiley.

"Simpson," shouts a six-foot-five pig standing outside the bus.

"Nine One." I rise from my backseat and struggle with my chains to move down the aisle and leave the bus.

Another CO calls, "Simpson. Step over here, please."

I step toward him and he removes the shackles from around my waist and the cuffs from my wrists and ankles. I maneuver around a group of Nazi prisoners covered with swastika tattoos. I have purchased an unobstructed view of the inmates surrounding the bus. As I search the crowd, a familiar voice shouts, "Cee."

"Sad, whassup, cuz?" Sad and I were in Soledad together.

"Cee. You went home and came back?"

"Yeah. He did," another voice interrupts.

I look past Sad and there's Smiley standing behind Sad the entire time, waiting for his opportunity to surprise me. I inspect his face for answers.

"Cee Loc," he doesn't smile. He doesn't meet my eyes, either. "I apologize for that shit at the county, cuz. Homies wasn't supposed to do you like that. I'ma come holler at you when you get to Fish Row."

I remember the last time he said someone was going to "holler" at me and I frown. I stare in Smiley's face, curious and confused, studying the lidded eyes, the lifting of one eyebrow, the shift of his weight, and the crossing of his wrists. I hunt for signs of sincerity, a sense of love or sorrow or guilt. Nothing. He reveals nothing.

If he's lying to me, we're adversaries. And I don't want us to become enemies.

"Cee Loc," Smiley continues. "Man, I know you don't think I told those niggas to get at you like that. Cuz, I . . ."

A pig escorts me and the other prisoners into a building, down a corridor, up four flights of stairs to the fifth tier, A-Side. This is orientation row, "Fish Row." I'm housed in a two-man cell. Prison policy prohibits different ethnicities from being housed together for security reasons, which benefits the minorities in prison—the Mexicans and Whites—and is a disappointment to the Blacks who are the majority. In the L.A. county jail, Blacks oppress Mexicans and Whites. Life is turned upside down and they're the weaker ethnicities, and so they are robbed, beaten, raped on a regular basis. Some have been raped and robbed so many times during their county stay, they dread the sight of a Black man. The Whites are preyed on the most. At last the Blacks have their "get back" for the centuries of White oppression.

Prison housing policy means the Whites can sleep and do their time in relative peace. For Blacks it means we can no longer turn the wheels of slavery back and do the White man as has been done to us for four hundred years.

I think about the streets, our families, our friends, which seem a million miles away. I think about Gina and figure by the time I get out she'll be married and have more kids. She probably won't give me the time of day. Even so, I dream of being with her.

The day after my arrival, I'm dressed, standing at the cell door and waiting breakfast release when the emergency alarm roars. Before it reaches its full decibels, I hear running feet and two gunshots.

I never make it to breakfast. The institution is placed on lockdown. We're fed sack lunches for the next month. A twenty-six-year-old brotha was stabbed to death for fraternizing with the pigs, who are being shunned for their shooting of a Black inmate.

This is what I enter when I'm sent to Folsom. Before I had been there a day, a murder takes place and we're on lockdown. A warm welcome.

So I number the squares on my chessboard and play with other Crips over the tier. I don't win more than ten games out of a hundred—a symbol of my accomplishments in the ever so serious game of life. One morning, Vertis, housed below me, tells me to send him a line. I tear sheets to shreds and tie them together and send it down to his tier. He ties a book on the end and shouts up, "Cee. This'll help get your game back."

When I pull in the sheet rope, I retrieve a book on chess. "Good lookin' out, Vert," I shout down to him.

"You know how we do it, cuz."

During the month lockdown, I'm moved to my new cell on the third tier on B-Side. There are four other Crips on the tier and they brief me on the Crip rules: Quiet period with no talking or playing the radio after nine o'clock Sunday through Thursday. For security, no wearing shower shoes outside of the cell. No fraternizing with the pigs. No "taking off" on enemies without notifying a homie first. No socializing with the Mexican Mafia or Southside Mexicans. Stay strapped outside the cell. Keep security on homies in the shower or on the telephone. No using the word "nigga" over the tier or in public. I can handle this.

My cell provides me with a view of the visiting-room patio. When bored, I sit on the edge of my bunk and gaze at the people from the free world. The visitors wait in the long lines before entering the inside visiting room or patio where I study their interactions with their loved ones. I can't see the women's faces, but can tell by their clothes who they're coming to see. Those with long dresses and hair past their shoulders are here for a White; those with khaki pants, inexpensive jewelry, and tons of makeup are here to visit a Mexican; those in designer clothes, 14-karat gold, and no makeup are here to visit a Black; those with long hair in ponytails and wearing Indian national attire are here to visit Native Americans. When I see a sista, I scoop her with critical attention, wishing like hell she's coming to visit me. Each one does her hair differently, each set of breasts, outlined by a sweater or hidden in billowing fabric, is different. I wonder if her nails are polished and note how she tilts her head, or leans forward on her elbows toward the man she visits.

No one had visited me during my last term, and only Gina visited me in the L.A. county jail. No one at all visits me here. I never understand why, but I don't ask, either. I assume people don't give a fuck about me. What else can I think?

Looking out the window at a sista with a pink sweater and jaunty walk that accentuates the balls of her ass is exactly what I'm doing when Smiley stops by.

"Whassup, Cee Loc?" His voice is soft but wary. Blue bandanas hang from both his back pockets.

Part of me surges with joy at the sight of his broad, brown face. But I shoot him a glare. "Man, don't give me that shit. You know what's up."

"Ah, homie, I—" he starts to apologize.

But I cut him off. "Why'd you have them niggas do that shit to me?"

"They wasn't supposed to. I tol' Don Don to get down wit' you 'cause you stole those shoes and Big T said you gave him a snitch jacket."

"I didn't take those fool's shoes. T-Dog took 'em. I got the buster's shoes back for him. Ask Bomb. As far as Big T. Come on, cuz, he's soft. Point blank. And he may have ratted me out." We've been over this before.

"You can't just trip on T with no facts. Cuz is the only one out there keepin' shit goin'. You know how many guns cuz put in the hood?" Smiley's lips form a straight line. I'm not warmed by his affection and bounteousness. His charisma is spent.

"Doesn't make him a rider. Or above the law."

"I'm just saying cuz is loyal and deserves a fair shot like everybody else. Now if you got paperwork with his name on it, he'll be dealt with. But you can't be putting him under the gun like that."

"I never said he snitched on me. But it's him or Li'l Dog. One of 'em. G thinks it's Big T."

"G's biased. Cuz likes you more 'en T." He steps back and crosses his arms.

My eyes burn, but I turn them instantly cold, hard, dry by narrowing my lids. He's always gone out of his way to protect Big T. Perhaps there's some sort of dark secret between them. I shake my head, unable to figure out why he chose Big T over me, praised him like he's a king when I know him to be a coward. "I'm tellin' you, something'll happen in the 'hood and fool'll crumble and you'll get another complaint. Watch."

"I'll get at Bomb and ask cuz 'bout the shoes. If that's true, then the homies lied to me."

"That's not the point." I punch my palm. Rage obliterates my sadness and clouds my mind. I inhale. *Don't show nothing,* I tell myself. "The point is, how could you believe them without asking me first? How'd you decide my fate without talkin' with me? How'd you get so close to them niggas?" *It would be easy for me to hurt Smiley,* I think. I'm a man now, as strong as he is, now. I study his folded arms bulging his biceps, his shoulders stretching the fabric of his tee shirt, the knuckles protruding on his broad hands. I could punish him. I swallow to control my temper.

But I love him.

We stare at each other, my head jutted close to his face. I see the bursting tension in his arms, the readiness. *If I hurt him, how would I remain with his, our family?* *G and Gina. How could I live with myself?*

He clears his throat. "I only did what I was supposed to, being in charge. I couldn't let the fact we're road dogs bias my decision. I couldn't show no favoritism. I didn't tell them *all* to jump you." He looks down, shakes his head slowly, his lips slightly open and moist. He seems remorseful, but he could be playing me. His expression is new so I can't read it.

"When you're in charge, you're supposed to do what's right," I bark at him. "I was disciplined unjustly and you were used as Monster Ken's and Big T's tool. He paid those niggas off." I point my forefinger to the ceiling, holding it up like a warning. "Big T'll show his cowardice."

"You gotta let the other homies see Big T's softness. Once they see it, if they see it, they'll deal with cuz."

"No one should tell you shit about me." We're inches from each other's face. "You know me better than anyone. Anyone in the world." And as I say this I realize how true it once was and I how disappointed I am in the limits of his knowledge. *That's his betrayal. I thought he knew me, but he didn't. How little our time on the street together means to him.*

"You have to let the county shit go. You can't bring that shit up here."

"Hey. You. Get away from the cell and clear the tier," a pig bellows from the gun walk.

Smiley steps back. "Let me roll. But I'll get at you on the yard, Loved One." He throws the Harlem Crip sign, waits for me to respond.

"Yeah." I turn away.

The blue flags sway with his glide.

I climb on my bunk and resume watching the visitors, rolling his words in my mind. *Once they see it, if they see it, he'll be dealt with.*

The visitors straggle out, drifting away from the gate, disseminating in the parking lot. I watch a sista wipe a tear with her hand, reach in her purse for some tissue, and blow her nose. She hitches her purse strap higher and walks away looking at the ground. She reaches her car, a gray sedan, throws her purse on the passenger seat, and gets in. The sedan backs up, stops as though reluctant to continue, and then rolls toward the free world. She's going to miss somebody. She knows it already. A piece of me goes with her.

A few days later in the yard, Smiley gives me the information on the Crips and introduces me to the members of the set. Smiley is in command of the Crips. He explains there's a conflict between various factions of the Crips occurring. Big BJ, who I heard about from Pup when we were in Palm Hall, had been stabbed by two members of the CCO. He was disciplined for snitching on one of the generals of the BGF who had been a comrade of George Jackson's in the 1970s. A trial was held by the central figures of the CCO during which he was found guilty, forced to step down as general, and a hit ordered. Rumor has it that the story was contrived to get BJ out of position because he was gathering too much power and threatening to leave CCO and take his soldiers with him. Talib, my homie and also a member of CCO, voted for BJ's discipline. Smiley thought Talib should have lost voting privileges because he and Big BJ had been road dogs and were from the same set. Once you join CCO, you are no longer a member of a set and are no longer privileged to certain information regarding your old set, but those loyalties die hard.

Both Smiley and Yog are extremely loyal to Big BJ. Yog had even put in work for him two days before his release date. This act of loyalty earned Yog enormous respect. Because of this, Smiley and Yog are allied against Talib. They decide a hearing should be held to decide Talib's fate.

The meeting is held in the month of July. The screaming sun scatters knife-edged shadows over the yard. It's so humid we're shellacked with sweat and irritable as hell, looking to vent anger. Talib cannot get to the rec yard so he sends a letter in his defense. It's noon and the shade is narrowed to sporadic slivers, so we drip sweat dots that spread on the cement. We stand together in the blinding light while Talib's letter is passed around to be read and considered. Two people have read it.

Smiley snatches it from the third man's fingers, kindles a match with his fingernail. The letter's corner burns blue, then explodes in orange flames. "Fuck what that nigga got to say." Burnt paper trembles before floating to the ground.

As the final carbon fragments hover and sink, the emergency alarm roars. In another section of the yard, a pig has been assaulted. Everyone on the yard is strip searched, escorted to their cell, and placed on lockdown until August.

In prison, August is celebrated. During August, Marcus Garvey was born (August 17, 1887), Jesse Owens won the gold medal in Berlin (August 9, 1936), Alex Haley, author of *Roots* and *Malcolm X*, was born (August 11, 1921), Edith Sampson was appointed first Black delegate to the UN (August 24, 1950), Ervin "Magic" Johnson was born (August 11, 1959), the March on Washington and Martin Luther King's dream speech occurred (August 28, 1963), the Watts riot ignited (August 11, 1965). But what turns August into Black August is the August 7, 1970, seizure of the Marin County courthouse by Jonathan Jackson, George Jackson's little brother. He entered a courtroom, attempted to free three Black convicts, one of whom was on trial, armed the convicts and took five hostages, and died a few minutes later in a hail of bullets. Only one man survived: Ruchell Magee, still secreted in solitary somewhere in the California prison system. One year and two weeks later, George Jackson was killed by prison guards for an alleged escape attempt.

Crips celebrate Black August by forming study groups and reading George Jackson's writing. During this Black August, the Black August of 1986, Smiley stabs Talib as discipline for Big BJ's assault, justifying it as a sentence given during the hearing in the yard. While walking away from the act and toward the basketball court, two goon squad COs cuff Smiley, who's caught with the weapon and hauled to the Security Housing Unit—the hole. Later that day, I pass Talib in a long line of prisoners shackled from the waist down being transported to SHU. Talib has gauze taped around his left arm. Other than the bright white tape on his brown arm, he appears uninjured.

A few weeks later, I receive an order from Smiley to stab two Crips for going against his decision to discipline Talib. I'm in the crossfire. I lay on my bunk, flipping through my photo album, and there's Gina's picture next to a photo of Huckabuck, Tina, and Li'l Huck, all with wide grins.

I turn over Smiley's letter. It's written in pencil, each word initiated with a flourish of high triple loops and ended with a swirl. I don't think Smiley should have disciplined Talib, especially without allowing all of us to read his defense letter. He repeated with Talib what he did to me in the Crip Module: judging without investigation. He'd become so arrogant in his own power, he thought he was above the law. I don't want too rip the fragile cord between us but can't blindly follow him.

I reread Smiley's note and print my reply. *I will not have any member of the set stabbed behind a decision that you made without everyone's input. You were my road dog on the street. But here, I have to stand for what I believe. I won't get involved. You're completely wrong in stabbing Talib. Plain and simple.*

A few days later, I receive another kite with his flowery handwriting. This time the loops on the paper almost eclipse the letters. *Once a Harlem. Always a Harlem. CCO or not. Talib's in violation for his part.* It's unsigned.

Doesn't he see this as a duplication of what he did to me? Is he testing me, hoping I'll accept his order, thus acquiescing to his authority to have had me beaten? Is he checking if my loyalty to him continues and my desire to please him prevails over self-protection? Or is he playing a version of Al Capone's game and assessing if he now owns me? I let these possibilities revolve in my mind as I light a cigarette and turn his letter over, no longer seeing the treacherous sway of soft curlicues.

What if this request is his testing the depth of the rift in our relationship? And what is his commitment to principle and honor?

Ultimately it doesn't matter. He's right. *Staying true to your own principles is more important than relationships.* I touch the ember of my Camel to the center of his letter and let it curl into ash.

I don't agree, I print back.

We sever all ties.

THIRTEEN

Reality Hits: War and Depression

My vanity is as vast as the scope of a dream, my heart is that of a tyrant, my arm is the arm of the Executioner. It is only failure of my plots that I fear.
—Eldridge Cleaver, *Soul on Ice*

IN ORDER TO RESTORE UNITY AND PREVENT SITUATIONS LIKE Talib and Smiley from recurring, I remove myself from the influence of the CCO and the BNO and simultaneously separate myself from tribalism. By severing ties with Smiley, only my set and the ideals of Cripism connect me with others. If we reaffirm our ideals, stick with goals, follow rules and regulations, our loyalty and team love will return. All fall, each evening, I inform homies about my decision, writing letters to the men I know in other prisons. My goal is to stabilize the Crips, to set down principles that govern our behavior. To my surprise, Don Don joins us. Jockeying between the various factions occurs as each set mends alliances. A number of stabbings, resignations, and rejoining transpires. Eventually, every member of the Harlem set joins with me except for Talib. Soon we're united and strong. Peace reigns. There's no tribalism. CCO has disbanded and Crip unity is restored. We concentrate on ensuring everyone is educated about the movement.

Principles will make us strong, I say. Loyalty and love to your own. Don't talk about your homie behind his back. Don't tell others our business. Don't disagree in public. No snitching. Exercise. Keep security for yourself. Keep security for each other, including standing post if someone is on the phone. You'll see, I tell them, we'll be united. Everyone else will fear and respect us.

Some of the fellas don't like my strict, principle-oriented approach and plant a knife in my property. An officer finds it and I'm sentenced to a twelve-month SHU program and taken to the hole.

The next day, I receive a letter with unfamiliar handwriting on the envelope. Inside is a beige folder with a picture of a skyline of bright lights on the cover. I open it to see a photograph of Huckabuck, smiling. On the other side is his obituary.

Huckabuck dead?

I read the prayers and mention of his parents, Tina, and Li'l Huck. Immobile in the middle of my cell, I grip Huckabuck's photo and let the tears wet my face, my tee shirt. His sister encloses a note saying he was shot in front of Tina's house. *Me and my mother were told that a guy named Way-Out put a thirty-thousand-dollar contract out on Huck for robbing him. I'm not sure if it's true though. None of Huckabuck's homeboys will tell me anything cause they think I'll go to the police. My whole family is stressed out behind what happened. But me, I can't believe it. It doesn't seem real that my little brother is dead.*

I hold Huckabuck's obituary, staring at his picture, and cry.

I don't know how long I stand. Vaguely, I hear joot balls slide in my cell. Vaguely, I hear rats rush the food. My tee shirt is chilled with my tears. And then I kick out the food, lay on my cot, and sleep.

I wake in a fury. Muthafuckin' Way-Out. I remember when he offered me ten thousand dollars to break a man's legs after I was released from prison. I wish I had told Huckabuck. Would Huckabuck have robbed him then? Probably not. But if he had, he would not have let Way-Out live to put a contract out on him. I could have done something to save his life. Huckabuck dead. Loyalist and an elite soldier. The nicest person you'd ever want to meet, but if you crossed him, he'd get you. He was a killer. A real killer, not some cat perpetrating the fraud.

Now what? I want to go on a search-and-destroy mission. I want to avenge his life.

Huckabuck dead? I still can't believe it.

But I'm in the hole, isolated from the enemy, trapped in a mass of steel and concrete. No one to talk to. I cannot even vent my anger. All I can do is gaze at the obituary; I can do nothing but cry. Huckabuck was only twenty years old and had just fathered a son.

I begin to warehouse my thoughts and look at those around me more carefully. Once I felt so united with the set, as though we were fingers on the same fist; now I struggle to figure out the similarities between me and my homies. A few of the men stay true to the ideals and avoid favoritism, homosexuality, and cowardice. But there's something missing. As a unit we lack goals and aspirations. We're not bonded. We don't put Crips above self. Now that I've reestablished unity, we're at a standstill, our energy unchanneled. In spite of remaining physically fit and reading books on Black history, we fail to evolve. I struggle to figure out what's wrong. My only answer is remaining faithful to the rules.

I start drafting a list of goals, but as I do this, two officers force me from the cell, search it, find the list of goals, and confiscate it. Three hours later, I'm told to roll it up and am transferred to New Folsom Security Housing Unit.

New Folsom opens in August 1986. The worst of the worst are sent there from all over the state of California. At twenty-one, I'm one of them, sent on the second bus. My cell's concrete walls are so thick my own voice bounces around and returns to me in a slight echo. The door is made of steel, six and a half feet high with a small Plexiglas window. It's electric, with a pressure-controlled mechanism. Fresno Shorty moves in my cell the next week and with his property in the cell, voices no longer echo. Since Shorty is a Crip associate, we know some of the same men. He's finishing up the last four months of a three-year bid, sentenced for dealing crack, and then to a SHU program.

True to his name, he's short, about five feet two inches and stocky. No scars. No tattoos. He's brown skinned, hair cornrowed. He breathes with his mouth open and, in between his words, I hear rattles in his chest, bubbling up his throat. "You have asthma?" I ask.

"How'd you know, cuz?" His cheeks are puffy.

"You sound like my brother. He has asthma."

"Yeah, my medicine's in the gun tower." He jerks his head toward the tower, then picks up a stack of pictures and starts showing me his collection of women.

Shorty and I create a routine, exercising every morning, studying, writing letters, and reading until dinnertime. After dinner, we practice our Kiswahili and share old war stories. I can do my own cornrows, but Shorty's fingers fly through my hair. We're allies, so we braid each other's hair as we tell stories. Mine are about my exploits with Huckabuck. As I talk, the reality of his murder dims. It's just like it always is when I'm in prison, except I don't get his letters. Shorty's war stories are invariably about women who initially aren't interested in him, but because of his flashy lines, creative tales, and persistence inevitably succumb to his charms. And just as he gets them, trouble starts. An ex, crazy mother, or collection agency. Some of his stories are hilarious; some have a moral at the end.

One night, we're watching TV, a preview comes on for *New Jack City,* and there's Ice T. "Hey. Look. There's Tray. Ice T. He's my homie."

"Hey, I know him," Shorty's breath rasps.

I'm not shocked to see him on TV. "He always had so much talent," I say. "Him makin' it, feels like all of us have made it."

Shorty watches the preview and nods.

At eight P.M., it's time for Shorty's medicine—his usual pills and the inhaler. A Medical Technical Assistant (MTA), Sam, arrives with his pills. The inhaler, encased in an aluminum canister, is a security risk housed in the gun tower under the watchful eyes of the pigs. When the pills don't keep his breathing easy, we bang on the steel door for his inhaler. Some officers come quickly and respectfully give him his medicine. Others refuse to be bothered. Then, we bang on the door for hours. Peering out the small window, we see them look at us like two animals in a cage and fall out laughing. It's hilarious to them, but not to Shorty, whose wheezing deepens. One night, he falls on the floor and pleads, "Please, man. Please. I can't breathe."

"Shut the fuck up and go to sleep," the officer, Berger, screams back.

The pigs target Shorty because he stabbed a White boy. Shorty had been talking on the phone and the White guy, waiting his turn, disconnected the line and called Shorty a bitch. Shorty retaliated by stabbing him four times with a nine-inch piece of steel. But that's inmate prison politics and should not involve the officers. Racial identity takes precedence over status, I guess. Every morning, Sam, who's White, about forty-five and a happy-go-lucky sort of guy with a tentative smile and a huge potbelly, brings Shorty his medication. Sam and I usually have an extensive conversation about sports. One day, I complain about the guards in the gun tower.

"I can't do nothin' 'bout them," Sam shrugs. "Don't worry 'bout them, they'll get justice in the end," he adds.

"Life ain't like that," I tell him.

The next morning, Sam brings Shorty an inhaler to keep in his cell. "Tired of your complaining," he says as he tosses it to him.

To keep the gun tower sadists from becoming suspicious, we continue our ritual of pounding on the door. They point at us, continue laughing and joking. They don't know the joke is on them.

Prison politics shuffles the security of our routine. The unity between the White pigs and the White prisoners is destroyed when a White pig manhandles a White Aryan Brotherhood shot-caller. War is declared, which escalates to the point that the pigs beat Blue, the leader of the ABs and kill his second-in-command. The ABs strike back by shooting a correction officer on the highway. The pigs then pass out false passes, ducats, to the dentist and law library. Once the prisoner is outside of the building where there are no witnesses, the officers Taser him and beat him bloody. The Taser is a stun gun that leaves no evidence. White men refuse to leave their cells.

The pigs retaliate by searching cells. Everyone's cells. One night, Shorty and I are cuffed and ordered out of our cell. Officers completely trash our personal property. Shorty's color television is smashed; my new radio is broken to plastic shards under the heel of a boot. Most unfortunate of all, they find Shorty's hidden inhaler and confiscate it. I write Gina and she sends money for a new radio, which I order immediately but don't receive for three weeks. Shorty has only three months left and decides not to order another television. He's more concerned about his health than his entertainment.

Every night, we have to pound on the door for Shorty's medication, his wheezing increasingly frantic. Meanwhile, the anger between the AB and the officers spreads to all of us. Since everyone's property was trashed, no one has the materials to make a piece. We begin saving plastic ice-cream cups, which can be melted and crafted into a shank. The pigs pillage our cells again and the plastic cups are seized, the man holding them written up for conspiracy to manufacture a weapon.

We protest our treatment by flooding our cells and day room with water from the toilets. In response, they cut off the water. We refuse to eat and throw our food trays on the building floor, walls, everywhere we can. They end our protest by forcing us to lie on our bunks, face down. Then they open the tray slots and toss sack lunches inside the cells.

We're in a no-win situation, so we let things slide back to normal. The pigs still ransack our cells. For Shorty and me, eight P.M. is banging-on-the-door time.

One night, Shorty rehearses his lines to use on women when he's released. He picks up his stack of photos, remarkably intact in spite of the persistent destruction of our property, points to a White woman, and says, "She didn't wanna go for me. But I brought her 'round. 'You never had a man like me,' I tol' her. 'Don't know what men can be till you have me.' I guess it worked 'cause it got her curious. She'd never been with a brother before." He flips to another one, a brown-skinned woman with a jeri curl. "Your father musta stolen the stars from the sky when he made your eyes."

We both bust out laughing and he falls to the ground. I figure he's playing. "Come on, man, get up from the ground."

"Bang on the door."

I pound the door; the steel resounds with thuds that start to echo a chime but terminate in dullness.

Shorty rolls on the ground, wheezing.

"He needs his inhaler. He's having an attack," I yell.

In the gun tower are Berger and a new officer. Maybe the new man will respond. I bang faster.

Shorty starts coughing like a child in a house fire. I kick the door as hard as I can and shout, "Hey my cellie's dying in here, man! Please man, he needs his inhaler."

Berger rises from his seat, walks over to the control panel, and cracks the door. I prepare to exit the cell and walk to the tower. He slams the door shut and busts out laughing. "Fuck off," he screams.

I increase the tempo of my hammering, hoping he'll show some compassion, but he ignores me. Shorty's sweat leaves dark spots under his arms, on his chest. Drops bead on his forehead, his upper lip as he gasps, his mouth opening and closing. "You alright, homie?"

Strangled by his coughs and rumbly gasps, he whispers, "I can't breathe."

"Help. Help." I pound on the door, keep pounding on the door. I search for something harder than my hand, but there's nothing. Shorty lies on the floor. I beat it for three hours. Finally four officers come to the door. "What's wrong?"

"My cellie's having an asthma attack. He needs his inhaler."

One of the officers notifies Sam, who brings his medication, but Shorty's condition worsens. Sam says he's too far into the attack and needs a different medication.

I resume hitting the door. Finally, the pigs return. They make me stick my hands through the tray slot and cuff me. I move to the rear of the cell before they rack the door. They pick Shorty off the ground, tussle him onto the stretcher, manhandling him. They cuff him to the stretcher.

Shorty's talking crazy, crazy partly 'cause he's so hard to understand between the wheezes, the gasps, the sucking of air in the middle of a word. "Whats'all. Let me. Die. In here?" he pants.

A pig tugs at the cuff, fastening him to the stretcher.

Shorty takes in all the air he can. "You guys going to let me die in here?"

An officer grabs him by the throat and starts choking him. "Shut the fuck up."

"I got asthma," Shorty wheezes.

One pushes his shoulder as they start carrying him. I watch as they lug him out of the section door.

The guntower CO looks down at me and grins.

"Po-lice killer muthafucka," I trumpet back at him.

I lay on my bunk but can't sleep. Instead, I toss and turn, thinking about Shorty.

The next morning, I hear a voice through the vent. It's the Mexican guy in the next cell who always treated me like a person. "Ey, Cee."

I'm not supposed to speak to members of the Mexican Mafia, but I get off my bunk and stand on the toilet so I can talk into the vent. "Whassup?"

"Hey, homes. I'm not trying to get in your business or nothin' but wha's goin' on?"

"Hear us banging?"

"For hours, homes. I'm not wishing nothin' bad, but, I saw how the pigs did your homeboy last night. Last time I saw something like that it was my homeboy they dogged out. Took him out of the cell after midnight and never brought him back."

"What you mean?"

"He died, man. They killed him. They took him out real late. He was having a seizure, transported him to the hospital. He never returned. Heard he was killed by the pigs for assaulting a cop, the case that sent him to the pen."

"What? Shorty gonna be alright. He just has asthma."

"I'm not wishing nothing bad on your cellie, homes."

I push away his warning as paranoia and then hear sounds of jangling keys as doors open and close and prisoners are escorted to the yard. I start my push-up burpy routine. The pigs make it to my cell and inform me I'm on CTQ (confined to quarters).

"Why?"

They shrug and walk away.

"You punk bitches. Stupid rednecks. Tell me why."

"You'll get ten more days CTQ for that."

"Fuck you and CTQ," I shout.

I finish my burpy routine and do some additional push-ups. I'm calm now and figure I'm CTQ for trumpeting "Po-lice killer" at the gun tower the previous night.

The following morning, I wake to the sound of "pill call" announced over the PA. Shorty has not returned from the hospital. *Somethin' ain't right,* I think. An hour later, the lieutenant comes to my door. "Hey. Simpson. Do me a favor."

"What's that?"

"I need your cellie's phone book. He got a phone book in there?"

"I think so."

"I need you to get it."

I start searching through Shorty's property.

"Why? What happened?"

"He's going to be alright. You might as well roll it all up. He's going to be alright."

I roll up Shorty's property, taking special care with his gallery of women, and hand it to the lieutenant.

That night, Sam walks right by my cell and I call his name. He backs up. "You alright, Simpson?" His face is serious as he crosses his arms over his belly, his legs slightly spread, and his demeanor withdrawn and cautious.

"Why'd you ask me that?"

He closes his eyes and grimaces and starts to walk away.

"Where you goin', man?" I say it with a pleading tone in my voice.

He returns, his face now very pale, looking over his shoulders to see if anyone watches him. "You didn't hear what happened? No one tell you?"

"Whadaya mean?"

He twitches like he wants to run and says, "I'll let the officers tell you."

"Fuck all that shit. I ain't no muthafuckin' kid. You tell me."

"Calm down. Calm down." He places his finger to his lips. His hair is a fringe above his ears.

"You gonna tell me what's up?" But my voice is low now, almost a whisper that comes out as a hiss because of my coiled anger and fear.

He stands close to the door and whispers. "You didn't hear this from me, Simpson. Your cellie died yesterday. You saw an officer choke him. By the time the ambulance got to the prison, your cellie was dead."

"What?" I shout.

"Calm down." Sam steps back from the cell, faces his palm toward me. "I didn't have anything to do with it." He marches down the tier, looking back and forth over his shoulders as if I could open my cell and chase him. All I can do is sit on my bunk.

Shorty dead. Gone. He was so close to freedom. He only had a few more months. I hear again his chuckles while telling about one of his girlfriends, the soft, helpless sound of his wheezing. His voice surrounds me in our cell as I stare at the wall. I cry for all he didn't get to do. And cry for myself that I'll never see him again. *They killed him.* But I don't think it with anger, just loss.

Eldridge Cleaver's *Soul on Ice* is on my bookshelf. I grab it, absentmindedly, and as though a message to me, it opens to page sixty-nine. There I read James Baldwin's quote: . . . *the white man is himself in sore need of new standards, which will release him from his confusion and place him once again in fruitful communion with the depths of his being.*

Shorty was killed by White sadistic callousness. Then I think about my own life and see once again Pete's twisted face as he beats me with his belt. Pete, my White stepfather. I intensified his beatings, my mother's beatings, the Crips initiation, the Bloods shootings. My violence cleansed me of my victimization. And now, disarmed and caged, I have no recourse. I begin to cry. Cry for Shorty. Cry again for Huckabuck. *Why are so many people around me dying? Why isn't my pain ever considered? Doesn't anyone think I feel, too?*

My sadness changes to anger. I think about the violence that Whites have done us, resounding throughout Black communities where we retaliate against each other. We use the violence we learned, violence, learned from the White man, and just like we escalate the violence perpetrated on us to feel invulnerable, safe and strong against the Bloods, we escalate the violence shown us by Whites. It originates with the White slave master, like the sadistic torture of busters in the Crip module, of Loco done by Al Capone. With nowhere to go but our own communities, we vent our rage at the Whites, at their racism on each other. And then as it gathers momentum, it takes on a velocity of its own.

It's how I escape from reality. But you cannot fight reality's violence with more violence. We're not innately more violent or murderous than White people. Yes, the murder rate is higher for Blacks than for Whites in the United States. But you know what? In Africa, the murder rate is the same as it is in Europe. In Ghana, the part of West Africa from which we were stolen, the murder rate is 2.1 per one hundred thousand. In Denmark, it's 4.9.

So, we're not innately more violent than any other people. Something happened to us. It was slavery, and following that, a century and a half of unremitting racism and increasing income disparity between Whites and us, because income disparity is associated with crime. The pace of income inequality is growing faster in California than the rest of the United States, and the gap between the rich and poor is greatest in L.A. County.

A week later my Aunt Bertha dies of blood cancer. A few days later, a homeboy is killed in a drive-by. I'm trapped in prison. *Trapped and cornered. My life is in their hands. The pigs can take a life and it's nothing. They won't even have to answer questions.* My strength, my courage, my bravery can't keep me safe. I put Cleaver back on my shelf.

The next day, the very next day, I receive a letter with an obituary telling me my Aunt Deedee died. Deedee tried to show me life by taking me to Knotts Berry Farm and to amusement parks. Once we drove north from Los Angeles and walked around in a forest of such thick trees it was dusk in daytime because no sun could get through. Deedee opened her house to me when I was released from prison, grinned her welcome, her arms wide as she sat in her wheelchair. She was the only person who understood the Colton side other than Grandmother Louise. Now she's gone, too. *I'm so far away from home, any home.*

I give one of the officers her obituary to prove she has died so I can use the phone. Later that day, when I'm in the yard, I see a trail of the obituary. Little bits of beige paper, crumbs trailing from my cell to the yard. The officer ripped and sprinkled Deedee's obituary from my cell to the prison yard. The pieces stun me in their meanness and his inability to feel compassion, to even define me as a human being, and I realize once again how vulnerable I am in this place of cold steel and concrete.

I sink to my bed and stare at the books on my shelf: Malcolm X, Eldridge Cleaver, Mao Tse-tung. I just stare at the books. For hours. I get lost in examining the turquoise and cobalt words, on the spines, on the covers. Blue. The color of the sky, the sea, Crip colors. Finally, my body can no longer sit and stare, so I pass out, and what seems like days later jerk awake in the middle of a dream that vanishes with the thought, *What's the point?* And I light a cigarette.

I can't eat. I quit exercising. I stay in my cell. I'm safe here. Some days I don't sleep until my body gives out and I sleep for days. Then wakeful for days till the cycle repeats itself. I cry.

I light a cigarette and get absorbed in my thoughts, thoughts I now can't even capture to remember. The cigarette burns until its ember hits my fingers and rouses me from reverie. I stab it out and light another one and continue my examination of my books. I'm still on CTQ. That's okay. No one pays attention to me.

I stare at the steel door, smudges on the polish from Shorty's pounding, my pounding. The door becomes a relic, as though Shorty left a part of himself on it. One smear seems to resemble his puffy face with his firm jaw. His sweat, his flesh is on that door. I cry some more, not even bothering to wipe away my tears.

Then, two months or so after Shorty's death, I'm escorted to the yard. Men corral around me, "Cee, you all right, man?"

I sit.

"We worried."

Everyone's concerned about me, but I can't quite figure out why.

"You okay, cuz?"

I can't digest what they're saying. Or why they're saying it. So I don't answer. Then it's time to go back to the cell where I look at the spines of my books, examine Shorty's face on the steel door, think about Huckabuck and Deedee. Finally I fall asleep. I'm like that, that depressed for four months. Maybe a little more. But I don't realize I'm depressed. I just float between the covers and letters of my books and study the smears on the steel door and smoke. No one visits me. Even Gina does not visit me. There's no point for her to drive five hours for a five-minute visit behind glass. Now, I'm glad. I don't want her to know how I am. She would think I'm weak.

My pants slide down me. One day, I look at my arm and notice, vaguely, how narrow it's become. I'm wasting away. But don't care. I lie back and examine the wall. A glob of paint wrecks the smoothness of the concrete. Little whirls form ripples around it. I study the pattern the ripples make as they edge outward, wondering if they cover the wall, pondering how far the consequences, the influences of that glob of paint travel. Does it affect the air currents that are forced to bump slightly to move over it? That's what I think about when I'm not thinking over and over about Huckabuck, Shorty, Aunt Bertha, Aunt Deedee, and my home-boys' deaths.

Meanwhile, months go by and it becomes winter 1987. During my absence, two other Crips, Big Poppa from Long Beach Insane, and Big Donut from Nine-O, handle my responsibilities conducting exercise and study classes in the SHU yard. While I watch the paint bump, the ABs surrender after months of cell ransacking, beatings. The pigs win. The ABs turn around and declare war on the Blacks.

I struggle out of my depression to face a war. What sparks the war is a tier-tender, an AB who steals a hacksaw blade from a Blood named Hurk. The ABs are desperate for weapons because of the continual cell ransacking. Hurk threatens to kill the AB. The next day, two ABs stab Hurk twice in the chest. He resists, takes the

ABs' knives, and beats both of them unconscious. Hurk is hand-cuffed, thrown on a stretcher, and transported to the hospital.

After the botched attack on Hurk, the Bloods hit back and gore an AB. The ABs retaliate.

Then the shit gets crazy. Everyone madly fabricates pieces. I'm still in and out of my daze. Not crying through each day, but not up to masterminding a war either. I inform Big Poppa of my situation and watch from the sidelines. The pigs side with the ABs and take the scrawniest Black prisoner, place him on the yard with the biggest White prisoner armed with buck knives the pigs purchased. The Whites place bets, using anything from money to push-ups. When the battle starts, pigs take potshots at the Black prisoners; they aim not only at the prisoners involved in the fighting, but those in the general vicinity.

The establishment, rather than hold the guards responsible, brings additional charges against the prisoners. Family members raise questions and file complaints about these unjustified shootings. The pigs reply that they're simply keeping the peace and securing the safety and security of the institution. The media broadcasts it; the government has its excuse to do nothing. The incidents are never investigated by outside agencies and no one is required to confirm the legality of the shootings. But I'm here. I see it. I witness it all. My depression is sufficiently lifted and I realize it's not a crazy dream, but a crazy reality. Pigs, murderous racists in disguise, get off scot-free. Crips and Bloods are shot, killed, charged with violent crimes. Domino, my homeboy, is shot in the leg; a young Crip from Hoover is shot in the face at point-blank range. Both survive.

Before anyone knows it, the entire SHU has erupted into a war between the Blacks and Whites allied with the pigs. I must protect my brothers; I must protect myself. I resume my exercising. Once again, violence is my refuge, my antidote for sadness. Once again violence rouses me from victimhood, from the seduction of obliterating unawareness.

The Whites in our building tell us that they have no beef with the Crips, just the Bloods. But I have settled into a pro-Black mindset; a Black man is a Black man—Crip, Blood, BGF—it doesn't matter any more to me. A brotha is a brotha. I tell everyone that.

Rock, a Blood in prison for killing a Crip, tells me he's going to take off on an AB and when the White boy is "booked," I can have his tier-tender job.

"Check this out, Rock. I'm a Crip. But I'm also Black and therefore I do not allow other brothas to divide themselves from me in racial situations. Deception is war," I tell him. I'm in my cell and he's talking from outside my little window. And for a moment, everything I'm reading is with me, in my head, speaking through my voice. "I believe once they're through with the Bloods they'll start in on us. Divide to conquer. The White man's way. Like what the FBI did to the Panthers and the United Slaves. Remember?"

Rock stares at me in amazement.

"So I'm with you one hundred percent. I'm not going to let those clowns put a piece in my neck."

"Cee. You sure you wanna get involved?"

"You never let another race touch one of your people. You're my people. I'm wit' you. Rather, I'm wit' the brothas."

"Righteous," Rock says as he goes off about his business.

Later that morning, we rush three ABs and dust them. A pig fires a round from his state-issued mini-14 assault rifle at Rock and yells, "Get down." The victims are removed on stretchers. I'm handcuffed, beaten, escorted to my cell. The entire building is placed on lockdown. No showers, no yard, no canteen, no law library, no visits.

And then I'm transferred to C Section. I miss Shorty and my steel door as soon as I'm told to roll it up.

FOURTEEN

Candy and a Stamp

...discover your humanity and your love...pass on the torch. Join us.
—George Jackson, *Prisons on Fire*

WHILE CARRYING MY PROPERTY FROM A SECTION TO C SEC-
tion, a gunshot blasts. The emergency alarm blares.

Blam. Another bullet.

I'm forced to lie on the floor, searched from head to toe. Then, I'm locked inside the C Section shower for three hours before I'm moved to my new cell. My cellmate tells me the pigs armed two ABs, released them to the yard, then escorted Peabody and Row there. The ABs took off on them; the gun tower officer fired two shots. Those were the two shots I heard on my way to the C Section. One bullet hit Peabody in the leg; the other hit Roe in the thigh.

Before my cellie finishes his conversation, the C Section door grinds open. I peek out of the cell window slot to see two officers escorting a man to the shower. They lock him inside and stroll from the section. When they reach the day room, a voice bellows, "You racist pigs. You'll reap what you sow." The words aren't spoken in the usual urban threatening tone; they're said as a statement, a matter of fact, and with such extreme confidence there's no need for the additional bluster of swearing.

The pig responds by giving the finger to the entire section.

A few days later, I learn that the person who spoke with such certainty and calm is political prisoner Ruchell Magee.

I learned about Ruchell Magee during Black August and knew he was in the California prison system somewhere and had been since August of 1971, when Jonathan Jackson broke him out of a Marion County courtroom in San Rafael, California. Jonathan armed him and they took five hostages, including the assistant DA and the judge, still attired in his robes. They attempted a getaway in a rented van, but it was hit with a hail of bullets that killed those inside, including Jonathan Jackson. There was only one survivor: Ruchell Magee.

The entire incident was an attempt to free Jonathan's older brother, George Jackson, who was a Black revolutionary serving a one-year-to-life sentence for a seventy-dollar gas station robbery.

The year after Jonathan was gunned down, George was killed by guards at San Quentin. The convicts who were with George, like Lafayette Rainey, have asserted that he sacrificed his own life to save them from a massacre.

Ruchell Magee is an original member of the Soledad Seven, George Jackson's comrade, a member of the Black Panther Party. His name rings volumes. When it comes to Blackness and prison politics, he's the man. He's been through it all. He received his life sentence for his part in the escape attempt and has spent the years since in maximum security.

When I hear he's in my section, I send him a kite, politely requesting his help in obtaining plastics to make knives. The war with the AB rages and the ransacking of our cells by the pigs has depleted our weapons. We are fighting a two-front war—against the AB and against the White pigs.

A few days later, a manila envelope slides under my door. Inside are a letter, a book, and two pieces of Jolly Rancher candy. I remember the letter saying, in part:

Abaragani Ndugu Cee,

I am sorry to inform you that I am not simply a political prisoner, but also an enemy of the state and the racist pigs. My new program, Saving Lives, prevents me from donating any material to you that may be fashioned to a point. However, I do not intend to stagnate your movement or prevent you from handling what, in your eyesight, needs to be handled.

I have come to realize that every man must first explore on his own before he can appreciate the wisdom of another. Thus, I have vowed to save lives. The most important thing to me is your freedom. Enclosed is a book and two pieces of candy. Inside the candy wrapper you will find two stamps. The stamps can be used to contact your family and the sentencing judge in your case. They are the only people who can better your situation.

Violence is not the answer. It cannot get you out of jail. The candy should wash the bloody taste from your mouth. Feel free to communicate with me when you get the urge.

In struggle:saving lives

Ruchell Magee

The book is *Blood in My Eye* by George Jackson. I place it in between *Soul on Ice* and *Malcolm X*. My comprehension is limited, my reading still laborious. Each word, each sentence hits a snag, but slowly I realize that vaulting each hurdle amounts to winning a race of new ideas, ideas that make sense of my environment. The books are not just covers and spines with Crip-blue lettering silently mocking me while they wait for my courage. I reread Malcolm X's autobiography. His life as a youth is much like mine. He, like me, had a thirst for money and power; he, like me, lived on the streets. When he talks about his life as Detroit Red, I'm reading about a close friend, a brotha I've grown up with. *The first step to change is accepting the fact you need to change. The second is putting trust in God.* He sounds like my Grandmother Louise. Malcolm finally gets her thoughts across.

Ruchell Magee never comes to the yard. He never goes to the shower; he does everything in his cell. Several nights a week he's greeted over the radio by station KPFA out of Berkeley. "Ruchell Magee, political prisoner, power to the people," the DJ says. So I write Ruchell my thoughts about Jackson and Malcolm. Our letters lengthen as we correspond. He asks me questions and guides my reading, which forces me to ponder and wonder. Ruchell expresses his anger at the government and its systematic institutionalized racism and the destruction of Black men.

I begin to get a vision, a vision of legions of stalwart Crips educated in social studies, our history, trained, and united. If we understood Black history, we would love each other and trust each other more. The war with the Bloods would end and we could unite to take over Los Angeles with our own businesses—grocery stores, produce markets, clothing stores, bakeries, beauty shops, attorneys, doctors, banks—and vote in our own mayor. Then Crenshaw and King would truly be our 'hood. The image is so clear to me, I can touch it.

For months, I read and write letters. Meanwhile, I stop swearing. I stop saying "nigga." I quit drinking and doing the drugs that filter to me in prison. My mind slowly clears from the marijuana and the alcohol I've taken since I was eight. I dream more. I write longer letters to Ruchell and Gina.

Then one day, Ruchell comes to the yard to talk to me. He exits his cell to talk with me about what I'm reading. He's a lanky guy with long hair that's without a touch of gray twisted into a braid dangling down his back. He's all sinew and tendons and stringy muscles, as though he doesn't need to bother with the strength of his body; it's all in his mind.

He comes right toward me, this man as tall as me who walks straight ahead with no urban sway, just straight-on walking as though the yard is his and everyone will get out of his way, which they do. He locates me and walks a direct line. His hand is bony and hard when he shakes mine. First we discuss *Soul on Ice*. And then he says, "You still have a life in front of you." His voice is a raspy baritone and his accent is slightly Southern and easy.

I look down, not wanting to meet his eyes, giving him the respect due an elder.

"Change the way you think and don't allow your anger to affect your future or your present."

Now he sounds like my father who warns me of the dire possibilities that can come from my temper. "I see your temper, 'cause it's mine. I have it," Pops told me.

"Don't dig the hole deeper. There's other ways of dealing with the White man and with his politics of hatred. I'll send you some more books, Brotha Cee." Ruchell shakes my hand again and as he returns to his cell the men divide before him, yielding him his road.

He sends me law books and refers me to Mumia Abu-Jamal and the book he wrote, *Live from Death Row*, which points out case law that remains on the books from the Dred Scott case, in which the Supreme Court stated that Africans and their free descendants have no rights that a White man is bound to respect.

In November of 1987, the war between the Blacks and Whites ends. By its conclusion, twelve prisoners have been stabbed. Eight of them are White; the other four are Black. Four prisoners are shot and one killed. All of them are Black and three of them are Crips. What does that tell you? Those statistics? They tell me volumes about America and the prison system.

I work hard to increase the unity among the Crips. We stop cursing. We don't say "nigga." We exercise. We read. Discipline. Love. Loyalty. Understanding, I tell them over and over. I'm voted in as a Crip stabilizer. But the earth signs start shifting as word gets round about my relationship with Ruchell.

An officer asks me about the kites going back and forth. "He came out of his cell to talk to you. Hasn't left in years."

I shrug his questions away, but the twinge of anxiety expands. Then, I hear that I'm considered the orchestrator of the war between the Blacks and Whites. At first I'm bemused by this rumor, then I understand that simply by siding with the Bloods, I changed the nature of the war. The pigs and the AB want the Crips to spill energy fighting the Bloods. Divide and conquer. I united us.

Sure enough, I'm stripped down and ordered to cuff up by extending my hands from the cell door slot, then ordered to back out of my cell. A six-foot-four-inch officer grabs me by the neck and jerks me. I don't say a word. I pull the other way, my muscles taut. I don't know where I'm going or why.

"We hear you starting shit." He shoves me, tugging my chains against my waist. The earth signs warned me once again, but what could I do?

"Creating shit. You started a war between the Blacks and Whites. You fucker."

A short, muscular officer punches me in the chest and I'm yanked the other way.

"What war?" I focus on tightening my muscles to lessen the pain of the punches and yanks.

The tall pig chokes me, stops when I gasp for air. "Fuck the Crips," he hisses. "You wanna be a Crip. We gonna take your ass. We gonna show you 'bout being a Crip." They heave me back and forth between them all the way to another building. I flex my muscles so they jerk me like a taut pole between them, choking and punching me as we go.

"Spread 'em," the short officer orders and begins to remove my handcuffs. "Okay, Simpson, or should I call you Cee? The first thing I'm gonna do is take off these handcuffs in case you wanna get physical."

By now, more officers have arrived. Eleven surround me. I'm ready to fight; I'm in the middle of the circle. *How do they want me to take them on? One at a time?*

Then one of them, a medium guy with gray eyes, says, "I heard all 'bout you. You're a Harlem Crips, Rollin' Thirties. You one of the head figures over there in the other building. Writing back and forth to Magee. You out there making knives, got people exercising, stabbing people."

I play stupid. I try to decipher what's going on and why. *I'm being moved away from Ruchell. They're afraid of my power and are trying to weaken my influence. They're afraid of Ruchell spreading his gospel, the gospel of Black unity.*

The gray-eyed one says, "I'm gonna tell you right fuckin' now that we don't play that bullshit down here."

Two pigs step closer to me. They're aching to beat me senseless. "Man, I—"

He interrupts. "I'm gonna let you know right now that I hate Crips. You have a problem with that?"

They're poking me with words to goad me to fight. Setting me up.

"You think you're a smart-ass, uh? If I catch you doing anything, if I hear your name ringing, if I see you looking like you're up to something, I'm going to bust your ass."

I've heard this spiel a million times. I don't dignify this with a response.

"Simpson?" calls out another officer.

I hear the wind from the short pig's punch. And duck.

He misses. "Oh, you think you're fast, huh?"

Whap. He slaps me across the face.

The odds are against me, but I could go down fighting, feeling powerful. My temper, my rage churn. Adrenaline pumps my arms, my legs. *I'm ready.* I clench my fists, tighten my jaw.

He tries to slap me again, but this time I grab his arm in midswing.

In that tenth of a second, there's the *zzzzsht* of a round being chambered above my head. I look up. Over my head on a catwalk is a man pointing a rifle at me, hoping to blow my brains out.

With that *zzzzsht* sound something clicks. Everything I've read about racism, about the institutionalized hatred of Black men, about slavery, about the redlining and the collusion between the banks and the real estate agents that formed the ghettos in the first place, about the use of prisons to reestablish slavery and diminish the threat of vigorous, powerful Black men, about how Whites killed Shorty, George Jackson, and Fred Hampton, becomes brilliantly obvious right then. Right then with the weapon aimed at my brain. Right then in my own life. In my very own life. Just like those books warn. They want to kill me; Whites with control want me, and those like me, dead; they're pushing for an excuse.

I'm a threat. I'm a threat simply because I'm Black. I'm a threat because I listened to Ruchell. I'm a threat because I'm beginning to think instead of react. I'm a threat because I united the Blacks for a war against the Whites. That's the greatest White nightmare of all. Just think what would happen if we united with the Hispanics.

It's true. It's all true, I think and a warmth and a terror flood me simultaneously as I think about our nation and my beautiful, powerful, and bedraggled Black people and the trials that lay ahead for all of us.

"Go ahead. Move. I'll blow your motherfucking brains out," he dares me.

I still inspect the pig with his rifle aimed at my skull as all these thoughts soak me. I look down and I'm punched in the face. But I know better than to react. They want to kill me. They saw me trying to organize and they made me a target. Just like they did Jackson and Malcolm and King. And I'm just li'l me. No one would bother to investigate.

I am terrified, and amazed by my own importance.

Just then a Medical Technical Assistant comes to the door. When they see him, everyone freezes. The MTA might tell. The pig with gray eyes looks at me and continues as though nothing unusual was about to happen, "You know what? You respect our house and we'll respect you. Leave us alone and we'll leave you alone. Whatever you got going on with the White boys, don't put us in your shit."

The war must have separated the White pigs from the White AB. We've divided and conquered, but won nothing.

"Don't bring that shit down here and we won't fuck with you," he continues.

They rack the doors and release me to my new cell in the second tier. I stick my arms through the tray slot and they remove the handcuffs and swagger away. I toss my things on my bunk and drink a cup of water. My throat is dry as toast.

I've been in the SHU for two years and some change. I've got thirteen more days in the hole. Just thirteen and then I can join the mainline.

The next morning a female officer strolls by. She's about five foot three, one hundred pounds, and of all things, White with deep blue eyes. Up to this point, the only White woman I'd been attracted to was Lindsay Wagner, who played the bionic woman. She was petite but powerful. I watched the show and lusted on her body, beauty, and brains, developed a crush on her and became star struck. My crush lasted until she married my uncle, became mother of his two sons, and divorced him. I hated her for a while after that, hated her for marrying another man, but, as the years passed, I realized I was being wacky. And forgot her.

And then along comes Ms. Harris reminding me of her. And here I am a prisoner and she's a guard. Here I am twenty-two years old and I haven't had sex with a woman for three years. I've managed to push the thoughts of women and sex aside and she messes all that up.

Harris's position at the prison is watch office security and escort, but she walks like a hooker strolling down Sunset Boulevard; her blonde hair reaches the middle of her back and sways back and forth with each stride. She stops to talk with the prisoners, asking about their girlfriends, families, and case appeals like we're human beings. Yeah, we're sex objects because she flirts her ass off, but she acknowledges that we're people, too.

There are other female officers; some of them flirt, and I check out their breasts and behinds but ignore their faces. But Ms. Harris is a decent-looking woman, pig or not. White or not. When she comes to my building, I scoop her up from head to toe and don't take my eyes away until she leaves. She quickens my imagination.

One morning after breakfast, I'm in the shower down from my cell and I hear the section door open. I look out the steel bars and, low and behold, here comes Ms. Harris twitching her booty with a clipboard in her hand. She stops at my cell.

"Simpson?" she calls.

"I'm in the shower," I shout back to her.

She walks down the tier to me, the tiny chain holding the pen to the clipboard swinging with her stroll just as I know her ass is switching from left to right. Looking at her, I become aroused and it begins to show. By the time she arrives at the shower door, I'm hard as a brick.

"Hi, Simpson. You got institutional mail. What's your last two?"

"Nine One." I say it quickly to cover my embarrassment.

"You want me to put it in your cell, or take it now?"

What's she talking about? Oh, the mail. "You can put it on the floor. I'll pick it up when I get out of the shower."

Right then, right in front of me, she bends completely over. She doesn't bend her knees. As she slowly leans down, the cheeks of her ass spread, her uniform trousers cling, the seam accentuating her butt cleavage. She remains open for me like that as though waiting for me and then reluctantly rises.

I remain wide-eyed, hard-on and all, and enjoy the view of her body with a huge grin.

She looks at my hard-on, then my smile, and says, "You have a lot to look at, too."

I'm shocked, exuberant, shy, nervous, overwhelmed, and completely taken aback all at once. I don't know what to do. She has disarmed me. I stand there, dick throbbing, with my mouth open.

"I'll see you when you get to the mainline, Simpson." Her eyes measure my body, survey my legs, thighs, erection, stomach muscles, arms, and face. She nods approval.

For a minute, I consider pulling her into the shower and making love to her. But I know, as does she, that prison is not the place.

After that, Ms. Harris and I become friends. We continue a teasing, secret flirtation. And then, I'm finally released from the SHU program.

I'm sent to New Folsom's Facility "B" mainline. My new home. I unpack my things: jeans, sweatshirts, Nike tennis shoes, Right Guard deodorant, Crest toothpaste, toothbrush, the new *Vibe*, *Hustler*, *Ebony* magazines, books, my green photo album, which I open on my desk to a picture of Gina, my twelve-inch TV, radio and cassettes, letters, pen, pencil, paper. All that stuff is my psychological link to the life I lost. My connection to the street.

My new cellie is from Seven-Four Hoover, under paperwork. He immediately whips out a hacksaw blade and cuts pieces of steel from the window frame. "The Blacks and Mexicans are on the verge of war," he mumbles. "I'd rather get caught with it than without it."

I like his style.

The Mexicans are in the majority here, then the Blacks. The Whites are the smallest number of prisoners. I look around at the numbers and I know we can't be bothered with set-trippin'. We can't even pay attention to the Blood-Crip war. We have to have Black unity.

Don Don and N-Dog are running the car and I'm appointed stabilizer once again. In this position, I counsel people, ensure there's no personality clashes, that each of us fulfills our obligations to the set and conforms to the rules. We can't be unified without harmony.

I settle into my new home, writing letters to Gina, and continuing to hone my body and mind. In the yard, I meet Talib, who is in the company of Monster Kody from Eight Tray. They have both broken from CCO and are functioning as Black Nationalists, having joined a new movement, the Republic of New Africa. (RNA). Together, they have adopted similar rules for their comportment as I have: no smoking, no use of the word nigga, no cursing. They exercise and read Black literature. I'm surprised seeing Kody like this because we've been bumping heads since we were both in Central Juvenile Hall and he's always exerted himself as a cat who lived to die a Crip. His reputation is based on his destruction of other Crips and not Bloods, as mine is. Talib and I have never met. I know he's Hawk's older brother. He's an OG from my set, he had been a central figure in the CCO, he voted to have Big BJ blasted at Old Folsom, and Smiley tried to stab him.

He and I talk about books. We greet each other as comrades and talk about our 'hood, laws, and politics. He lost his taste for gangbangin', he tells me, and hands me his photos of the gang. He and I are both in Vocational Electronics and sit across from each other, kicking it together during lunch break. After class, we lift weights—-all he does is chest inclines—and catch up with Monster Kody, Don Don, N-Dog. On weekends, I play basketball. Talib does burpies and attends study class with ex-members of the CCO. My life falls into a routine.

One Sunday, I'm told I have a visitor. *Who has driven all the way from South Central to see me? Grandma Louise? My father? No, he's never visited, and Huckabuck is dead.*

When I enter the visitor's room, there's Gina, wearing a yellow shirt that brings out the glow in her cheeks. She faces the door, watching for me, her fingers smoothing her hair, a bracelet of blue beads encircling her wrist, matching dangly earrings caught by her hair. She's more dressed up than I've seen her except when she's on her way to church. Her face is as slender as before the birth of her babies, so she looks like she did back when we were teenagers.

When I see her, I hesitate, then walk toward her and sit across the table.

"I wanted to surprise you." She doesn't say "Hi," she doesn't greet me, she launches right in, but her voice is whispery.

I laugh. "You my first visitor." As soon as I say it, I want to erase the words. It might seem like I feel sorry for myself. Or maybe she'll think I'm not worthy of a visit.

But a shy smile tugs at her mouth. She doesn't know what to do next. Her hair is freshly straightened and a soft bang covers one eye. She flips the strands of hair away and blinks.

I look at her. *I can't be hurt any more than I've been and here I am and here she is and we're facing each other once again.* "Well, glad you came." She's always been a good friend.

She looks away.

I contact the tip of her finger. The last time I touched her was when my hand grazed her arm as I grabbed Marcus's diaper bag. Then the helicopters came whirling, buzzing.

She looks down, embarrassed by proof of her caring and coy from my assumption of intimacy. Her shape is petite, but her bicep is evident under the smooth brownness. I know the power in her body in spite of the tiny frame and slender bones.

"So what did you do, just get in your car and drive all the way here?"

She laughs, snaps her fingers and shakes her head, and instantly she's the Gina with the bold personality and buoyant manner. "Got the thought and started driving north. Just like that."

"You sure dressed pretty for a sudden thing." I touch the end of her earring that almost hits her shoulder.

She jumped our relationship onto a new plane. We've just met instead of growing up together. Or maybe it's just that I'm so hungry. Hungry for a woman, hungry for home. And Gina always has been home.

As though she reads my thoughts, or is it that she's changing the subject and avoiding the fragile feeling trembling between us, she tells me of Marcus, who is in kindergarten now, and Antoine who is already out of diapers. She tells me how everyone is since Aunt Deedee's death. We talk of Huckabuck and G.

At first, neither one of us mentions Smiley; we avoid him. Smiley is in the hole for stabbing Talib and is on his way to do some federal time for that bank robbery. But me, not one to be too hesitant too long, just starts telling her the entire story from my point of view. I spend some time going over the events with Big T and Li'l Dog.

"Li'l Dog still using that pipe," she says and shakes her head. "Turned himself useless."

"One of 'em, Li'l Dog or Big T, ratted me out."

I go over again Smiley's betrayal. "He knew me better; we were like brothers." As my anger builds again and my voice rises, I realize I still haven't reconciled it. I tell her about Talib and how Smiley was doing the same thing to him as he did to me.

Gina listens, her face solemn, nodding. "Colton, he did wrong. Simple as that. But he's my brother and I love him. Just like you was wrong not listenin' to me and I'm here, visiting." Her eyes flash with determination.

"You not apologizing for him?" I ask.

A shadow passes her face. "He ain't me. Only I am me." Her polished thumbnail bounces off her chest. "I figure we be separate from all that."

Gina has a blithe way of resolving things, just getting rid of them like trash from a basket. Dump and forget. She changes the subject to Grandmother Louise. As she talks about Louise, I realize they've become a team working together. Each respects how helpful they are to me.

And me, I'm eager for news of home, to hear her voice, to capture every image of her, the hard muscles under the silky skin, the shining eyes, the way she nibbles on the corner of her lip when she's not sure what to say next.

At one point, she touches my face and says, "You didn't get no scars."

"Just a tiny one here," and I point to a dot that graces my jaw, slightly whiter than the rest of my skin. "You did a good job getting that glass out." It seems so long ago when she leaned over me. It seems so long ago when Huckabuck and I were gangbangin' in the jungles.

And before we know it, the visit is over.

I watch her walk away. Her slender hips move under that dress like two suns dancing together.

After that visit, I write her every day. She writes me. Our letters are my nexus; I weave my life around them, addicted to them. If I don't get one, I'm crestfallen. But I never mention that to her. Instead, I tell her casually, almost off-handedly, as a PS, that I like her letters.

She tells me she loves me. She had those kids because she likes having sex, but she loved me, always me. She didn't think to protect herself the first time. The second time, she was on the pill, she didn't know what happened, but she didn't believe in abortion. Oh, how she wishes they were mine. And then in one letter she confesses, "I've been in love with you all my life, all my life. I know I have a lot to prove, but I'll be here for you. I'll prove it by waiting for you even though you're in prison."

She visits every two weeks, driving six hours here, six hours back, leaving early in the morning, returning late at night. Sometime she flies to me and takes a taxi from the airport. She spends a lot of money, a lot of effort. She's busy demonstrating things will be different this time. Her constancy wins me and, after all, I have nothing to lose.

On her visits weekends, I escape the traumatic feeling of being trapped behind the fifteen-foot walls and constant war. The visiting room is like the end of a round to a boxer. Monday through Friday, the fighting; the chaos is nonstop. On the weekend, a bell sounds and I go to my corner, the visiting room. Then I'm in the company of someone who cares and attends my bruises.

The visiting room has vending machines with fresh water and food. Once the visit is over, I tighten up my gloves, put my mouthpiece back in, and go back out to the middle of the ring and fight some more.

During the week, I write my love for her, my loneliness, but warily. I must be strong. I maintain my hard attitude.

And then on February 11, 1989, Gina and I get married. I'm twenty-three, she's twenty-six. By this time, the paper doesn't mean anything to me. It's no big deal. I love her, loved her already. I figure she'll always be in my life since I can't seem to lose her. And I guess I'll be in Smiley's family one way or the other. She wears a sleeveless beige dress with a sheen to it that matches her fluffed hair. Her eyes are luminous when she sees me. I'm wearing a new white state-issued sweatshirt and navy pants. My hair is trimmed short, my sideburns long. No one is here from our families. Just me and Gina and End-All, a homie from my set, as a witness. We get married in the visiting room; a priest performs the ceremony. She's my clearest vision of security. The only thing that doesn't change, sift away, float in the wind. Her and my set. The only thing I still have. My reason for seeing and breathing.

We're given a five-hour visit to celebrate our wedding. We sit at the table holding hands, staring in each other's eyes, laughing, talking, hugging, talking. We remember a fight she got into when she was a girl, one I watched as her arms pummeled the other kid with precision and speed. We kiss. I cannot get enough of the cinnamon of her lips.

"We can't get any closer," I tell her.

And then our special five-hour visit is over. She'll visit me in two weeks, she promises. She'll bring the kids then.

"My boys now."

In four months, we have our first conjugal visit. The state notifies me of the date. Four months. As soon as I get the letter, I mark the date on my calendar and cross off each day before I sleep, like a child waiting for Christmas. Except when I was a child, I never wanted Christmas like I want to spend the night with Gina and watch her eyes twitch under her lids and wonder what she dreams.

Four months seems forever.

But what's four months when I've waited twelve years? Our letters go back and forth, fast and furious. She brings Marcus and Antoine to visit me. I concentrate on seeing her in them, concentrate on seeing G in them, Curly in them. When I hint at my arrest and the helicopter, Marcus's face clouds in a frown and solemn mouth and he shakes his head. I'm glad he doesn't remember. I wonder if Antoine cries so furiously he passes out.

I fill out the forms for a transfer to a prison closer to home.

As I work, study, exercise, reinforce the principles with the Crips, another layer inside me hums with eagerness for Gina. Little thoughts bubble unbidden. I bench-press two hundred pounds and there's her smile. *Only forty-five more days.* In between sentences about Ruchell Magee, I think *thirty-six more days.* My letters start, *Dear Gina, only twenty-three more days* and end with the same prayer. *Twenty-three more days, less than a month. God bless you and the boys.*

She's a secret splendor amidst all the gray, steel, concrete, fighting, and raging sun.

And then the day arrives without a fanfare, just like any other. My cell slowly lightens. But I've been up for hours, listening to the noises of the sleepless men, dozing and waking with each sound, watching daylight seep in its gray. My bag was packed the night before. A few more hours. I can tell it's going to be a hot day. And once again the institution doesn't turn on the air-conditioning.

I take my bag to the office for Ms. Harris to search. As she rummages through it, she teases, "You're goin' to have some fun, uh?"

She senses my eagerness to have sex, but she doesn't know, can't possibly imagine how long I've waited for this particular woman and this particular day.

I smile back at her, the flirting Cee playing her diversion game, and hold my hand out for my bag.

"Why don't you ever come see me? Why don't you come by my office?"

I grab my bag.

The visit is in a small apartment on the institutional grounds. Gina has brought food so she can cook for me. She wears a royal blue dress. She smells of roses and some smell that I can't define that must be her musk. We don't talk. We stare at each other, me smelling her, that musk, her want, as though we can't believe our own wonder. And then make love. Talk afterward. And make love some more.

I didn't think we could get closer, but we do. But instead of feeling at all vulnerable, I'm stronger, empowered. She's crazy after the first time we have sex, clings to me like a second skin, grips my clothes as I move around our apartment. She won't leave my side; she has to touch me.

"You want some water?" I ask.

"Okay, Colton," her voice slidy-soft, her lashes shadowing her eyes. She looks up at me and then glances away as though she can't get over the sight of me. Me, naked. Me, her husband.

I like this new her, this womanly her. The perky bitter personality is gone, the testing girl who bristles and pushes away. I've gotten through her defenses. But she can't own me; the prison and the gang have competing priorities.

To me, she's the finest woman in the world, the slight curve of her nostrils flaring, the gentle arc her cheekbone carves in her face, the knobby jut of bone in her wrist, her nipples the color of blackberries, the satin-brown flesh taut over her round ass. She's my love life. Everything else is hate and war. She's something to look forward to a couple times a month, and enjoy totally three times a year. An oasis.

She forgets to cook for me.

She brings some sad news with her. Big Mel had gotten hooked on premos—tobacco-and-cocaine cigarettes. He tried to rob his dealer and the dealer shot him. Big Mel died. Big Mel with his outgoing personality and businessman acumen supplied the set with stolen cars for retaliatory shootings and quick comradeship. When I was with him, I always felt like I belonged. He was the cat with intuition. I remember his giftwrapped sledgehammer when I was released from prison.

I don't think how quickly life turns; I think instead, *Big Mel never had that fighting edge to his personality. Easy to catch him slippin'.* Then Gina remembers to cook the tacos she promised.

And I figure I better have the delightful while I got it and eat her food and plunge back into her body.

We've finished making love and her head is on my shoulder, her eyes open. Her finger traces an imaginary line from the tip of my chin, down my neck, circles my nipple, gets stuck exploring a scar on my chest, then proceeds down to my navel. It's a lazy, easy motion, a motion of learning me, appreciating me, and soothing me. I let her travel around; a sense of accomplishment fills me.

I tilt her chin up so she can see my eyes, see how serious I am. I wet my lips. "Gina."

"Yeah," she slides the word with the same sensual motion as her finger and then stills her hand.

"I know this may not be enough for you."

"It's enough, baby."

"No. I know that having a man once every three months, four times a year is not enough. And you're out in the free world."

She tries to turn her face away, but I move it toward me again so our eyes are on each other.

"Just don't get pregnant with another man's baby. Don't be carrying no other man in you."

Her eyes wet and she blinks.

"Hear me?"

"Promise." Her eyes are steady as she looks at me.

Sure enough, just like I said, she's love. All the rest is war and hate. That Monday, the day after my conjugal visit, the day after Gina and I consummate our twelve-year relationship, war breaks out between the Blacks and the Mexicans. An all-out war that rages over the next half year and results at its end in the stabbing of one hundred seventy-two prisoners. Some of those wounds require no attention; others end in death.

Here's what happened. The Monday after my conjugal visit, I go to the yard, check its safety before joining the inmates. The yard is essentially a slanted oval cup, so I stride to the high end. This day, the customary pattern is different. The Mexicans outnumber the Blacks by a large margin. Usually, everyone stays in their own ethnic group and everything is segregated—weight piles, basketball courts, everything. We can't lift weights next to each other. Blacks have their own basketball and handball courts, their own weights. So do the Mexicans.

In the past few weeks, arguments have broken out between the brothas and the Southside Mexicans over the use of weights and the basketball court. The brothas want to use Mexican weights and the basketball court because they don't use them; Mexicans spend their entire time playing handball. The brothas wait to play basketball and lift weights, eyeing the vacant court and motionless weights of the Mexicans. The Mexicans wait turns to play handball, eyeing the empty Black handball court. Everyone stays on their own side and stabs jealous eyes at the unused equipment.

But this day, the yard is crowded with three hundred inmates, and groups of three or four Mexicans are scattered throughout. Three Mexicans stand near one corner, several crews of four Mexicans walk the track, and a cluster stand by the weights, leaning against the fence. A few groups huddle around the perimeter of the basketball court. There's about two hundred Mexicans, but no group larger than five. All the Mexican shot-callers are in the yard.

Don Don passes and I shout to him. He climbs up the hill to me.

"Somethin's goin' on. Look at this shit." I point to the sprinkled bunches of Mexicans.

More homies join us, "Yo. Whassup?"

"This shit don't look right. We need our pieces," I say.

We send a comrade to get weapons, and another one to run to the weight pile to inform the Crips and Bloods. Just as he reaches the weight area, war ignites.

Knife fights all over the yard—the buildings, the work areas, the gym, the weight pile, the courts. The flash of quick arms, blades, the moans of hurt men. Everywhere. All at once. A completely planned attack by the Mexican Mafia and Southside Mexican against unarmed, unprepared Blacks.

Almost as instantly, guards in the towers start their bombardment. Shots ring out throughout the yard.

In ten minutes, one hundred prisoners are stabbed; seventy-two are Black. One Black man is stabbed in the chest and dies; he'd been in Folsom a month, had no gang affiliation, and was serving a four-year sentence for robbery. Ten people are shot or hit by ricocheted bullets; they are all Black as well, which is another interesting statistic, especially when the Blacks are outnumbered by the Mexicans and they're the ones who are armed and start the fight. Are the guards aiming for the Blacks? Are the guards taking the opportunity to do things they've always wanted to do? Can this be coincidence?

As quickly as it starts, the fighting stops, as though a whistle is blown and the round is over.

Three hundred prisoners are ordered to lie on the ground.

Bodies are carried off in stretchers. At least four dozen inmates undergo surgery in the hospital; four are in critical condition, shot in the abdomen and legs. We're escorted back to our cells and strip searched.

It's the fourth death in Folsom for the year. Two men died from strangulation, and a bullet from a correction officer's weapon killed one inmate. The newspaper reports the incident, but their numbers are underreported. Well over a hundred men are injured in the fight. The great majority take care of their injuries in their cells. They use tape to push torn edges of flesh together; if they have access to needle and thread, they suture their own wounds. We don't want authorities to know of our involvement and we're used to caring for our own war wounds. Repercussions for being in a fight are often harsher than the injuries.

Just like that the peaceful goodness love of Gina is wiped away. Another domino has fallen. More events pile up, one after another, and I have no time to savor the aftertaste of her in my mouth.

We're on lockdown for six months. State-of-emergency plans are activated. There's no canteen, no packages, no visits, no Gina, no air-conditioning. We baste in our own sweat, smelling each other in spite of deodorants. The prison heats up, we're caged in the heat, sweat, annoyance. No nothing for six months. Except my books. My letter writing. My cell exercise.

During this time, I learn how the incident started. The day before, while I was on my conjugal visit, the Mexicans were playing handball on the Black court. A Crip, Tata, walked over to them and said, "Hey man, whatya' doin' on our court?"

"We only got two more points. Can we finish?"

"This is our court. Our court," Tata insisted.

The Mexicans kicked at the court and grumbled as they walked away.

"Don't bring your ass back," Tata shouted after them. "We can't go to your court and play."

"Yeah, okay, tomorrow." The Mexican cat turned around and shook his fist at Tata.

"All right. Tomorrow." Tata said. But Tata didn't tell anyone. He shrugged it away like bullshit bluster. But there's no bullshit bluster in prison. Everything has dire consequences.

Now the weird thing about this was what happened next. All of us are supposed to be searched before we hit the yard. The Blacks were all searched. But the Mexicans weren't, or at least not very well, because they came strapped and ready. Now, were the pigs in on it? Did they have a vested interest in the Blacks being beaten down?

The day we come off lockdown, the Blacks strike back. This time we have the advantage. Ten Mexicans are stabbed. The institution is placed back on lockdown.

Normal program resumes two months later. I write Gina our good news. As soon as I seal the letter, a Northern Mexican takes off on a Southern Mexican and the institution is back on lockdown.

The prison responds by moving the entire Southern Mexican population and placing them on a modified program. Then they're taken to another facility. Their bed space is filled with Northern Mexicans who are allies with the African Americans.

A few months later, the warden of the prison writes a memo to the Black inmates. By now it is 1990, the spring of a new decade. His memo tells us that Southern Mexicans will be released to the general population in April. They'll be coming from Tracy and Soledad and had nothing to do with the melee on May 25, 1989. It's imperative that these Southern Hispanic inmates be allowed an opportunity to program here, he says. Our cooperation will be appreciated.

The first Southern Mexican that hits the mainline is greeted with an eight-inch piece of steel by a Crip.

A week later, I am transferred to Tehachapi Max under Assembly Bill 1291, which allows prisoners to be housed closer to home. My transfer has finally come through and Gina's trips to visit me will be much easier for her. I've managed to stay clean for two years.

FIFTEEN

Transformation of a Crip

Viewed within the context of...policy developments and the life course data for these violent offenders, our findings lend support to the search-and-destroy hypothesis—the notion that African American males in Los Angeles have been...the systematic target of discriminatory treatment, especially in the public education system, the labor market, and the criminal justice system.

> Bobo, Oliver, Johnson, and Valenzuela,
> *Prismatic Metropolis: Inequality in Los Angeles*

THE TUMBLING DOMINOES OF MY LIFE EVENTS LOSE THEIR VE- locity. Ironically, as the compression of events lessens, time quickens. Days, months, and then years flip by. There's time for life to become routine; routine makes the days fold together. Life at Tehachapi is predictable, rational. I'm in a yard without a war. Of course, peace is relative but my yard, 4-B, is not as violent as the ones at Folsom or San Quentin. It's like leaving one world and entering another. All over the yard, I see Southern Mexicans and Mexican Mafia—who in other places and other times tried to kill us—hugged up with brothas, playing cards, shooting the breeze, sharing cigarettes and coffee, drinking pruno, and smoking weed.

I have space to sort through my thoughts. I'm drug and alcohol free so my brain begins to grasp my actual surroundings, a different reality than the one hazed by marijuana and Hennessy. Besides, I've learned that a low profile protects me, gives me greater freedom, since the staff doesn't key in on me and scrutinize my moves. *How can I deal with my surroundings with the pigs on my back? What if I have to defend myself against someone below my level of Cripism? Anonymity bestows freedom.*

I design myself a program to remain clean. Three and half days a week, I work in Prison Industry Authority (PIA). When I get off, I shower, eat, read, write letters to Gina and Grandmother Louise, watch TV. On the half day, I work out, play chess before I shower. On my days off, I play racquetball, lift weights, chess, and then read until I sleep.

The PIA is the immobile slave ship designed by the prison to benefit capitalism. We work for slave wages; the profits from our work go to the prison and to the companies. We're barred from selling directly to the public; we can only sell to government agencies, schools, libraries, hospitals, and overseas. Our blue jeans and denim jackets stenciled in dayglo orange with "California Department of Corrections" are sold to Japan.

I make wooden tables, chairs, sofas. Initially, I stand on my feet for seven hours and glue chair legs together, but I move up quickly to be a tablesaw operator and cut legs from slabs of wood. This is considered a good job because I can make from thirty-five to ninety-five cents an hour. Compared to yard crew workers, tier tenders, or culinary workers, who earn seven cents an hour, I'm a rich man.

I learn later that the large sheets of urethane foam we fashion into cushions in our unventilated shop pose a potentially lethal health threat. The fragments floating in the air are carcinogenic and, after accumulating in our lungs, can cause a condition similar to asbestosis. The California Furniture Association doesn't approve this foam for use in furniture. But I spend seven hours a day for two years breathing those urethane particles without being issued a mask. God knows what time bombs I carry in my lungs.

The work, though it's the same day after day, week after week, speeds up my time. Every new day is so much like the one before I don't notice it has changed.

I work under my shield, cutting wood, sawdust flying.

"Simpson?" Freeman, my White boss, calls out.

Here we go again. "Yeah?" I lift my shield.

"I gotta joke for you and Vincent." Vincent, the brotha who works with me, nudges me in the back and winks.

"Okay. What did the man say to the grown man when he caught him hitting on the dog?"

Vince and I put on our usual expression of pretend dumbfoundedness. "I don't know," Vince replies.

"Oh," Freeman says, already laughing at his joke, "you like hittin' on things, huh, boy? Well you can hit this"—he grabs his crotch—"and I'll turn your black ass blue."

"Ha. Ha. Ha." Vince and I fake laughs and glare at Freeman, both of us wanting to kill him.

He moseys off like a stray dog. But we know next day he'll try another racist joke. I wish I could slap the humor out of him.

The next day Vince and I don't pretend to laugh. Freeman gets red when his joke falls limp. "I expect you boys to cut out two thousand today. Two thousand chair legs."

Freeman walks away.

Vince and I work our asses off to fill his quota.

In the middle of the day, he's back at us again. "What the fuck's wrong with you boys? They're the wrong fucking size."

I pull out a protractor and measuring tape and evaluate the legs piece by piece. They're perfect.

"Hey, Freeman," I call out.

"What. You ready for another joke?" The sawdust has turned his hair fuzzy beige.

"Naw, man. I measured those legs and they're all perfect."

"Lemme see your tape."

I hand it to him and he checks the legs. "Fuck no, boy, They ain't the right size. You did them according to Kurt's size." Kurt is the other supervisor. "That's not how I like mine. You gotta take one-fucking-sixteenth off the width and length." He slaps the tape on the saw table. "And hurry your asses up. You only got two hours."

Vince and I get White Boy to rig the machine so it stops. Freeman calls the repairman, who is Romeo from Eight Tray. When we tell him the story of Freeman's racist jokes, Romeo informs Freeman it'll take a day to fix our saw. That buys us enough time for Kurt's shift and he, of course, accepts the chair legs.

When the racist supervisor isn't annoying, the economics of the situation are. The chairs sell for five hundred. I make well over four hundred chairs and earn forty dollars a month; the state makes six figures. Locking people up and forcing them to work for the Prison Industry Authority is big business, so other prison industrial complexes are built. Several corporations use prison labor. The prison industry now employs more than half a million people—more than any Fortune 500 corporation other than General Motors. Today, some prisoners are paid minimum wage, but they don't see the money. More than half is siphoned off to reimburse the state for the cost of incarceration and to the victim-restitution fund. Meanwhile, their families are going without benefit of their labor. So criminals pay for their crimes twice—once with time and again with labor, and, given the conditions of the complexes, often with their health.

But for me, PIA is good news: it makes time swift; it keeps me away from trouble. I do my program and look forward to the oasis of Gina's visits every other weekend and my conjugal visits every three months, the highlight of my life.

"I want you to have my baby," I tell Gina during one of our conjugal visits while we're eating steak and fried potatoes that she brought.

She glances at the bed. "We can start now."

"Not now. I want to be part of his growing. If you have him while I'm in here, he won't be a reflection of me."

She takes a deep breath as though to fill herself up with air since she can't fill herself up with me. "I got my hands full as it is," she agrees.

I'm eventually written up for a "failure to work" and not allowed back on my job. I start hanging out in the rec yard. I've suffered repercussions of associating with destructive people for over half my life, so I avoid the cats with negative outlooks on life. But it's hard. I get the urge to hang with the fellas, but they pull me into regressive activities and conversations. When the pull becomes relentless and I begin to participate, I fib to the yard pig, saying I'm sick, and return to the building. Then, I call Gina and ask about Marcus, Antoine, reminding myself of my responsibilities to her and my stepsons, take a shower, and pick up a book. Cats come by my cell, but I pretend I'm asleep, stretch out on my bunk, and consider my situation.

The homies think I'm getting soft. They think I don't have craziness in me anymore. I spent my entire life striving to be reputable and respected in the gang world. Li'l Cee Loc, a well-known thug, ghetto celebrity.

Now I'm a reader, a thinker. Laid back. I've lost my gang motivation. I want to construct something but don't know what. Just something, anything, to touch the Crips and the Bloods, African Americans. Something to let them know the reality. I go back and forth within my different layers, my Colton layer and my Cee layer.

I pick up some paper and start writing down my thoughts, looking for answers to why things are as they are and what I can do to change them. My writing becomes another oasis.

Then, what I've been afraid of happening happens. I'm lying on the weight bench doing triceps and I notice several Bloods behind me. Using a dumbbell to shade my face, I see Li'l Man slide a piece in his shoe. "Look at that nigga, Cee. He's a buster now," he says to one of his buddies.

Here's the day, the day I've feared, the day when someone tests me. My temper is triggered. And I'm forced to make a decision I don't want to make: to do the rest of my time with a bad reputation, or harm another Black man.

All I've worked for is on the line. The layers of Colton and Cee crash and collide inside me, fighting as fiercely as my temper yearns to fight Li'l Man.

I have only four years left before I make parole.

I'm off the bench steaming toward him. "Brotha, I don't know you. I don't want no problems, but disrespect will not be tolerated."

"What? Fuck you, crab."

Crab is the most disrespectful epitaph that you can call a Crip. In one motion, I pull the piece from my sleeve and stab him in the face, knocking him unconscious. I spin and pace past the tower steps.

A friend runs over to me. "Cee? What's up, cuz?"

"I had to blast on that fool Li'l Man."

"You still got the piece on you?" he asks.

"Yeah. Damn." I melted down garbage bags to make this piece and it shines like obsidian. I heave the knife in a trash can. My friend gives me his jacket as a disguise and I fake like I'm sick to return to my cell.

My escape is short-lived. Later that night, I'm shackled from the waist down, taken to Ad-Seg for assault on an inmate. I fight the charges for five months, but I'm found guilty and 180 days are tacked onto my time. Five days after that, I'm told to "roll it up" and I'm transferred to Tehachapi 4-A.

Four-A isn't different than 4-B in terms of atmosphere. No war is being waged; inmates get along, and there are the usual racist pigs. When I'm sent for classification, I tell the counselor I want a daytime job. I need a job that'll keep me off the yard. I'm assigned to silk screen in the prison industrial complex where I make United States flags, California flags, police stickers, and patches. A few months later, I'm transferred to yard crew.

I establish my routine. This time I play more chess. By now, I'm one of the best players on the yard. Those who want a challenge want a game with me. Chess helps my concentration. I avoid conversations surrounding the war and tensions between the Crips and the Bloods. I stay focused.

During this time, I receive an article from the *Los Angeles Times* from Gina. It reports that Taylor, the White superhero who tried to hold me for the police, has been awarded over eighty-three thousand dollars for his injuries. A jury found the jewelry store responsible for the bullet wound to his lung, liver, and colon. However, the jury also found him liable for 30 percent of his injuries. "We want to discourage this kind of behavior. He should not have tried to interfere or resist a robbery," the foreman said. Taylor is reported as saying, "I wouldn't do it again. Nothing is worth getting shot." He married his fiancée and returned to work as an electrican. They now have a baby girl.

I'm glad he recovered and got some money from his injuries. Even the jury and jewelry store agree with me that he shouldn't have interfered. I shouldn't have been doing what I was doing, but he made both our lives harder.

In pill line getting medication for an ankle problem, the man ahead of me says, "You look familiar, man. You look like somebody I know."

He's an older man, neatly groomed, with a serious expression and blazing eyes. Average height, average muscular build. I don't recognize him.

"Who's your family, man? What's your parents' name?"

I tell him.

"I know your uncle, man. He's an attorney. No wonder you look familiar. He's a good friend of my attorney, Johnny Cochran, I'm Geronimo Pratt." He holds out his hand. Geronimo was the minister of defense for the Black Panther Party in Los Angeles. After Bunchy Carter's assassination he became his successor and quickly became the target for "neutralization" by the FBI. He was falsely accused and convicted of charges of murdering a twenty-seven-year-old elementary school teacher in Santa Monica, California, on December 18, 1968. During the commission of the crime, he was in Oakland at a party meeting, but because of a conflict that developed over policy within the Black Panthers they refused to testify on his behalf. He's been in prison over twenty years, framed by the LAPD and the FBI and betrayed by his own men. We stand in the line and talk about his case and my uncle.

The next day I see him on the basketball court and we shoot some hoops, and then that night we're back on pill line again. This time we discuss books. He has every book one could think of, from revolutionary material to autobiographies of Black athletes. He lends me Huey Newton's *Revolutionary Suicide*. When that's devoured, he laughs and hands me *The Spook Who Sat by the Door* by Sam Greenlee.

He doesn't drink, curse, or smoke. He verbalizes his anger and reiterates his point from different angles, articulating clearly. I listen carefully to his speech, admiring his self-control and patience. He accepts struggle as part of life and not mere happenstance. He suggests I keep a diary, and my writing becomes where I am most me, where Colton and Cee are at last united. When I express sorrow for his situation, he smiles. "I'm going home. It's just a matter of time."

I look down.

"No, man. They're working on my case. It'll be any day now."

"You lost a lot of your life," I say.

"We all have." Geronimo glances away and then meets my eyes. "No point in crying about that because I can't get it back. But, at least I'll receive a huge reprieve. You just watch." He hands me Sun Tzu's *Art of War*. "Since you're an OG now, you need to read this."

He's right about his own future. His case is overturned; he sues the FBI and LAPD for framing him and he's awarded over three million dollars in the settlement. He returns to Louisiana where he grew up.

———

And then one night, while reading the Bible, I stab out a cigarette and I think, "That's it." And I quit. Quitting cigarettes is harder than stopping alcohol, marijuana, or cocaine. Much harder. I dream so vividly of filling my lungs with smoke that I wake with a start. But I have more free time to read, to think. So much of my time in prison was wrapped around figuring out how to pay for cigarettes.

Every night, I replay the entire day in my mind and analyze it, looking for verbal and physical actions to explain myself to myself, to grasp all the different layers that shift, twist, turn, swallow each other up inside me. I'm living inside myself, in my own mind, thinking about me and Gina and the boys and Grandmother Louise instead of the set, defense, retaliation.

On one visit, I tell Gina I'm reading W. E. B. Dubois and explain his idea of double consciousness. "This cat says that Black people have a sense of looking at oneself through the eyes of others, and through the eyes of the world." I'm trying to explain to her my two sides, the Colton and Cee side. I'm trying to figure it out for myself.

Her brows slide together, not in a frown, but in confusion.

I try again, "He calls it two unreconciled strivings. An internal conflict. We all have it."

Now she pushes back from the table. "What you talkin' 'bout? I got me a million strivings. I need a new car, Marcus needs new shoes, and Antoine wants a new bike. And not no money for neither. Those my unreconciled strivings."

"You should read, it. Try to buy it. It's called *Souls of Black Folk*."

"Don't need nobody to tell me about my soul. I don't have no time. Too busy comin' here." She points down with a red polished nail. "Too busy being a single mother." Her anger escalates as she lists her burdens. "Too busy working to support two kids. Too busy pushin' away being lonely."

"I know." I spread my arms to indicate the limits of my province. "But I'm here."

After that, we write less; I give her less of myself since she doesn't want the me I'm developing.

On our next conjugal visit, I try to explain what Ruchell Magee taught me about Black-on-Black violence. I tell her that we need to unite, put our energies into our own communities, our children.

But she looks away, turns back, and says, "Put your energies into my sons. My sons. Protect them."

"I am, that's what I'm talkin' 'bout."

She drums her red nails on the table.

I try a different tactic. "Don't you see the violence just escalates? Each retaliation is fiercer, more brutal than the one before." I use my hands to show the ascending brutality. "Now they're killing families as a threat. Little babies. We're building a tower of terror."

"You riding a high horse."

"I'm learning, Gina."

"Cee, you acting White."

I lean back. "You think I'm some bourgeoisie Negro? My changes aren't negative and White. They're positive and pro-Black. To better me," I point to myself, "you and our children." I point to her and smile, but a growing sorrow weights me.

She doesn't have a high school diploma, but she has a job. While she's working day after day, taking care of her sons and using her leftover energy to maintain our relationship, I study myself, life, books, my homies, her.

"I know things are hard for you out there. We have choices. Even me, even in here. Realistic ones, irrespective of being Black, a convict, and a banger."

"See? You even talking White. Irrespective? Fucking irrespective? How the fuck you learn to talk that shit?" She angrily snaps her purse on her shoulder, rotates, and walks away. *She doesn't accept that I thrive on my hunger to understand. She thinks I'm setting myself apart and rejecting her. So she rejects that part of me, the new me I'm forging from Colton and Cee. She has street mentality and I've transcended that.* I see all this. But I can't seem to halt it. And I can't bring her with me.

I stop writing her my thoughts. They go into my journal. I don't tell her what I'm reading. But I don't give up. After all, she's my family. Seems like she always has been. So, I ask her gossip about the set, but the news she relays is about people I don't know. I tell her about the people in prison, but she's tired of anything to do with prison.

I hear from a new arrival she's seeing other men. I'm doing thirteen years and she's on the street, and at one point or another I've anticipated that temptation will be too strong. I don't even mention it to her. I continue writing, trying to tell her about me.

The visits lessen. Gina can't drive up to see me; she's busy with Marcus's baseball game, her sister's shower, working.

But as the months go on, and become years, as I do my time, write my journal, talk with Geronimo, read my books, do my job the "I love you's" peter out, then dribble away. One night, I realize months have passed without even an "Hello, I love you."

And then one Saturday Gina comes for a visit and brings Grandma Louise and my brother Curtis. My mother couldn't take care of him and so Louise is raising him. The four of us sit around talking of old times. My grandmother tells me I look just like my father and is overjoyed by the changes I've made. Gina just looks away. Louise's hair is completely gray, and she's lost so much weight she looks fragile. Then she smiles at me, "Don't worry none 'bout me."

But I wonder what she's been through that she hasn't told me.

She pats Curtis's arm and I see in her eyes how happy she is to have another kid to raise. She'd raised six, not including Damon, me, and now Curtis.

During that visit, while Louise and Curtis get some Snickers and Mountain Dew out of the vending machine, Gina tells me she has a boyfriend and that she's pregnant.

That night, I write in my journal: *Today I received a visit from my family. From each of them I learned something valuable. From Gina I learned she has a boyfriend. This helped me realize that aside from her connection to my gang past we no longer have anything in common. As Geronimo has told me, history repeats itself. She walked out on me pregnant with another man while I was in Youth Authority and now again in prison. From my grandmother, I learned that she's doing well now that she has another child and although her age shows, she's still the Louise of old. Thank God. From Curtis, I learned that although nine years have elapsed quickly in my life, it's still a long time. The last time I saw him he was four years old and riding a Big Wheel. Now he's thirteen. He is today where I should have been sixteen years ago. Please Lord, keep me focused.*

Gina doesn't want to be married anymore and files for divorce. The divorce is like the marriage in that the truth of the matter has long been established. We've been married six years. We've known each other for eighteen. I still love her but I can't be romantic with a woman pregnant with another man's child.

Meanwhile, the homies feel let down by me. That's-It accuses me of betrayal and wants to fight.

I'm beyond my old emotional self, reacting blindly out of my temper; my fight with Li'l Man was the last flare. Now, I interpret That's-It's annoyance as a way to reclaim me, reinitiate me.

"Cuz, I'm still Crazy Colton, I still love the set." I use my wit to help him see my side. "But I can help you from outside the walls better than in here. I can look after our families and loved ones. We don't want our little brothers and our kids to follow in our footsteps and have lives of prison and destruction, do we?"

He clenches his fist and maintains his mad-dog stare. "You can't just quit being a Crip."

"There's lots of ways of representing the set. Look at Ice T." I open my arms to embrace him and he steps toward me.

Since making my break from the set I have no support from

anyone at Tehachapi except Geronimo, and he only knows part of my life. So, other than my books and my journal, I'm alone. No family other than Grandma Louise. Every year, though, Gina sends me a birthday card.

And then, after four and a half years in Tehachapi, I'm transferred to Calipatria to do pull my final stretch of two and a half years. I don't know why I'm transferred. Just to shake things up a little. The guard booth at the main gate is unmanned, as are ten of its twelve perimeter gun towers. Instead, there are three fences; the middle one stretches thirteen feet and is armed with fifteen strands of wire charged with five thousand volts. Since this is ten times the lethal amount, it guarantees that any inmate touching the fence will be toast. Ironically, animal rights activists and the Audubon Society have insisted it be surrounded by warnings—a signal for curious rodents, antiperching wire for birds. Now, droning with voltage, it's ecologically sensitive death wires. California shows more concern for the animals than the human beings. But I knew that already. Since I've been in the California prisons over the past decade, guards have killed thirty-six inmates, more than triple the number killed in federal penitentiaries and the six other states with the highest number of prisoners combined.

Each of Calipatria's twenty housing units is designed like a two-story horseshoe with a guard station. This is the "270 plan," which is named for the 270-degree of vision afforded the guards and is a panopticon designed to provide our continual surveillance and control. We are always watched. And we are crammed together. The six-by-ten-foot cells are built for one man, but as the prison population escalates, another man is stuffed in. The California Department of Corrections prison system is more expensive ($5.6 billion) than the University of California system ($4.3 billion). When the "three strikes and you're out" law comes fully into effect, it is estimated that twenty-three more prisons will have to be built. California incarceration rates are the highest in the world at 626 people per 100,000. In the rest of the United States it is 517. Only South Africa at 355 is even close.

Ironically, the crime rate has dropped during the last decade, as have the absolute number of crimes. The crime rate since 1991 has gone down 16 percent, but 33 percent more people per 100,000 are incarcerated. More men are being incarcerated for less violent crimes for a longer periods of time. Of the top ten reasons for incarceration, four are drug related, five are robberies or burglary, and one, the sixth, is for a violent crime—assault with a deadly weapon. So most of the prisoners when they're sent to prison are not in for violent crimes. But prison is an excellent place to learn violence.

I notice the murderous electric wall and know I'll have to establish my reputation once again. The earth signs tell me instantaneously of the tension between the ABs and Nazis versus the Bloods, and another between the Crips and the pigs. It's like a step back in time. Except this time, I've walked into two wars and I don't want to be a soldier.

I'm greeted on fish row by Al Capone, who has matured since our days on LACJ. He, too, has distanced himself from bangin'.

Sure enough, two months after I arrive, the Nazis and ABs take off on the Bloods, beating and stabbing several. Just as predictably, the Bloods retaliate and stab an AB, who is hospitalized in a coma. My cellie and I stay armed and keep tight security on each other. Then the ABs and Bloods call for a treaty.

By early spring of 1995, I'm ducated for the in-grounds crew job, cutting grass, picking up paper. I don't have to deal with the yard chaos—the rumors, fighting, stabbings, and gunfire. I watch staff drive back and forth to work and scope out the female visitors as they make their way to the gate. I shake everybody except for Al Capone and my cellie. I work, lift weights, write, and read the dictionary or the Bible. Only a few more years to go.

By early May 1995, the second war explodes as tensions be-

tween the Crips and pigs escalate. A corrections officer pulls a
Crip from the track, insists he raise his pants. Now "sagging" is a
sign of Cripism. The Crip refuses this humiliation and the officer
pulls his pants into his butt, roughs him up, cuffs him, and drags
him to the hole. The very next day, as I am putting gasoline in the
lawn mowers, the institutional alarm breaks out with a roar. A
hundred pigs storm the facility in full riot gear. I watch in amazement as twenty retreat, carrying officers covered in blood and
screaming in pain.

"Get down. Get down. Get down," shouts one of the pigs
carrying a correction officer.

I hit the grass head first and remain there for three hours before being escorted to my cell. Every prison in the state is placed
on lockdown status. State-of-emergency plans are activated. The
incident makes world news. What happened was this: Frustrated
and furious by the verbal and physical abuse, the beating of the
Crip for "sagging" becomes the final straw. Five Crips seize the
prison's program office, armed with inmate-manufactured
weapons, and attack the pigs. Eight officers are stabbed, including
sergeants and lieutenants. A female officer's breasts are slashed.
The message is, "You fuck with us, we'll fuck with you."

As a result, several officers immediately quit their jobs and
move, leaving no addresses or phone numbers. We remain on
lockdown for six months during which time the officers picket
outside the prison demanding better security, gates dividing the
yards in half, and sectioning of the program offices, canteen area,
infirmary, and package room from the rest of the prison. They win
their demands.

The day we're released from lockdown, a Black female lieutenant pulls a Crip out of chow line for "sagging," has him handcuffed and roughed up. Two of his homies rush the pigs and kick
the lieutenant in her belly. The entire institution is back on lockdown status. That night around four A.M., fifty pigs storm the
buildings in full riot gear: fatigues, helmets, Taser guns, billy

clubs, handcuffs, loaded belts, guns. They round up three bus-loads of Crips under CCO and Blue Note constitutions and drive them directly to Corcoran.

The Crips are taken off the bus, shackled in a chain gang, beaten with hands, feet, and batons. "Welcome to hell," yells one of the pigs. He grabs a man by his braid and cuts it from the root with a box cutter.

"Fuck you, fuck this African bullshit."

All of the men's braids are ripped out.

After they're roughed up again, they're housed strategically between Mexicans. Hispanics now make up the largest single group of men. The Mexican-Black war is still going on—the one that started when I was in Folsom.

Once the prisoners are cleared for the SHU yard, they're set up by the pigs, who want revenge for the Calipatria incident. The Mexicans start stabbing before the Crips are even out of cuffs. The Nazi Low Riders and AB are armed with buck knives and hypodermic syringes loaded with poison and bleach. The Crips are outnumbered, outarmed. While being worked over by the Whites and Mexicans, the officers take potshots at the Blacks.

Once again retaliation escalates the violence. The slashing of the pigs accelerates to gladiator games and gunshots. The war continues, each side teaching the other increasing brutality.

Eventually one of the officers (Richard Caruso) at Corcoran, who refuses to participate in this brutality, steals prison documents and turns them over to the FBI, which sparks a federal probe into Corcoran, the "deadliest prison system in America." Thirty-one inmate shootings occurred between 1989 and 1995. Seven of them fatal. During one of the brawls, a guard says, "It's going to be duck-hunting season," and fatally shoots an inmate. In 1993, Corcoran guards deliberately set up a Black prisoner to be attacked by leaving him in a cell with a known White sexual predator for a two-day period and ignoring his pleas for help. Four guards are eventually charged. More prisoners are shot and killed by pigs in California prisons than in the entire rest of the country.

Meanwhile, in Calipatria I have my own war raging. It's my war to quit the Crips, quit all violence, which is made harder in this situation where I'm pressed to pick between being a soldier or a buster. It's extremely difficult to be nonviolent in prison. That's probably why Ruchell stays in his cell. It's a war inside myself. I remind myself that Sun-tzu says, "Though effective, appear to be ineffective." I stay low and hope I'm not pushed. But I am. By this time, my cellie is a Blood and I am not involved in the Blood-Crip war. But old reputations die hard and a Blood from Detroit makes an attempt on my life outside the chow hall. I guess he's trying to climb up a notch in the reputation ladder, because I see his quick hand movement and ready myself.

"Hey, Bro."

He keeps coming and I knock him unconscious with one punch and he goes into convulsions. I break my thumb and am rushed into an outside hospital. I'm returned to the prison with three pins in my thumb and housed in the infirmary.

My cell has a rectangular window providing me a view of the roadway. I stand at my window studying the stream of stabbing victims as they're brought to the infirmary by ambulance, carried on stretchers, or walking between two guards.

For the first time, I think about the people I have victimized during my stint as a banger. The people I beat, the people I shot, the people I terrified, the people I stabbed. All around me, moaning in cots in other cells, are the injured of the war.

One man has been stabbed six times. One slash, like a jagged S, scuttles from his forehead, over an eyelid, pivots down to his lip. A gash bolts from his cheek to his ear. The two cuts zigzag across his face like the arms of a swastika. The slices are red, outlined in purple, stitched with blue. Why? Because he's White. He'd been in prison for sixteen hours when a race riot blew up in the rec yard. He had never been to jail in his life and has been sentenced to fifteen to life for a crime he didn't do.

"Damn, man, What did you get stabbed with?" I'm amazed at the fury of his wounds.

"Scissors," he mumbles between groans.

"How can a person be so ruthless?"

And then I think of myself and a sick feeling fills me, that feeling I've pushed away and avoided since I was initiated twenty years before. From long ago I hear that silly Mr. Softee song, *Do to do, do to do do to doddle do to do. Men moan and clutch bullet-torn flesh. Hole-ridden bodies slump behind the dash of the red Buick.* Nausea waves over me, churns my stomach. I clench my eyes to obliterate the splashing images, but they play behind my lids. I feel sick at what I've done to others.

This time, it doesn't go away. I don't have marijuana and Hennessy to block the images. In the showers, I see the scars, the disfigured bodies, and the faces we wear. We've beaten, stabbed, shot each other because of the color of our skin or the color of our flags. Human beings of all races, real people's bodies, are transformed into unidentifiable shapes. One man's bicep is so demolished that the remains of the muscle is pushed to the side of his arm. Another has a leg with an excised quad. I see a man with no eye, waiting for a glass one. Another misses an ear. The tattoos do not cover the scars. Our bodies are the graffiti of our wars. Some of us cannot see anymore. Some of us cannot remember anymore. Some of us don't have two legs, many of us dead. These comrades remind me of my victims. *What have we done to each other? How am 1 going to purge what I've done?*

I tilt my face to the shower and open my mouth. The water is clear, empty. I swallow it without stopping for air.

But nothing changes.

I can't take back what I've done. I was only a soldier in the war. I'm located in this void forever.

My cast extends to my elbow and I'm helpless without the use of both hands. I cannot tie my shoes, my laces drag. Buttoning a shirt with my left hand requires concentrated effort as I use my cast to push the button to the hole and then try to fit it into the slit with my left hand. The nurse has to help. Even opening a book, propping it on my bent legs, and using my cast to maintain my open page requires adjustment. My writing with my left hand is barely legible, but I write anyway.

I think about the prisoners I've seen with only one arm. My crushing remorse pounds in my thumb, throughout my hand, up my arm. I can't sleep. Eating is physically difficult anyway. I stand at the window as another man is lugged into the infirmary. I lie down and close my eyes, my thumb, my wrist throbbing. Behind my lids, I see blood, spurting blood. I open my eyes and witness another person slaughtered. The cement floor puddles with blood. Red trickles like paint down the walls. Splatters on windows. Loco is tied again to cell bars that drip. A man clutches his chest and moans. Blood seeps from a slash of flesh. My shirt flies through the air, spinning my own blood as it falls. Finally I fall asleep. But sleep is no escape. Even my dreams ooze the pornographic images of murder.

After three days are up, I'm rehoused in Building One. My guilt recedes, then returns in waves. I see the men in the yard through new eyes, aware of the results of the war we wage. I wear my cast for six weeks. Each night, I have to force my eyes closed, go beyond the blood, and try to sleep through pain while my limb throbs. My aching muscles, though, provide a relief from my conscience. Or maybe it hurts so much because I can't escape my mental state.

Because of my fight, I loose my minimum-security status and am given ninety days loss of credit. In the first week of Black August, I'm taken to the infirmary where the doctor removes the cast and pins. My thumb is shrunk to the size of my pinkie and my forearm looks as narrow as my wrist. Once I return to the cell, I begin my own rehab.

I'm moved one more time, back to the mainline. Talib is my cellie and next door is Tim, who I haven't seen since Old Folsom.

Tim hasn't changed; he's still the stalwart soldier but has developed a quick, fascinating verbal fluidity. He's left the Crips but remains fixated on analyzing each unresolved issue within the set. We each make sure the other doesn't go off behind something petty.

I'm placed in a new job, working in the watch office writing memos. Lieutenant Hunt, my boss, is a White man who treats me like a human being. Not a prisoner, not a Black guy, just a human being. He encourages me to write my story and demands when it's published that I send him a copy.

One afternoon, I overhear him reprimanding another officer. "This is my worker. You don't talk to him like that." He enters his office, sits at his desk, writes a memo, and hands it to me. "Here you go, Colton. You need this."

The memo states I can leave my cell whenever I want.

I guess the problem with the set is that we know each other so well. We've lived life on the edge together—crime, drugs, sex, war, and murder. Together, we've gone from exhilaration to agony. We know each flaw and, with time and pressure, weaknesses grind, insensitivities or callousness stab. Like any other family, the history of injury, jealousy, competition ends up resounding. Add the pressure to prove by violence and the passion for vengeance and the set becomes a mix of love and security, hurt and hell. Slights become antagonisms that crawl under your skin and create an infuriating itch that swells into an ache that cannot be ignored and is only relieved by the scratch of retaliation. It's Cain and Abel over and over again.

When my own feelings churn, Tim reminds me, "You can do more for yourself on the street than behind bars."

He's right. I've learned what I needed. I don't need to do any more time. Ironically, I didn't learn what I needed to learn from the institution. Except for Lieutenant Hunt, the institution simply taught me carnage and reinforced the violence taught by

Pete, by Smiley, by the Bloods. Pervasive brutality, systemic and automatic.

Instead, I learned what I needed from the rare man able to rise above hellhole circumstances: Ruchell Magee, Lafayette Rainey, Geronimo Pratt, and the support of some of my brothers: Tim, Keitarock, Talib.

"Besides, Cee, how old are you now?" Tim asks.

"Thirty-two."

"Party's over."

SIXTEEN

Uhuru

The earth is but one great ball. The borders, the barriers, the cages, the cells, the prisons of our lives, all originate in the false imagination of the minds of men.
—Mumia Abu-Jamal, *Live from Death Row*

ON JUNE 10, 1998, I'M PAROLED. I'VE SERVED TWELVE AND A half years, two and a half in solitary confinement. Five California prisons have been my home. I'll turn thirty-three in six days, three days short of Juneteenth, a holiday in the African American community celebrating the emancipation of the last slave.

I shoot out of the prison and to a friend's car so quickly I don't look back and I hardly say hello. Once we're on the freeway, I relax. I'm no longer caged by cement and steel. I pull my typewriter from one of my boxes and begin typing the fourth chapter of this book while my friend drives me to my father's house. Then, I insist my Pops take me to the Culver City post office. I have two hundred dollars in my pocket; I send Tim a money order for a hundred. I am free, he's trapped. He needs it more than I do.

The second thing I want to do is visit Grandmother Louise, but she's in a convalescent home in Orange County and I cannot travel more than fifty miles. My parole officer informs me I have to be home for thirty days before he can approve a special visit. I ask my Aunt Audrey to tell her.

"You know, Colton, she insisted the nurse call me in the middle of the night. She said, 'I dreamt that Colton was home. Are they really going to let my baby out of prison? I told her, 'Momma, it's okay. Colton's gonna come home. Just take it easy.' "

"I'll be there. Thirty more days. Twenty-nine now."

"But she kept asking, 'Is he really getting out? Are they going to let my Colton out? You think he'll come to see me?' 'Yes,' I told her. 'You sure? I dreamt he and Damon would be by my bedside.' "

"I'll be there as soon as they'll let me."

In a way, things have changed since I've been away; in another way everything is the same. The games and hustles are the same; the players are different and wear different costumes. Filas have been exchanged for Rocawear and Phat Farm. White America has become urbanized in clothes and music; Caucasians are enthused by hip-hop. Tattoos and braids are acceptable. The speed limit has gone from fifty-five to seventy and I have the sense that I'm going to be hit by a car. CDs have replaced tapes. Cell phones, pagers, portable phones, text messages, computers, laptops are everywhere. At first I'm bewildered by these tech toys. Then I realize they allow me to expand my eyes and ears, enhancing my ability to read earth signs. I walk around wired by cell phones, pagers, text messages, a headset. I'm available. I can get what I want when I want it.

A friend helps me obtain a job working for Final Cut Multimedia. I write treatments to songs, deliver CDs to major record company productions, accompany the owner to celebrity parties, and network. My first major job is for Rick James in Bel Air. His music helped get me through prison and was the score for my life on the streets.

And then one day, I'm in the office learning Microsoft Word

when my new pager goes off. Beep beep. I look at the number but don't recognize it. Who's this, I wonder. I have to ask someone to show me how to use the cordless phone. The phone is answered on the first ring and a voice says, "Whassup, nigga?"

"Final Cut Multimedia Productions. May I help you? Did you page?" I reply.

"Nigga, you sound old as hell."

"Who is this?" I sit up in my chair.

"Oh. You don't know my voice no more, huh? Cee, this is Tray, your homie. Didn't know I had your number, huh?"

Tray is Ice T.'s gang name. "Ah, What's up, Ice?"

"You, sir. You the man."

"Naw. You the man," I say. "I hear you the rap star slash actor, Ice."

"Hey, Cee. You been knowin' me too long to be callin' me Ice. Just call me Tracy or Tray. I ain't went Hollywood on you or nothin'. I'm still your homeboy."

"Okay, Tray."

"So you gonna come see me?" Ice asks. "You still know your way 'round L.A., don't you?" He laughs. "I might just have a job for you. Come now."

"But Tray, how'd you get my number."

"What d'ya mean how I get your number? I'm still Tray."

"I'm in traffic."

Ice's office is on the tenth floor with a view of the city. His kick-it spot has a big-screen TV, expensive leather couch, glass table, a telescope pointing toward the skyline. Ice lounges on the couch, his hair in a ponytail, wearing a pair of jeans and a tee shirt. He introduces me to two rap friends and begins to tell me not to hang with the homies, that I need a job. I know this and tell him I have one, but he offers me another. When I was released, other homies suggest drugs and money. But not Ice; he offers me a job.

I lean back on the soft leather and celebrate the moment of kickin' it wit' my homie who was once in the trenches of negativity and bangin'. Now he's making legal money spittin' out the truth about the ghetto in his music. Ice is the only person I've grown up with who has kept it real and made it. He beat the odds of prison, bullets, drugs. There aren't many other role models. If he can make it, I can.

The Hollywood Hills lie under a veil of mist and blue sky. *I'm free. Here's Ice offering to let me be a part of his fame even though I'm an ex-con ex-thug. I can have a life in freedom. I don't really have a care in the world.* I watch the city, spreading calm before me, humming as people go about their daily activities. I take several pictures of Ice and me and send them to Tim, Al Capone, and other homies in prison. *Be inspired!* I write on the back.

I leave Ice's office that day an employee.

Coroner Records. Sounds like I belong.

On July 27, I'm approved to visit Grandma Louise, who's been transferred to a hospital because of a stroke. I drive out with Damon and his girlfriend, still flinching because of the velocity of our travel. I sit in the passenger seat, gazing out the window. The trip reminds me of my rides in the gray goose from one prison to another.

Once again, I use the quiet time for reverie. When I was still incarcerated, my grandmother told me she was ready to leave.

I knew she meant she was ready to die.

"I'm tired. I want to go see my mother and sister," she said. I pressed the receiver into my ear and pled with her, "No, Grandma. I'll be home soon. Wait for me to come home so I can see you."

The phone was quiet and I thought we were disconnected, but then she inhaled and said, "I'm so so tired. But I'll wait on you."

"Promise?" I pushed her.

"Told you, didn't I?"

Now here I am, zooming to hold her to the end of her deal.

My grandma is in ICU, fluids and oxygen from the life-support system run on all cylinders to keep her alive. I step to her side and hold her soft, Creole hands, and look at her face. She's beautiful. Light complexioned with the distinctive African American broad nose, ample lips tugging into a smile. All she needs is her Bible and the ever blooming African violets on the table beside her to appear to be sleeping back in our home in South Central.

"Grandma," I call her. "How you doing?"

Her eyelids don't flutter open.

"I love you."

Tubes are connected to her arms. I check the monitor and see the slow waves of her beating heart. Her chest moves in and out. I see no sign of pain. Just peace with that slight smile. She's my everything. My mother, father, sister. Damon stands beside me and puts his arm around me.

"Granny dreamt this, Colton. Us standing together next to her bed. Weird, uh?"

And in that instant, the machines change their song and she dies.

I look at Damon and we cry. I let the tears float down my cheeks. I quit hardness in prison.

I can't stay in that hospital and see her dead, so I walk outside and look at the sky, which is resolutely clear and blue.

At her funeral, I think how much I've changed. Grandma was always making me promise I'd quit the gang. "You and Smiley gotta stop. A lot of innocent people getting hurt."

"I will, Grandma," I replied, with every intention of quitting. I feel different now than the last time I was released from the lion's

cage. More in control of myself and angry at the ongoing destruction of my people, Black people. I don't want to watch other
brothas and sistas speed full throttle toward that fifteen-foot wall,
the sadistic prison.

It took me four years to quit the Crips while I was in prison. I
had to do the internal work, the hard work first. And then the
leaders of the Crips said I could represent the set and Crips best
by being out, by telling people what being a Crip is like through
this book. "Warn the children," one said. But that was there; this is
here. I realize I have to quit all over again. I know I have to get rid
of my gang tattoos on my face, neck, my hand.

The next month, I have another funeral to attend, Don Don's. I
haven't seen him since we were in Folsom in 1988. He'd been released and died from complications of diabetes. A homie tells me,
"Cee, Cuz, you know how Don Don would want you to come to
the funeral. Everybody's gonna be Cripped up."

I attend the funeral wearing a Zenetti suit. Everyone else is
dressed in gangbangin' attire. Since the funeral is in the territory
of another set with whom Harlem is at war, every attendee is a
target.

I walk to Don Don's casket and look at my comrade and one-
time enemy. He's dressed in a blue khaki suit with a Crip-blue flag
tied around his head, a flag hanging out of his shirt pocket. His
hands are sewn to reveal three fingers; the Rollin' Thirties
Harlem Crip sign. I clench my fist and bang it hard across my
chest three times. Then walk away. Another fallen soldier.

The others drive low riders and gangsta cars. I get in Grandmother Louise's Honda Accord. They drive into the 'hood. I drive
to Pops's house. Only I have changed.

I rarely go the 'hood. Not much has changed with the exception of
the set itself. Rollin' Thirties Harlem Crip still exists, but its members are even less productive than in my day. In my time, proceeds
of robberies and sales of marijuana funded the set. That's been re-

placed by crack and carjackings. We still held elders, neighbors, women, children with respect. Nowadays, elders are seen as easy-quick cash. Family members are viewed by other sets as fodder and manipulation points for the war that continues to rage.

I go instead to new events, events that may be commonplace and ordinary for some, but are novel for me. One such event is the auto show; at thirty-three I attend my first one. While I'm scoping out the cars, I see a familiar face: Correctional Officer Ireland, who worked at Calipatria. I remember him well. It was summer and I was returning to my cell after a hot day of work carrying a bag of ice. He made me pour the ice on the ground. "Ice cannot be taken to the housing unit," he insisted. It was a hundred degrees that day.

I poured the ice on the ground.

The next day, I was working for Lieutenant Hunt when I stumbled on Ireland's time card. All officers were required to have their cards or they wouldn't receive credit for the day and wouldn't get paid. I caught up with Ireland in the dining hall and handed him the card. "Here, man."

I'm sure he felt small about making me toss the ice. Seeing him at the car show reminds me of that incident. And then I thought about Fresno Shorty and a promise I made to him. If I ever caught a CO slippin' on the street, I'd take off on him for the sadistic cruelty with which Shorty was treated.

I meet Ireland's eyes and say, "What's up, man?"

He frowns, trying to figure out who I am, and then notices the "30's" under my left eye and fear crosses his face. His hands start shaking. He spins around and takes off, walking as fast as his short legs can carry him. I get satisfaction out of watching him march to his car, jump in, and speed away. If I want, I can write down his license plate number, run a make on it, and call on him at home.

But I don't bother. No point taking out on him what Berger and the others did to poor Shorty. Nothing will bring him back.

I visit Crip Alley where I was initiated. A crack addict sits next to an open bag of garbage, shuffling through some cartons and parts of a smashed TV. Our graffiti, carefully sprayed by T. J., has been scrubbed off and replaced. I drive by Smiley and Gina's old house, Grandma Louise's. Her shrub with the bright red flowers and barbs blooms. Now it reaches the top of the window. I catch myself about to stop at Huckabuck's house, ring his bell, and see if we can go to Skate City. I visit the sites of my shootings.

Grandma Louise saved everything and, sure enough, she has a box of my stuff. In it are the blue flag and Dodger bat I received from Big Mel and T. J. when I was initiated. I throw the bat in my car, carefully and customarily fold up the flag like the sacred object it once was, and go to Inglewood Cemetery to pay my respects. Li'l T served over eight years and, once released, returned to the 'hood, and within three months was gunned down by a Blood. With his murder, Big T went crazy and checked himself into a mental institution where he still lives. Li'l T's grave stands off to the side, alone.

And there's Huckabuck. I stare at his nameplate, feeling for a moment guilty that I'm alive and he isn't, as if my continued life diminishes my loyalty to our comradeship. I remember our good times, tears on my cheeks. When I was the in O-Car, we wrote a Crip prayer:

> Crip is who I am, but God is who I love.
> Death is what life brings, but life is what I bang for.
> Harlem is my dedication, but faith is my obligation.
> If I die, let my life not be in vain.
> Five-two whatever I do.
> Six-O whereever I go.
> Tray-O is all I know.
> Let no man judge me but God.

I say that prayer and as soon as I say the final *God* I see flashes of people in panic scampering for cover while muzzles burst. Bodies, hole-ridden and covered in blood, scatter across the city like footprints. Men slump in car seats with bullet wounds in their chests, lives spewing from wounds and pouring out of the open car door where streams of blood join and drip into the sewer drain like rain. Mothers faint at the sight of their children lying in open caskets. Sirens sound, alarm lights twirl. Helicopters hover above the palm trees that dot the battlefield. Small children gaze down at bodies, eyes confused, but solemn. Girlfriends and family fight over the victims' money, cars. Shell casings line up like land mines. Black men in slave chains walk into courtrooms, on trial in front of twelve nonpeers. Prison walls shadow the recreation yard. Officers, assault rifles hanging from their shoulders like purses, patiently wait for an excuse to rid the world of another Black man. Blue and red bandanas drape from pockets, wrap around heads like armor. Churches jam with mourning soldiers. Cars miles long are escorted into cemetery gates.

I wipe the wetness from my face, reach into my pocket, and remove the blue bandana. Carefully I unfold it and hang it across Huckabuck's nameplate. I motion the sign of the cross and walk away.

I slowly start Louise's car and pull to the gate. But I'm reluctant to leave the cemetery and sit there, the car purring.

And behold, here come four Bloods. Spider from Denver Lane, dressed in gang attire, flagging red bandanas, quickly surrounds my car with his homies. I haven't seen Spider since our brawl in Chino. He's put on a little girth, but his long limbs and popeyes still justify his name. He never snitched on me but never before had an opportunity for his revenge.

He walks over to the driver's window, and before I can react, he points a .45 Magnum in my face.

"What's up, Blood. You remember me?"

The thing I fear is taking place. The enemy has beaten me to the draw. Ironic that just as I say good-bye to my loved ones and bangin', I might be saying good-bye to myself, my own life. I do not fear death. I embrace it with pride and dignity. I compose myself as Spider stands there, death fury in his eyes, murder rage in his voice.

"Nigga, you remember me?" He spits.

"Yeah. I remember you, brotha. How you doin'?" My voice sounds gentle to me, but weary.

"Don't try that brotha friend shit, crab. You ain't no brother."

"I don't have a beef with you. I don't bang no more."

Spider cocks the hammer.

It's coming now. My death.

"Who's this nigga?" one of his homies asks.

Spider turns and my window of opportunity opens. I reach to the floor and grab the L.A. Dodger bat.

"This nigga Cee," Spider tells his homie.

Spider turns back to me, the gun points toward the ground. *I can easily grab his arm, crack him in the head with the bat, and win once again.*

But then Lafayette Rainey's voice warns, "Consequences. Consequences."

I sling the bat out the window, look Spider in the face, and say. "It ain't worth it."

I shift the car and drive. As soon as I'm out of the gate, I hear shots ring.

Boom. Boom.

Anxiety charges my heart, pours through me.

I check the rearview mirror, but there is no one in sight. No cars are following. There is only cemetery road winding through serene green, trees lining each side of the road, sticks with nameplates bursting through the earth, catching sunbeams and spurting them back as diamonds. There's only graves and grass and sky. And light shining from the sun.

The sound of my death was mere imagination.

My war is over.

Epilogue

And so the story goes. . . .

TWO POLICEMEN, ONE IN UNIFORM AND ANOTHER IN PLAIN-
clothes, pound my front door and insistently ring my bell.
Alarmed, I answer their clamor. A black and white police car sits
in my driveway. Instantly, I fear my daughter, driving home from
a nearby city, has been in an auto accident. The detective asks if
I'm Ann Pearlman. When I say yes, he hands me an envelope.
"Here's a subpoena," he says firmly.

The district attorney in Riverside, California, summons me to
appear at the trial of Colton Simpson charged with being a getaway driver in a robbery. The book you have just finished reading
submitted as part of the evidence against him. If found guilty, the
prosecutor has alleged Colton's prior plea bargain as strikes pushing the judge to use this crime as a third strike. At stake is Colton's
freedom. He faces life in prison.

My heart pounds. *How can I testify against Colton? More than*

*my coauthor, Colton has become my friend? What mean irony if
the most positive thing Colton has accomplished with his life is
used to stab him in the back.*

The crickets begin their nightly hum and the fireflies stroke
their embers on this Friday in early July, 2005. The officer in the
corporate-casual summer outfit suggests I may want a lawyer. They
look around my porch at the flowering roses, heavenly blue morning glories, and the metal sculptures. The detective shakes his
head and asks, "How does someone from Ann Arbor get involved
with a gangbanger from Los Angeles?" He pronounces "Los Angeles" as though it exists in a different country, oceans and continents
away. His eyes narrow as he wonders how a middle-aged, mid-
American white woman living in the middle of a forest in a
middle-class suburb got involved with an O.G. from a Black gang.

"Now I know where to have my copy autographed," the uniformed cop jokes.

After they leave, I read the subpoena. In March, 2003, two
men committed a robbery of a jewelry department of a store in
California. No weapons were used. They stole one earring worth
eight hundred dollars. Following the robbery, they fled to a vehi-
cle waiting in the parking lot. Allegedly, Colton drove this car.

In March 2003, Colton stopped at the San Clemente border
patrol station. With a gun at his head, the police arrested him for
attempted murder and parole absconding. After searching
Colton's car, the police confiscated pages from a draft of this
book. Then, they turned Colton over to the Riverside Sheriff's
Department. There were no warrants for his arrest. Instead, they
were for Damon, Colton's brother. Ironically and unbelievably,
Colton faced charges for his own attempted murder. After the authorities resolved the confusion, they charged Colton with driving
a getaway car.

In October 2003, Colton posted bail and returned to work for
Ice T and various musical groups. In February 2005, bondsmen
revoked his bail. Since then, for a year and a half, Colton waits his
trial in jail.

Clipped to the pages of subpoena are a check to cover the fifty-five miles I must travel to the nearest airport and a reservation for a plane to California. The publication date for *Inside the Crips* is August 1, only a few weeks away. Instead of touring around the country talking to teenagers about the tragedy of gangs, instead of talking to reporters and being on TV trying to publicize a national problem and disgrace, Colton sits in jail. Is he accused of smashing the case, of holding a gun and threatening the customers, of grabbing the loot and running through the mall as described in these pages? No. No one has seen him or accused him of being at the robbery. He is accused of driving the getaway car. The two men who snatched the earring have not been found.

I follow the officer's suggestion and hire a lawyer, calling one the next morning. By the time I'm in his office, he's on the phone with the ACLU. "This abridges the sense and purpose of the first amendment," he tells me. "It hits at freedom of the press. Such a thing, a book admitted into evidence would not happen in many states. It would be considered pejorative and prejudicial. But California, well, California is different."

I know how different. California incarcerates at a higher rate than any place in the world. There are 626 people out of every 100,000 in jail or prison in the Golden state. In the United States, 517 of every 100,000 people are currently in custody. The next highest country is South Africa with 355. We imprison at an increasingly high rate even though our crime rate declines. The crime rate decreased 16 percent, but 33 percent more people serve time. Fanned by politicians' manipulations, our culture responds with fear. If violent criminals are locked up, we are safe. Thus, we buoy a sense of control over brutality and aggression. But, of the top ten reasons for incarceration, only one, the sixth, is for a crime of violence (assault with a deadly weapon). The others are for drugs, unarmed robbery, or burglary.

I appear before the judge that Monday morning. The prosecutor in my city says that the book shows a pattern of behavior; Colton has been a getaway driver before. I jerk at his statement.

As far as I know, he's never been a getaway driver. My lawyer later tells me, maybe that's what the California prosecutor told him. Maybe he's lying to convince the judge. The surprise must register on my face because he says, "Defense attorneys and district attorneys can mislead. Only *you,* the witness, cannot lie."

The judge peers through his glasses at the pages, scanning each one. He says the subpoena seems to be in order, I must go to California. It's part of being a citizen. The California judge will decide if the book is inflammatory and prejudicial to Colton's right to a fair trial.

When I talk to Colton, he tells me that the jail personnel intercepted our letters and passed them to the district attorney's office. A letter from him explained his arrest. A letter from me accompanied one of the drafts of the book proposal. Both are evidence. I thought that the United States protects mail as sacred and inviolable that it's a federal offence to open someone else's letter. But this shelter dissolves if one person is in jail. Then, from the time it arrives at the jail until delivered to the prisoner, mail belongs to the state. Allegedly, this is to protect the safety and security of the inmates and workers. I guess it's also to gather evidence against the accused. Colton seems energetic and anxious as the trial comes closer. With a half hour free from his cell each day to shower and make crucial telephone calls, his words erupt a mile a minute. "I love you. God bless you," he says his customary good-bye before ducking in his shower.

I met Colton through my agent in the spring or summer of 2002. "I have a fabulous project for you. It's the story of Colton Simpson, an OG of the Crips. Altogether he's served eighteen years in prison, six in solitary." Her voice sailed with excitement.

"I don't want to write someone else's story. You know I'm working on another project."

"Write the proposal. Just the proposal."

"I don't know anything about L.A. Get someone there."

"You're perfect. You worked in prison, you worked with gangs in Cincinnati, you know about race, and you're a therapist. Who better? Just meet him, talk to him."

"I'll think about it."

"Meanwhile, talk to him."

"Okay," I reluctantly agreed.

We talked and he sent me his manuscript. I realized his story reveals the America we seldom see: racism, police brutality, use of prisons to house the Black poor, what goes on inside our ghettoes and prisons, the civil war that rages in our cities. Two million Americans are currently in our prisons. Three quarters of them are Black. Colton is a face behind the numbing statistics, a person behind the gloomy headlines.

The weekend of Super Bowl in 2003, I flew out to L.A., and interviewed Colton, his father, his friends, ex-wife, girlfriend. I toured the houses, schools, alleys, corners of his South Central, the 'hood of the Rollin' thirties. Before New Year's of that year, he visited me with my family and we completed our interviews. Then, I showed him my world. He met my children and grandchildren, went to a party with my friends. When in New York, my daughter, a student at a university, and he spent time together. Over the course of the four years I have known him, we have become friends, included with my family.

An ironic tragedy in Colton's life occurs now. *Inside the Crips*, which may be the most redeeming and positive act of his life, is exploited as a weapon to put him in prison for the rest of it. If found guilty, the three-strike law may doom him to twenty-five to life in prison. The third strike law in California is not without controversy. Passed in 1994, it allows courts to sentence defendants to life if they have two violent felony convictions and an additional serious conviction. Already, the cost strangles the California taxpayers. Corrections consumes more money (5.6 billion) than higher education (4.3 billion). Designed to hold 100,000, 178,000 inmates stuff the California prison system. Twenty-three more prisons must be built to cage the inmates. This overcrowding provokes increased violence and troubled medical care (34 percent of inmates are over the age of fifty requiring additional medical treatment. Forty percent of men have unprotected sex in prison spreading AIDS not only in the prison, but throughout their communities).

Though originally intended to protect citizens from repeat violent offenders, the three-strike law has increased the sentences of more than 35,000 people who *never* committed a violent crime against another person at a cost to the taxpayers of more than $800,000,000 (FACTS Families to Amend California three strikes). A man whose previous strikes were for residential burglary received a life sentence when he stole razor blades. For another man, the third strike was for perjury. The crime: lying on a driver's license application. The sentence: life.

The ballot in the presidential election of 2004 proposed to change the three-strike law. The corrections union, the most powerful union in California, spent their advertising budget to defeat the law. A correction officer in California can earn over $100,000 per year. The governor backed the union. The proposition limped to defeat.

The L.A. County district attorney recommends restricting the law to those whose present crime is violent. L.A. County has followed his suggestion for the last two years. If Colton's arrest took place in L.A. County, the third strike would not be considered.

As you know from reading this book, Colton took a plea on his previous cases. Both of his previous charges resulted from one incident and he served twelve years for that particular crime. During the plea negotiations, agreements and waivers he signed, the state promised Colton that a future felony conviction could result in a one- to five-year enhancement. The three-strike law alters five years to twenty-five to life. The courts have made it clear that all plea agreements be construed according to state contract law. Thus plea agreements are contracts between the state and the accused. When the state unilaterally changes previously agreed contracts made during plea bargains, it violates its own promise. In fact, the 9th Circuit Court of Appeals has said, "As a defendant's liberty is at stake, the government is ordinarily held to the literal terms of the plea agreement it made . . . so the government gets what it bargains for but nothing more." The state of California disagrees. Recently, the courts at the state level (in fact in Riverside) handed Riggs, halfway through a twenty-five-year sentence for stealing a bottle of vitamins, a get out of jail free card. "He struck a deal with prosecutors and dropped a hearing before the U.S. 9th Circuit Court of Appeals. . . . If Riggs had won, it could have opened the way for some inmates to get a similar second chance at an easier sentence. Prosecutors were concerned enough to make their offer" (Press Enterprise, June 16, 2006) rather than allow his case to set a precedent on which others could climb from similar circumstance.

So here we are: a book on its way to the stores, one coauthor in jail, the other coauthor subpoenaed in his trial. St. Martin's Press, the publisher, is in a quandary. They prepared a wide, sweeping publicity campaign with Colton at the helm using his life as an exemplar of the evil, danger, the agony of gang life to stop its spread. In respect for Colton's right to a fair trial, they pulled back publicity. But the local press in California picks up the story. A barely recognizable photo of Colton appears. A sidelong hostile glance, clenched jaws, sucked-in cheeks, and turned-down mouth portray an alien expression. Headlines describe the book as boastful. Select passages bolster the perception of Colton as lacking regret and illustrate his mentality as a nineteen-year-old who had not yet transformed from the gang. Written in the present tense, the lines sound as though he thought this way, felt this way yesterday.

Publicity, negative publicity, has started. The book is the star witness for the prosecution. As I fly over the Grand Canyon, I think I am a two-edged-sword witness. I reinforce the case for both the defense and prosecution; I damage each one. I am no one's witness. And Colton, my friend and coauthor may be buried in a cell for a nonviolent crime at the cost of well over a million dollars to the citizens of California.

At the airport, a man from witness protection meets me and drives me to a hotel. It's noon in California. He instructs me to wait in my room for the prosecutor's call. Instead, I give the witness assistant my cell phone number and tell him I'll probably be climbing the nearby hills. The prosecutor calls around four to interview me in my hotel room that contains nothing but a queen-size bed. I am uncomfortable with this, so we talk in a Starbucks for two hours. With a warm, congenial, comforting demeanor, the prosecutor argues that *Inside the Crips* proves Colton's intent to participate in the earring theft. I cannot mention the name of the book on the stand. He quotes lines admitted as evidence from the book describing Colton's thoughts and deeds from a quarter of a century ago to prove his lack of remorse and his intent for the current crime. We review the admitted text as I try to tease apart which are my words and which are Colton's. Part contains a rap song. "You mean I'm supposed to rap on the stand?" I ask.

"I'll sing the backup," he jokes.

Very funny.

At the end of the interview, he says, "You know this is an amazing story from everyone's point of view."

I think how right he is. Each of us has his story, a culmination of our values, stereotypes, individual histories, and beliefs in personal transformation. Each of us reads the book and interprets the lesson. To him, it is the bragging of a cold-blooded gang member. To Colton, it is a way to try to do something positive with his pain and to help curtail gangs. To me, it is a tale of redemption, proof of individual growth and change that details the factors creating gangs and the cruelty in American prisons.

Colton's attorney interviews me by telephone. At the pretrial hearing that day, Colton broke down on the stand and began crying, trembling. The tears and his cracking voice seemed authentic. The newspaper adopts a cynical tone describing the scene.

The next morning, while dressing to testify, I receive a call that Colton's attorney quit. Information, revealed on the stand the previous day, indicated a conflict of interest. The trial is postponed.

As I fly home, I pick up *Entertainment Weekly* at the airport. *Inside the Crips* received an excellent review.

Colton ran out of funds and a public defender must represent him. The months wear on. At each hearing, the prosecutor summons the media. The trial is repeatedly delayed as the new lawyer must investigate, and file motions. Subpoenas arrive in the mail every few months. I receive calls in the fall, in the spring, in early summer asking me my availability. Then the public defender quits beginning a private practice. A new lawyer, Colton's third, is assigned. They start all over again. The judge transfers to another court. While writing this chapter, I learn the prosecutor receives a promotion and a new one is appointed to the case. Colton has been in jail twenty-three months. The cast of characters has entirely changed except for Colton (and me).

Television wants to interview Colton. These interviews are cumbersome to organize, but each one is blocked. In one, Anderson Cooper arranges interviews: Colton's uncle and aunt wait in their home. I am supposed to be interviewed via satellite. But the interview is suddenly cancelled. The producer was informed there'll be a plea and the case settled. Later, I hear the prosecutor told the public defender he didn't want a liberal interviewing Colton. Cooper might make Colton look good.

Using *Inside the Crips* as evidence displays Colton's previous crimes to the jury and may be unprecedented. As John Pomfret from the *Washington Post* states: "While U.S. law forbids the mention of prior convictions in the prosecution of a new crime, (the prosecutor) convinced the judge that Simpson's book—about crimes that occurred more than two decades ago—was relevant to the current case because it showed a behavioral pattern."

"'Simpson's case appears to be the first in which prosecutors have relied on a defendant's book as evidence of intent to commit a crime,' said Laurie Levenson, a professor at Loyola Law School. Prosecutors have used journals and letters to attempt to show criminal intent . . . Santa Barbara County prosecutors *unsuccessfully* tried to use holiday cards (Michael) Jackson wrote the alleged victim to prove the singer's guilt. But the Simpson case, Levenson said, 'is the first I'm aware of in which some of the key evidence against a defendant—*the most damaging*—is in his own book.'" (Italics mine.)

Thus, the book Colton and I wrote appears to be the best evidence the DA has against him. *Inside the Crips* may be exploited to put him away for the rest of his life in a retroactive ambush to his prior contracts with the state in spite of the fact that no violence, no weapon was used in the crime of which he's accused. Never before has a book been admitted into evidence in this way, and this would not be happening ninety-four miles farther to the west where the third-strike law is restricted to violent crimes. In other words, one particular court in one particular county establishes an enormous precedent. And the ambitions of a publicity-hungry prosecutor benefited from Colton's situation.

There's a principle that's at stake here and a freedom that may be lost that will affect publishing. *Inside the Crips* is a story of redemption; it details crimes that Colton committed and for which he paid with a total of eighteen years of his life. If admitted into evidence, it would curtail publication of biographies that deal with stories of recovery and personal change. Certainly Malcolm X's *Autobiography* in which he discussed being a pimp and a burglar, Bill Ayers's *Fugitive Days* in which he discussed his activities in SDS and the Weather Underground, Nathan McCall's *Makes Me Want to Holler* in which he discussed his participation in a gang rape and other misdeeds would not be published. This is contrary to Justice William Brennan who wrote in *New York Times v. Sullivan* in 1964, the First Amendment provides that "debate on public issues . . . [should be] . . . uninhibited, robust, and wide-open." Books such as this one produce a positive social good as well as impact on individual hopes and aspirations. Cautionary tales serve as warnings to some and give hope to others suffering from similar circumstances that they, too, can transform their lives.

The use of *Inside the Crips* as evidence against its author and the chilling effect it would have on biographies proving transformation would be another in the list of lost personal freedoms. That Colton's attempt at amends and our effort to do something positive to curb gangs and urban violence could result in grave consequence provides an excruciating mockery.

Colton and I know that everything we write each other is copied. When I write about my family, or make small talk about the weather, I assume he understands I'm letting him know I think and care about him. My message is the medium.

In a recent letter to me, Colton wrote, "It's almost as if people in jail get angry and become violent toward law enforcement or they become depressed and turn to suicide. Prison has nothing to offer, no educational opportunity, no programs—nothing. For many, opting to commit suicide rather than take yourself and your family through a lifetime of expense and grief is a quick and easy way out. Others ingest every kind of drug and homemade drink to get high and escape the time.

"The cell I'm housed in has a bug/pest problem. I'm told two people hung themselves in this cell. Apparently their bodies were found hours later.

"Just two days ago Big BJ, one of the founders of the Rollin' thirties who had pieced together the first Crip Car in prison, a General of C.C.O., and highly respected in West L.A. and prison, committed suicide. He had accomplished everything that the parole board requested. His sentence was seven to life and he'd been eligible for parole since 1983. Imagine. A quarter century of parole eligibility. He had done decades of time without a write-up. Apparently, he appeared before the parole board a few days before and was denied again. This year marked his thirtieth year in prison. Thirty years and he hung himself. He left a wife and kids behind and many men who admired and loved him. Ann, many people are tripping off BJ committing suicide as a way to escape doing time. But I'm not. I understand the pressure he had to deal with. The pains. I'd never commit suicide because of my faith in God and all I have to live for. But I do understand how sorrow can defeat people.

"Meanwhile, I pray God puts a spirit on the court and releases me."

A year later, it is all eerily familiar. *Inside the Crips*, this year in paperback, is going to press. Colton is still in jail, beginning his twenty-fourth-month. Now, he has high blood pressure and takes medication. Attacked while he slept, Colton lives on a different floor, in solitary. He prefers the solitude and quiet. Still, the admission of this book may hurt its author and change the face of American publishing. And I wonder when, once again, I will be summoned to fly across the Great Plains and mountains to be a witness in the trial of my friend and coauthor.

Afterword

EVERYTHING YOU READ IN THIS BOOK IS A TRUE AND ACCU-
rate reflection of the people and instances that have impacted me.
I did not exaggerate or romanticize my life. Many of the people
who I have loved are now dead; others are behind bars. It's kind of
a joke that a Crip never has to worry about getting old.

I've told you terrible things, things that may have made you
sick, things that may have made you hate me. No one wants to be
hated. But there was no point in writing this if I was not honest.
Every Crip, including myself, started out as a child open to love.
Most of us never found any love except what we gave each other.
We used that as an excuse to do what we did. The Crips became
my family and I gave them my loyalty, my life. I thought it was the
right thing to do. I did prison time for this family, honored them,
and kept the code.

But now I'm almost forty and everywhere I look I see destroyed lives. I see kids in every state in this country looking up to

the Crips, ready to join. I read the statistics. Blacks are six times more likely to be murdered. South Central L.A. all by itself accounted for 50 percent of all homicides in L.A. In 2003 Allen Beck, chief prison demographer for the Bureau of Justice Statistics, an arm of the Justice Department, reported that while 1.6 percent of White men between 20 and 34 are in prison, 12 percent of Black men 20 to 34 are in prison, and it is calculated that 28 percent of all Black men will be sent to jail or prison in their lifetime. My people are still enslaved.

I am haunted by the things I did and saw. Every time I turn around I see another person slaughtered. I see blood drenching the ground. I close my eyes and see blood. Even in my dreams. For most of my life, I pushed people violently away from me, my homies, and our space. It was not out of anger but obligation. I sincerely thought I was a soldier in a legitimate, necessary war. But now, the thought of pushing someone's child to extinction has made me an insomniac. I don't think I'll ever sleep till this stops. That's why I wrote this book. I'm crying for help, hoping you will listen and care, hoping all of us together will work to stop the sources of the gangs.

And yet every day another child joins a gang and it starts all over again.

A few months ago, I read a quotation from a study done by Donald Rumsfeld's office. He said, "Military doctrine and forces are created in the image of the economies that spawn them; military forces, although multi-purpose by nature, are formed around a core of threats that they are designed to defeat; asymmetric confrontations have historically generated decision outcomes, whereas symmetric confrontations tend to be exhaustive."

I realize now, he's right. His comments describe the war I shared with you in this book, the war that I was in, but didn't know it. The war between the Crips and the Bloods is a symmetric confrontation, like the Protestants and the Catholics in Ireland, the Bosnians and the Serbs, and the Hutus and the Tutsis. I didn't know it then. I was caught up in revenge and protection.

We are doomed to fight until we were all exhausted or dead. Or make a paradigm leap and quit.

You may wonder what has happened since I was released from prison in 1998. The dominoes started their colliding as events stacked up on each other. I lived only a few months with my father before settling into a one-bedroom in a middle-class neighborhood. It was small, but after spending most of my life behind bars in a six-by-nine-foot mass of steel and concrete, it seemed like a nice-sized home to me. I finally had my own space to concentrate and gather my thoughts without distraction.

My thoughts ran mostly around my looming future. What was I going to do with my life? Who would I allow in my space? Who would I trust? And where in the world did I now fit?

I worked for Ice T as his personal assistant. As Ice T told me, "You meet a lot of interesting people in this business." One such person was Tony, who then owned a production company and happened to be the little brother of a schoolmate of mine, Jennifer. Tony and I started a small business, writing treatments for videos, finding promising recording artists, and creating promotional packages to get major record deals. This brought Jennifer and me in each other's presence. She had written to me several times while I was in prison, and once she went so far as to send me photographs of her in a bikini. The craziest thing about Jennifer is that she was born the exact same day and the exact same year as I was. We had a thing for each other throughout junior high and high school, but shortly after graduation she married a friend of mine, so our fondness for each other never developed. She divorced three or four years into their marriage.

She was single, as was I, and just as sexually frustrated. Her sexual frustrations came from her not having sex due to her lack of trust for men. She believed that once she slept with a man he'd leave her because all men wanted was to score. My sexual frustrations came from my being held captive all my life and missing out on my twenties, and half my thirties—the sexually fun years. Eventually we talked about our old fondness for each other and, one day, we ended up spending the night in each others' arms pouring our guts out to each other and then making passionate love. After that we were inseparable. Whenever we weren't working, we were together. We even moved in together.

My life was developing. I had a job and a love life. Working with Ice T brought me to the realization that in the music industry the independent labels and distributors are the ones who make the money. Ice T gave me enough information to go out and start my own label, and he offered his services and assistance in teaching me the ropes. Tony and I discovered a lot of talented artists and we were eager to get our hands deep into the music business, but none of the major labels wanted to take the risk of investing a million dollars on an unknown artist. We decided to go independent and looked for the capital to get it off the ground.

Son, an acquaintance of Tony's, decided to invest twenty thousand dollars for a demo tape. A demo of three songs would give us a solid product to shop and, once a deal was secured, we'd all be rich. Or so we thought.

One night, I was sweeping the courtyard when a Black man, dressed as a business professional, parked next to my driveway, got out of the car. He told me Son had passed twenty thousand dollars of counterfeit money. I told him it was between him and Son and thought that was the end of that.

A few weeks later, when I was visiting a friend in the hospital, I got a phone call and learned that Son had just been shot. That night the police came to my house and arrested me for the shooting, saying I was the person who had shot him. I was booked on attempted-murder charges and given no bail.

I was back in the county jail. I stayed in that nasty L.A. County Jail for two years fighting that case. I went to trial three times. I got two hung juries the first two trials and was convicted on all counts in the third, even though I had several witnesses who testified as to my whereabouts during the crime, including a hospital pass and a clerk placing me at the hospital. I was sentenced to life in prison plus twenty-eight years and shipped off to Salinas Valley State Prison. Immediately, I filed a notice of appeal.

Ice T hired an attorney for me. When my appeal was heard, all three judges in the Second Appellate Court ruled in my favor and my appeal was granted. They ruled that my conviction and incarceration were unconstitutional, and ordered that my sentence be vacated and I be given a new trial. A few weeks later, I was shipped back to the L.A. County Jail.

I was housed in the New Crip Module in the Lynwood Jail and placed on single-cell status. Ironically, my next-door neighbor was Smiley, waiting trial on a case he didn't do. After seventeen years without seeing each other we were back together, this time both of us innocent! His hair had started to recede and was gray, and he'd put on at least fifteen pounds. I was two inches taller than he, but only a few pounds lighter. Musclewise I was bulkier also. We were both middle aged. We looked at each other and laughed at how things panned out.

The Crip Module hadn't changed, though. They were still tying up busters and using that threat to amp adrenaline. They accused Smiley of being a buster and threatened to tie him to a chair and beat him. For awhile, they got him going, but then everybody laughed. Their mockery provided an evening's entertainment.

Smiley and I talked so much it made our heads spin. We began each morning by saying, "Good morning, homie," and ended each night by saying, "I love you, cuz. God bless you. Good night."

Of course we went over the beatdown he ordered for me when I was in the Crip Module back in the mid-eighties. He justified himself by telling me he was beaten as a punishment, too. Apparently, he violated one of his own principles and ordered himself to be disciplined. "See how much I believe the rules need to be maintained? See how serious I am?"

"Yes, but that's different," I told him. "You had broken a rule and controlled the discipline. I hadn't broken any rules and you didn't gather the evidence."

"It's history." He turned to me. The scar on his neck was evident, but it seemed like a crease; it was now that much a part of him.

I guess he was right. Here we were. One way or another, we shared our lives together.

One night we got into a conversation about the many loved ones we'd lost to the Crip-and-Blood war, Crip-and-Police war, Black-and-White war, and Black-and-Mexican war. This compelled us to tally up the dead and captive. To date, of all the ex- and present gang members mentioned in this book, only five of them are alive and out of prison: Watt Nitty, Keitarock, Baby Rock, Three Finger Louie and Ice T. Six, including me. The rest are dead or locked away in a cell. Many reside right here in the California Department of Corrections, the biggest incarceration state in the country; Don Don, Li'l T, Cadillac Jim, Baby Bro, Huckabuck, Big Heron, Goofy Vee, Bird, and Big Mel are all dead. Al Capone, T. J., J Dog, Big Boo, Tim, aka Big H, Maxwell, Lefty Dog, Popeye, Li'l Eddie D, Li'l Tony Mac, Li'l Harlem, Lunatick Frank, Doc, Let Loose, Shyster, Li'l Quake, Drack, Tweety Bird (From Compton Crip), UT, and Hank (from Hoover), Big Pup, Big Silky, C Dog, Moe (from Pueblo Bishops), Spyder (From Denver Lane) and T-Bone (from BPS Bloods) are all in prison.

The faces of my dead and incarcerated comrades flitted before me. Our army, strong, brave men, all made powerless. "Man," I said to Smiley, "that's a lot of homies."

"No bullshit." His face bowed so all I could see was his gray head.

"Do you ever regret anything? You ever feel bad about some of the shit we did?" I asked.

He shook his head. "I don't know, Cee Loc. Sometimes I think I made some mistakes. What about you? How you feel?" His voice was almost a whisper.

"I don't regret shit because I made the decision to do those things back then, at that time, and, at that time, that's what I thought was best. But to do some of the things I did back then today? Hell, nah. That ain't me. I wouldn't do it, Smiley. I couldn't. I couldn't live with myself." The sick feeling turned my stomach, the sense of shame. What had Lafayette said to me decades ago? *It ain't in you; I see it in your face.*

We were both quiet, heads turned away from each other. I plunged into the terror of remorse. After a few minutes, I said, "You know what? Yeah, I do regret a lot of shit. I feel remorse because that shit wasn't fair to our family. The enemy is one thing. But we affected a lot of people, including ourselves. We have no idea how many people we influenced because many people know of us and we don't even know them. They follow behind us, thinking we did the shit 'cause it was cool or fun. Niggas don't realize we did it to stay alive. To breathe to tell about it. Nowadays people think it's hip and fly to be gangsta. Tattoos, sagging, C-walking, all that shit's cool now. People don't understand that in another time that could get you killed."

"Another time? Shit. Niggas are still getting killed behind that."

Thinking about what he said I had to respond, "Yeah."

Because of business ventures and other political aspects of life, society has socially accepted a part of the gang lifestyle to the point of it slipping into every neighborhood and household in this country. Parents are so out of the loop that their children are transforming right in front of their faces, making gangbanging more out of control and elusive than before.

But, yes, I have my regrets. I have remorse. I helped fashion something that is so violent and dangerous it could hurt me. I have to protect myself from my own creation, something I helped build. When these kids see me walk or drive down the street, they don't know who I am. I don't look the part anymore. To them I'm a potential victim. It bothers me that they could look at *anyone* in society as a potential victim, a buster.

I'm out here struggling to fight the causes of gangsterism, struggling to end something I once devoted my life to. So, in essence, to many, I'm a real hypocrite. Remorse and regret or not. No one really understands, except for those fortunate enough to live through the wars and fighting and still stand free, capable of making sense of it.

The violence escalated, just like I said. Escalated. Retaliation escalates violence. And instead of winning a war and protecting our communities, we increased the fear and tragedy, building that tower of terror. I regret being a part of that. I worked so many years creating something I now hate, that I see as destructive and deadly instead of protective.

Smiley and I were each quiet in our separate cells, listening to the racket of music and shouts and rapping around us in the module. I turned to him again. "I believe everything happens for a reason, Smiley. I went through the shit I went through 'cause God felt it was necessary for me to go through all that. All that made me who I am today." *I am now who I am. I can't regret too much or I'd regret myself. And then where would I be?*

"Yeah, I believe that, Cee Loc. But, for real-for-real, who knows? I feel fucked up 'cause I'm back in here for bullshit I didn't do, but then, look who I'm talking to? You, another brother who's in here for some shit he didn't do. I look at it like this: I know you're going home, but me, I don't know what these White folks are gonna do to my Black ass. And maybe that's why you and I landed here, in each other's presence, decades later. So we could kick it one last time and see where each other are mentally. To form some other movement and help bring other homies in. Something more constructive and positive."

Smiley leaned back and placed his palms on his knees. The flesh on his hard, scarred hands twisted like bark. Then he turned to me. His eyes had that solemn look that I know so well, with the slight twitch, almost imperceptible at one corner. "Cee Loc, I'm a grandfather now. I have kids that're having kids. And you, man, you damn near forty years old. We spent our whole life in here." He shook his head and then asked, "Have you talked to Gina and Moms lately?"

"Not lately. Gina always sends me birthday cards and I brought presents for the boys' Christmas when I was out, but I haven't talked to her since I've been back in. My prison shit wore her out."

"Man, Moms is getting old. Gina can't even tell her half what's goin' on. She can't take it no more, cuz."

I thought of Curly and Grandma Louise and my father.

"All I want you to do for me is look after the family. Please, cuz, just do that. Look after the family." Tears poured down his face. I'd never seen Smiley cry. Never.

Not two days after that conversation Smiley was told to roll it up. He grabbed his personal belongings and was transferred to another part of the L.A. County Jail. On his way out he hugged me and reiterated: "Look out for the family, cuz. I know you're getting out, so just look out for the family." And then he shined his generous grin. Even though we were parting I felt the warm light of his smile.

A week later I went to court and took a deal for probation on the case that had sentenced me to life plus twenty-eight years in prison. I took probation not because I was guilty. I wasn't. But because I was sick and tired of being in jail. I wanted out. I wanted a life. I wanted to finish this book and work. I was released in 2002.

Once I was out I resumed working for Ice T. Jennifer couldn't deal with my incarceration. So I was single again.

It's not all bad news out of South Central. Gina's sons, my stepsons, are well-mannered, disciplined young men. Marcus is playing basketball in college. Antoine is a high school senior. Huckabuck's son is a lighter-skinned version of him, just like he was as a baby. He has graduated high school and will be attending a culinary arts program. None of them joined a gang.

Neither Steve nor D'Andre got in trouble again. Steve is an electrician and D'Andre's wife gave birth to a daughter in 2004. Together, they have a housecleaning business.

Big T never recovered from his brother's murder.

Neither Gina nor I remarried. We remain friends.

Nearly a year after I was released, Smiley was found guilty of masterminding the murder of a known Crip who was a good friend of ours. Did Smiley do it? Hell no! Impossible! We were all friends. At sentencing he received two fifty-to-life sentences. Ice T and I pitched in and hired him an attorney. The same attorney that got me out of prison: Hurdle Clay Jacke II. He saved my life.

And what do I have to say about what happened to Smiley? Life, that's it. Life!

Life is something to live and do, not to verbalize. Sometimes there are steps in life that can be only baby steps. This demands a super amount of work, energy, and patience. Sometimes just when you've taken three steps forward, you take a giant step backward; just when you begin to see the light at the end of the tunnel, something blocks the view. But when this happens and you fall down, you must quickly get up and put one foot in front of the other to continue in a forward direction. Then one day, after much pushing, it's necessary to stop, turn around, look back at all the goals and objectives you have or have not accomplished. Accept yourself for who you really are, not who you portray yourself to be, or how others portray you. Once you've done this, then decide what you are going to do with the years that are left to you. Sometimes those years are many, and sometimes all too few.

What am I doing with the years I have left? First and foremost I'm adhering to Smiley's request; I'm looking out "for the family." The other thing I'm doing is praying daily that this thing called bangin' is somehow worked out from the root up. I hope this book will educate people so we work together to stop gangs. Thus, my pain will have some value and do some good. I hope you will want to help. Silence is condoning. Tell a friend. It's cheap. Please.

Everything else in life I've found the power to put in God's hands. What must be, will be. . . . And so the story goes.

In Struggle,
Little Cee (Loc, no more)

Index